D0830096

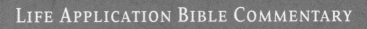

LIFE APPLICATION BIBLE COMMENTARY

life APPLICATION® Bible Commentary

HEBREWS

Bruce B. Barton, D.Min.
Dave Veerman, M.Div.
Linda K. Taylor

SERIES EDITOR: Grant Osborne, Ph.D.
EDITOR: Philip Comfort, Ph.D.

TYNDALE HOUSE
PUBLISHERS, INC.
CAROL STREAM,
ILLINOIS

Visit Tyndale online at www.tyndale.com.

Life Application Bible Commentary: Hebrews

Copyright © 1997 by The Livingstone Corporation. All rights reserved.

Contributing Editors: James C. Galvin, Ed.D., and Ronald A. Beers

Cover photograph of bridge and path copyright © by Alyn Stafford / iStockphoto. All rights reserved.

Cover photographs of woman with a laptop and man holding a pen copyright © by Dan Wilton / iStockphoto. All rights reserved.

Cover photo of man reading copyright © by Ronnie Comeau / iStockphoto. All rights reserved.

Scripture quotations marked NIV are taken from the *Holy Bible,* New International Version®. NIV®. Copyright © 1973, 1978, 1984 by International Bible Society. Used by permission of Zondervan. All rights reserved.

Scripture quotations marked NKJV are taken from the New King James Version. Copyright © 1979, 1980, 1982 by Thomas Nelson, Inc. Used by permission. All rights reserved.

Scripture quotations marked NRSV are taken from the New Revised Standard Version of the Bible, copyright © 1989, Division of Christian Education of the National Council of the Churches of Christ in the United States of America. Used by permission. All rights reserved.

(No citation is given for Scripture text that is exactly the same wording in all three versions—NIV, NKJV, and NRSV.)

Scripture quotations marked KJV are taken from the *Holy Bible,* King James Version.

Scripture quotations marked NLT are taken from the *Holy Bible,* New Living Translation, copyright © 1996, 2004, 2007 by Tyndale House Foundation. Used by permission of Tyndale House Publishers, Inc., Carol Stream, Illinois 60188. All rights reserved.

TYNDALE, Life Application, New Living Translation, NLT, and Tyndale's quill logo are registered trademarks of Tyndale House, Publishers, Inc.

Library of Congress Cataloging-in-Publication Data

Barton, Bruce B.
Hebrews / Bruce B. Barton, Dave R. Veerman, Linda K. Taylor ; editor, Philip W. Comfort.
p. cm. — (Life application Bible commentary)
Includes bibliographical references and index.
ISBN 978-0-8423-2856-2 (pbk. : alk. paper)
1. Bible. N.T. Hebrews—Commentaries. I. Veerman, David. II. Taylor, Linda K. III. Comfort, Philip Wesley. IV. Title. V. Series.
BS2775.3.B37 1997
227'.87077—dc21 96-53647

Printed in the United States of America

17 16 15
17 16 15 14 13

CONTENTS

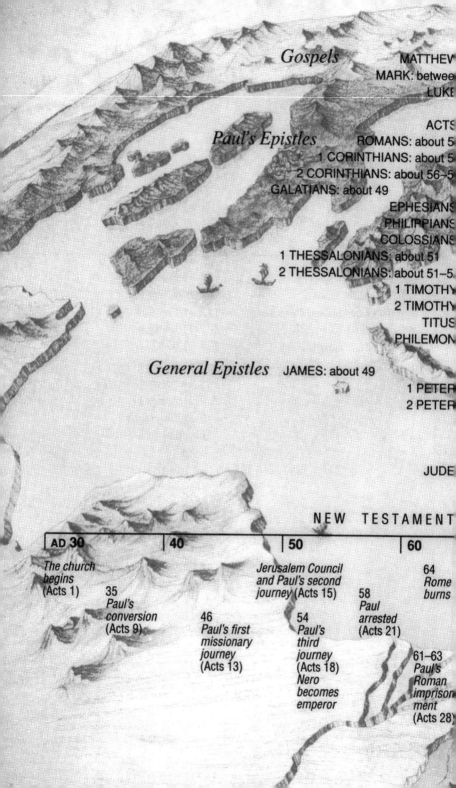

Gospels MATTHEV
MARK: betwee
LUKE

ACTS

Paul's Epistles ROMANS: about 5
1 CORINTHIANS: about 5
2 CORINTHIANS: about 56–5
GALATIANS: about 49
EPHESIANS
PHILIPPIANS
COLOSSIANS
1 THESSALONIANS: about 51
2 THESSALONIANS: about 51–5
1 TIMOTHY
2 TIMOTHY
TITUS
PHILEMON

General Epistles JAMES: about 49
1 PETER
2 PETER

JUDE

NEW TESTAMENT

AD 30	**40**	**50**	**60**

The church begins (Acts 1)

35 *Paul's conversion* (Acts 9)

46 *Paul's first missionary journey* (Acts 13)

Jerusalem Council and Paul's second journey (Acts 15)

54 *Paul's third journey* (Acts 18) *Nero becomes emperor*

58 *Paul arrested* (Acts 21)

64 *Rome burns*

61–63 *Paul's Roman imprison ment* (Acts 28)

etween 60–65
5–65
bout 60
JOHN: probably 80–85
bout 63–65
bout 61
bout 62
bout 61
bout 64
bout 66–67
bout 64
bout 61
HEBREWS: probably before 70
bout 62–64
bout 67
1 JOHN: between 85–90
2 JOHN: about 90
3 JOHN: about 90
bout 65
REVELATION: about 95
IMELINE
70
80
90
100
7–68 Paul and Peter executed
68 Essenes hide their library of Bible manuscripts in a cave in Qumran by the Dead Sea
Jerusalem destroyed
79 Mt. Vesuvius erupts in Italy
About 75 John begins ministry in Ephesus
75 Rome begins construction of Colosseum
About 98 John's death at Ephesus

FOREWORD

The Life Application Bible Commentary series provides verse-by-verse explanation, background, and application for every verse in the New Testament. In addition, it gives personal help, teaching notes, and sermon ideas that will address needs, answer questions, and provide insight for applying the word of God to life today. The content is highlighted so that particular verses and phrases are easy to find.

Each volume contains three sections: introduction, commentary, and reference. The introduction includes an overview of the book, the book's historical context, a time line, cultural background information, major themes, an overview map, and an explanation about the author and audience.

The commentary section includes running commentary on the Bible text with reference to several modern versions, especially the New International Version, the New Revised Standard Version, and the New Living Translation, accompanied by life applications interspersed throughout. Additional elements include charts, diagrams, maps, and illustrations. There are also insightful quotes from church leaders and theologians such as John Calvin, Martin Luther, John Wesley, and A. W. Tozer. These features are designed to help you quickly grasp the biblical information and be prepared to communicate it to others. The reference section includes an index and a bibliography.

INTRODUCTION

Faced with the choice of something good or something obviously bad, only a foolish or misguided person would choose "bad." Good should win every time.

At the next level, however, choices become more difficult—deciding between *good* and *better.* Again in this case, the logical choice would seem to be "better," but the choice is not as clear-cut as in the former situation: The differences between the two options may seem insignificant, the reasons for choosing what purports to be "better" may be unconvincing, and staying with the familiar "good" may feel comfortable and convenient. Thus, faced with keeping the *good* or moving up to *better,* many people stick with what they have, because, after all, it's not "bad."

The next choice is even more difficult—deciding between *better* and *best.* Again, the obvious choice should be "best" every time, but many miss what is best and settle, instead, for "better" or simply "good." For them it is better to stay with what they know.

The writer of the letter to the Hebrews had to convince the readers to settle for nothing less than God's *very best* for their lives. Jews were familiar with God's goodness and perfection. After all, they were his *chosen* people, and through them God had communicated his love and plan for the world. They were the recipients of the covenant, the law, the tabernacle, and profound religious rituals, and they had been blessed with prophets proclaiming God's messages and priests doing God's work. Judaism was God's way, and it was good.

But Jesus, the Christ, had come, fulfilling the law, making the perfect sacrifice, and initiating the new covenant. Christ was a better prophet, a better priest, and a better sacrifice. In fact, he was the ultimate, the *best.* Many Jews had embraced this new way, expressing faith in Christ ("Messiah") as Savior and Lord. Yet the familiar, *good* Judaism continued to draw them back. Some returned to the old way, and others attempted to combine the old with the new, forming a hybrid of Judaism and Christianity. And so they missed God's *best.*

Hebrews is a masterful document written to Jews who were

evaluating Jesus or who were struggling with the Christian faith. The message of Hebrews is that Jesus is better, Christianity is superior, and Christ is supreme and completely sufficient for salvation.

As you read Hebrews, catch the profound message of this important book. Judaism may not be calling you back, but many other gods and belief systems clamor for attention and push for allegiance. Regardless of their claims and promises, know that only Jesus is the truth, and only he brings life. Jesus is the *best,* the only way (John 14:6). Don't settle for anything less!

AUTHOR

The authorship of Hebrews has been in doubt since its publication. In fact, none of the early writers who refer to this book mention its author. And no one since early times has been able to identify the author.

Hebrews names no one as author. This is unusual for a letter, especially if Paul had written it. (His letters usually bear his name and personal greetings to the readers.) In fact, the only ancient title for this book is simply "To Hebrews," and that may not have been on the original, since all of the manuscripts with that title date after the first century A.D., the original having been written in about A.D. 60.

The inclusion of Hebrews into the New Testament canon came from the Eastern church as early as A.D. 185, mainly because of the traditional belief that Paul had written it. Clement of Alexandria described his teacher's (Pantaenus's) explanation for why Paul did not use his own name in this letter. Pantaenus surmised that Paul refrained from mentioning his name out of reverence to the Lord, who himself had been their Apostle (3:1). Clement accepted this explanation and proposed that the original had been written in Hebrew (Aramaic) and Luke had translated it into Greek. But this is conjecture.

What, then, do we know about the author for certain? Clearly the author was an early Christian because Hebrews was used by Clement of Rome in A.D. 95 (for example, 1 Clement 17; 36) and probably by Polycarp (for example, *To the Philippians* 6.12) and Hermas (for example, *Visions* 2.3.2; 3.7.2; *Similitudes* 9.13.7). From the content of the letter we learn several other things:

- The author was a teacher and a second-generation Christian: "This salvation, which was first announced by the Lord, was confirmed to us by those who heard him" (2:3b NIV).
- The writer had thought long and hard about a Christian interpretation of the Old Testament.

- The author was probably a Greek-speaking Jew, familiar with the Old Testament Scriptures and with the religious ideas of the Jews. The author claims to share the inheritance of their sacred history, traditions, and institutions (1:1) and writes of them with intimate knowledge and enthusiasm.
- The author seems to have known the Old Testament only in the Septuagint (ancient Greek translation of the Old Testament), which is followed even where it deviates from the Hebrew.
- The fact that Hebrews contains teachings that are "Pauline" along with the mention of Timothy in 13:23 seems to suggest that the author knew Paul or associated with those who were close to him.
- The author used Greek with a purity of style and strong vocabulary, and the style is unlike any other New Testament document. However, the fundamental concepts of Hebrews correspond fully with the writings of Paul and John.

Beyond this limited profile, the letter gives few authorship clues. A number of possible authors who fit the profile have been proposed over the years:

Paul. As mentioned, this has been the traditional view in many circles. For example, the introduction to the *Scofield Reference Bible* (original copyright 1909; copyright renewed in 1937 and 1945) reads, "The Epistle of Paul the Apostle to the Hebrews." Hebrews 13:23 and 2 Peter 3:15 are given as support for this view. Some have proposed that the epistle may actually have been a transcribed sermon by Paul; this, it is thought, would account for the differences in style with his other letters. Paul as the author has also been the official Roman Catholic view since the Council of Trent (A.D. 1545–1563).

The style of Hebrews, however, differs greatly from Paul's letters. For example, it includes none of Paul's Hebraisms, none of his long involved sentences, none of his rapid changes in thought, and none of his usual way of introducing Old Testament quotations. Also, Hebrews contains no personal allusions (a common practice of Paul), and the author aligns with those who have a *secondhand* knowledge of the Lord (2:3), something that Paul strongly denied (1 Corinthians 9:1; Galatians 1:12). In addition, the style of the Greek in this letter is the most elegant and pure in the New Testament, closer to Luke's writing and unlike any of Paul's letters.

Perhaps the strongest argument against Pauline authorship is the considerable theological difference between Hebrews and Paul's writings. Hebrews highlights the high priesthood of Christ, a concept totally absent from Paul's epistles. And many of Paul's most prominent teachings are absent in Hebrews. These include: union with Christ, justification by faith, the opposition of faith and works, and the tension between flesh and spirit.

The content of Hebrews does not contradict what Paul has written. In fact, Hebrews and Paul's writings hold many concepts and teachings in common. This led Origen to conclude that much of the contents of Hebrews was Pauline.

Barnabas. Paul's friend and companion on his first missionary trip (see Acts 9:27; 11:22-26; 12:25; 13:1–14:28; 15:1-41), Barnabas, "Son of Encouragement," was a Levite (Acts 4:36) and thoroughly familiar with the priestly services. Because of these Levite connections (Hebrews contains much Levitical ritual), Tertullian (c. A.D. 160–230) and scholars of North Africa supposed Barnabas to be the author. When introducing a quotation from Hebrews 6:1, 4-6, Tertullian wrote: "There is also an Epistle to the Hebrews under the name of Barnabas . . . and the Epistle of Barnabas is more generally received among the churches than that apocryphal 'Shepherd' of adulterers" (*De pudicitia* 20). Despite this strong endorsement, however, there is no other evidence or ancient support for Barnabas as author.

Apollos. This charismatic preacher is mentioned from time to time in the New Testament (see Acts 18:24-28; 19:1; 1 Corinthians 1:12; 3:4-6; 4:1, 6; 16:12; Titus 3:13), but we know very little about him. Apollos was a Jew, a native of Alexandria, well educated, and well versed in Scripture (Acts 18:24). It was also said of Apollos that "he spoke with great fervor and taught about Jesus accurately" and that "he vigorously refuted the Jews in public debate, proving from the Scriptures that Jesus was the Christ" (Acts 18:25, 28 NIV). Apollos knew Timothy and had been instructed by Paul, indirectly, through Priscilla and Aquila (Acts 18:25-26).

Luther proposed Apollos as the author, and many modern scholars lean in that direction because the epistle displays the kind of allegorical interpretations that were prominent in Alexandria.

Luke. Clement of Alexandria and Origen believed that Luke translated Paul's original writing or speaking. Parts of Hebrews are similar to the style and content of Acts, especially Stephen's speech (Acts 7:1-53), but that is the only proposed connection between Hebrews and Luke. This theory is quite speculative.

Others. Over the years, many other writers have been proposed. Each one has a bit of support: Silvanus (Silas), a member of both Paul's and Peter's circles and possibly the coauthor or secretary for 1 Peter (there are similarities in style between 1 Peter and Hebrews); Philip the evangelist (commendation of Paulinism to Jewish Christians in Jerusalem); Clement of Rome (nearly identical wording in places between his writings and Hebrews); Epaphras (similarities between Colossians and Hebrews); Priscilla (the anonymity of the letter—a woman author would have been difficult for the early church to accept); Priscilla and Aquila together (the use of the pronoun "we" in many places; for example, 5:11; 6:3, 9, 11-12; 8:1; 9:5; 13:18).

Having no known author is one reason that the early church was slow to include Hebrews as Holy Scripture. In the final analysis, Hebrews's own intrinsic worth won its place in the canon. We can only agree with Origen, who stated in the third century: "But who wrote the epistle, God only knows the truth" (quoted by Eusebius, *Ecclesiastical History* 6.25.14).

DATE

Written in approximately A.D. 60.

Because Clement of Rome used Hebrews, the letter must have been written prior to A.D. 95. An argument from silence is the lack of any reference to the destruction of the temple in Jerusalem in A.D. 70. Certainly in a book written to Jews, an event of such catastrophic proportions would have been mentioned, especially since it would have strengthened the argument for the superiority of Christ and the new covenant over the Levitical ritual. Thus Hebrews must have been written prior to A.D. 70.

An additional important factor in setting a date for Hebrews is the identification of the persecution referred to in chapter 10:

> *Remember those earlier days after you had received the light, when you stood your ground in a great contest in the face of suffering. Sometimes you were publicly exposed to insult and persecution; at other times you stood side by side with those who were so treated. You sympathized with those in prison and joyfully accepted the confiscation of your property, because you knew that you yourselves had better and lasting possessions.* (10:32-34 NIV)

Three Roman persecutions stand as possibilities: under Claudius in A.D. 49, under Nero beginning in A.D. 64, and under Domitian in the eighties and nineties. Note that the passage refers to "earlier days" and says nothing about loss of life. Many believers died under Nero and Domitian, but the persecution suffered by the readers of Hebrews does not seem to have involved martyrdom

("In your struggle against sin, you have not yet resisted to the point of shedding your blood," 12:4 NIV). In his persecution, Claudius expelled the Jews from Rome, including Jewish Christians (among whom were Priscilla and Aquila—Acts 18:2). During this expulsion, they would have been publicly mocked, and they would have lost their property. That treatment seems to match the description in chapter 10.

Considering all of the above, Hebrews was probably written in the early fifties or sixties, before the terrible persecution under Nero. This date also seems compatible with the statement that the readers had heard the gospel from those who had heard Jesus (2:3), and that Timothy was still alive (13:23).

AUDIENCE

Hebrew Christians who may have been considering a return to Judaism.

As mentioned earlier, the title "Hebrews" or "To the Hebrews" does not appear on the earliest copies of this letter. Nevertheless, the title is appropriate considering the content, which is narrowly focused on the Old Testament Scriptures and Jewish religious practices. The writer thoroughly discussed the worship in the tabernacle, the priests and the sacrifices, the covenant, and Jewish heroes including Abraham, Isaac, Jacob, Joseph, Moses, and others. References to "Abraham's descendants" (2:16), the argument that Jesus is superior to Moses (3:1-19), and the emphasis on "Sabbath-rest" (4:1-11) would have appealed to Jews and would have had very little effect on Gentiles.

Support for a Gentile audience comes from the use of elegant Greek in the letter. Some believe this indicates that neither the writer nor the recipients were Jews. The argument, however, fails to recognize that the Jews who had been dispersed all over the world were very familiar with Greek. The Septuagint, in fact, had been written for them. So Jews would have had no problem writing or reading "elegant" Greek.

The next question, then, is whether Hebrews was written for Jews in general or for Jewish Christians. This is not as clear, but the serious exhortations in chapters 6 and 10 against "falling away" and for maturing in the faith seem to imply that the recipients were part of the Christian community. Consider also the fact that the early church often had to contend with those who would push for a return to Judaism or who promoted a hybrid mixture of Judaism and Christianity (Acts 15:1-29; Romans 2:17-29; 4:1-25; Galatians 3:1-29; 5:1-15; 6:12-16; Colossians 2:11-23; Titus 1:9-16). Certainly the church needed to hear the message of Hebrews.

From the text, it would seem that the original readers of Hebrews were:

- *a specific group of believers*—They had received the gospel from eyewitnesses (2:3), had seen signs and wonders (2:4), knew basic Christian principles (6:1), were fruitful (6:10), and had ministered to people who had been mistreated (10:32-34). The writer wrote of their earlier days (10:32) and of previous persecutions (10:32; 12:4). The writer also knew of their present state of mind (5:11-12; 6:9-12).
- *a group known by the writer*—In addition to knowing all of the above facts about the readers, it is clear from the text that the writer had visited them and was hoping to return to them: "I particularly urge you to pray so that I may be restored to you soon. I want you to know that our brother Timothy has been released. If he arrives soon, I will come with him to see you" (13:19, 23 NIV).
- *a group that was part of a larger community*—The writer explained that by that time the readers should have been "teachers" (5:12). This could imply that the main recipients were a small group of believers within the church. Some scholars believe that they comprised a house-church and were a small enclave of conservative Jewish Christians.

DESTINATION

Rome.

Again, as with the author and the audience, the text provides no definitive word on the location of the original recipients of this letter. Certainly groups of Jewish Christians could be found in almost every important center of the world.

Traditionally, Hebrews was thought to have been sent to believers in Jerusalem. Jewish Christians there would have been under the greatest pressure to return to their former religion. And they had suffered severe persecution. The problem with this view, however, is that the strong Greek character of the book would not fit as well with Jerusalem readers as it would with those outside Palestine, especially since many of the Greek-speaking Jews had been driven from Jerusalem following the death of Stephen (Acts 8:1-3). Also, remember that the Jerusalem church struggled continually with poverty and would not have been capable of the generosity mentioned in 6:10, 10:34, and 13:16. In addition, Jewish religious life in Jerusalem was dominated by the temple, to which Hebrews makes no specific reference (contrast this with Stephen, who spoke of the temple in his speech before the Jerusalem Sanhedrin—Acts 7:44-50).

Another possible destination is Alexandria in Egypt. Support for this city comes from apparent signs of an Alexandrian perspective in Hebrews: similarities with the Alexandrian Jewish scholar Philo, the use of the Old Testament, and the dualism between heavenly archetypes and earthly copies. Yet this may mean only that the author was acquainted with Alexandrian thought, not that Alexandria was the destination.

Many other places have been suggested as possible destinations for Hebrews: Colossae, Samaria, Caesarea, Syrian Antioch, Ephesus, Galatia, Cyprus, Corinth, and Berea. None of these has much evidence or support.

A probable destination is Rome. That is where Hebrews was first known and quoted. In a letter written to the Corinthian church on behalf of the Roman church, Clement of Rome revealed his knowledge of this epistle. Certainly the references to persecution fit Roman readers (see the discussion under "Date" above). Also, the phrase, "Those from Italy send you their greetings" (13:24 NIV) points to a Roman connection. Quite possibly the author, writing from another location, knew Italian believers in that city and was sending their greetings back to Rome.

OCCASION AND PURPOSE

To present the sufficiency and superiority of Christ to Hebrew Christians who may have been considering a return to Judaism.

We don't know of a specific occasion for the writing of this important letter, but there is no doubt that believers of all backgrounds were subject to persecution and pressure to renounce their faith. Jewish believers were vulnerable to doubts about Christ and to thinking about turning back to their familiar rituals and old way of thinking. Many had been persecuted severely by their countrymen and branded as heretics (see, for example, Acts 8:1-3; 9:1-2, 20-25; 14:2-7; 17:5-15; 18:6, 12-17; 19:8-9; 20:3; 21:27–23:22) and had been deserted by their extended family. As they thought back to the past, their Jewish traditions and ceremonies must have seemed wondrously attractive. Primitive Christianity had no parallel ritual trappings and no replacement for the temple. Christians met in homes, with no large, central meeting place and no altar, priests, or sacrifices (Acts 2:46; 5:42; 20:20; Romans 16:5; 1 Corinthians 16:19). Thus they were tempted to hold on to the old while, perhaps, secretly professing the new. In this way, they thought, they could have both Judaism and Christianity.

The purpose of the Epistle to the Hebrews, therefore, was to remind and convince readers of the sufficiency and superiority of Christ (9:14), to warn them of the danger of drifting away from Christ (2:3), and to exhort them to faithfulness (3:6).

Although most Western Christians do not face severe persecution from family, friends, and society in general, at times they may look back longingly at their previous life "before Christ." Though not tempted to return to a former religion, they may feel the pull of an old lifestyle, materialism, or the cultural cult of self-worship.

Hebrews speaks to this temptation with the clear message that only Christ brings salvation, only Christ brings forgiveness, only Christ satisfies. And he alone deserves our adoration, worship, and praise.

MESSAGE

Superiority of Christ, High Priest, Sacrifice, Promise, Maturity, Faith, and Endurance.

Superiority of Christ (1:1-14; 2:5–3:6; 4:14–5:10; 6:13–10:18). Hebrews reveals Jesus' true identity as God in the flesh. Jesus is the ultimate authority. He is greater than any angel or religion. As the divine Son of God, Jesus is superior to any Jewish leader (such as Abraham, Moses, or Joshua). As the perfect man and mediator with God, he is superior to any priest. As one who endured suffering and temptation, but without sin, he knows us thoroughly. Jesus is the complete revelation of God. And he has been exalted to God's right hand (1:3), crowned with glory and honor (2:9).

Importance for Today. In our competitive society, everyone seems obsessed with winning and identifying with the "best." In our pluralistic society, we are aware of a wide range of religions and worldviews. In this age of technology, we are inundated with information about cultures, cults, philosophies, charismatic leaders, and alternate lifestyles. In all of this noise and clutter, however, we must keep our eyes on Christ, remembering that he *alone* can forgive sins and give eternal life.

Jesus has secured your forgiveness and salvation by his death on the cross and by his resurrection. You can find peace with God and real meaning for life by believing in him. Don't accept any alternative or substitute, no matter how attractive it may seem. Have you understood that Christ is superior in every way?

High Priest (3:1; 4:14–5:10; 6:19–8:6; 9:6–10:22; 13:11-13). In the Old Testament, the high priest represented the Jews before God. He would make blood sacrifices to atone for the people's sins before God. Once a year, on the Day of Atonement, the high priest would enter the Most Holy Place in the temple to make atonement for the sins of the whole nation. The high priest would approach God only once a year, but Christ is *always* at God's right hand, interceding for us.

Importance for Today. Jesus Christ is always available to hear us when we pray. He links us with God. In fact, there is no other way to reach the Father except through the Son. Because Jesus lived a sinless life, he was the perfect substitute to die for our sin. And he is the perfect priest, having offered himself as the sacrifice. Jesus is our perfect representative with God.

Jesus guarantees your access to God the Father. He intercedes for you, so you can come boldly to the Father with your needs. When you sin and are weak, you can come confidently to God for forgiveness and for help. What is keeping you from the Father?

Sacrifice (1:3; 2:9; 7:27; 9:12-14, 24-28; 10:5-22). Old Testament sacrifices had to be perfect: animals without any injuries or blemishes. These animals were killed on the altar, their blood spilled for the sins of the people. Jesus, the divine Son of God and the perfect Son of Man, died on the cross, shedding his blood to secure forgiveness for all people. Christ's sacrifice was the ultimate fulfillment of all that the Old Testament sacrifices represented.

Importance for Today. Because Christ is the perfect sacrifice for sin, our sins are completely forgiven—past, present, and future. Christ removed sin, which barred us from God's presence and fellowship. We don't automatically receive this forgiveness; we must accept Christ's sacrifice for us.

By believing in Christ, you are no longer guilty; you have been cleansed and made whole. His sacrifice cleared the way for you to have eternal life. What can you do to express your gratitude to Christ for his profound love for you and for his work on the cross?

Promise (4:1-11; 6:13-20; 7:18-25; 8:6–9:22; 10:15-16). God made a holy promise, a covenant, with Abraham. In this covenant, God promised to bless Abraham, to make of Abraham's descendants a great nation, and to bless all the world through him. God also promised to be with his people and to give them *rest.* Although the people often failed to live up to their side of the covenant, God always kept his: through Abraham came the nation of Israel, and eventually Christ. In addition, God brought his people to the Promised Land, and eventually he will bring them to their eternal rest. Now God has a new covenant with his people, which he has written "in their minds" and "on their hearts" (8:10 NIV).

Importance for Today. The old covenant made with Abraham

was tied to the nation of Israel. God's new covenant, secured through his Son, is available to *all* who place their trust in Christ. In addition, the new covenant offers total forgiveness and eternal life. Believers can have hope in the future because of what Jesus Christ has done for them. Eventually they will find perfect rest in heaven.

Regardless of your circumstances or difficulties, you can have hope in Christ. If you have trusted him for salvation, the covenant promises apply to you. This means that you have forgiveness, the Holy Spirit, and eternal life. How can you celebrate the new covenant? What can you do to share this good news with others?

Maturity (2:11-13; 5:11–6:3). Although God's people are saved from sin and given eternal life when they trust in Christ as Savior, they are given the task of going on and growing in faith. Too often, however, believers remain immature, feeding only on "milk" and not "meat" and arguing over the "elementary teachings" (6:1) of the Bible. Through a living relationship with Christ, however, believers can live blameless lives, be used powerfully by God, and mature in their faith.

Importance for Today. The process of maturing in our faith takes time and discipline. Daily communication with God through prayer and study of his Word produces maturity. When we are mature in our faith, we won't be easily swayed or shaken by temptations or worldly concerns.

If you find yourself disputing issues of lifestyle, faith, spiritual gifts, and the end times, you may be spiritually immature. Don't be content to remain a spiritual baby. What can you do to grow in faith?

Faith (11:1-40; 13:1-21). The Bible, from beginning to end, is a book about faith. Many believed God and received multiplied blessings on earth. Others believed God and were persecuted, tortured, and martyred for their faith. God expects his people to come to him in faith and to live by faith, regardless of the circumstances or outcomes. Faith is confident trust in God and his promises. God's greatest promise is that people can be saved from sin and have eternal life through Christ.

Importance for Today. Those who trust in Jesus Christ for salvation, God will transform completely, moving them from guilt to forgiveness, from death to life, and from despair to hope. A life of obedience and trust pleases God.

The more you know of God, the more you will trust him. The more you trust, the more you will hope in his promises. Consider the evidence of faith in your life: Do people know of your faith by the way you live? What can you do to demonstrate your trust in God when life is good and you are prospering? How can you live your faith during tough times?

Endurance (2:1-4; 3:1-19; 4:11-16; 6:4-12; 10:19-39; 12:1-29). It wasn't easy to be a Christian in the first century, especially a Jewish Christian. Believers who had come to faith in Christ out of Judaism were ostracized by their families and persecuted by the religious leaders. When the Romans began to persecute Christians, they seized their property, imprisoned and tortured them. These believers felt tremendous pressure to denounce Christianity, to combine Christian teachings with Judaism, or to be secret believers. Hebrews, therefore, warns against apostasy and against slipping back into old habits and beliefs; the message of this book challenges believers to endure to the end.

Importance for Today. Faith enables Christians to face trials. Genuine faith includes the commitment to stay true to God when we are under fire. Endurance builds character and leads to victory.

You can have victory in your trials if you keep your focus on Christ and don't give up. What pressures do you feel to return to an old way of life or belief-system? What can you do to keep your eyes on Christ and not on your struggles? Stay true to Christ, and pray for endurance.

VITAL STATISTICS

Purpose: To present the superiority of Christ over Judaism.

Author: Unknown. Paul, Luke, Barnabas, Apollos, Silas, Priscilla, and others have been suggested because the name of the author is not given in the biblical text itself. Whoever it was speaks of Timothy as a "brother" (13:23).

To whom written: Hebrew Christians (perhaps second-generation Christians, see 2:3) who may have been considering a return to Judaism, perhaps because of immaturity stemming from a lack of understanding of biblical truths; and all believers in Christ.

Date written: Probably before the destruction of the temple in Jerusalem in A.D. 70, because the religious sacrifices and ceremonies are referred to in the book, but no mention is made of the temple's destruction.

Setting: These Jewish Christians were probably undergoing fierce persecution, socially and physically, both from Jews and from Romans. Christ had not returned to establish his kingdom, and the people needed to be reassured that Christianity was true and that Jesus was indeed the Messiah.

Key verse: "The Son is the radiance of God's glory and the exact representation of his being, sustaining all things by his powerful word. After he had provided purification for sins, he sat down at the right hand of the Majesty in heaven" (1:3 NIV).

Key people: Old Testament men and women of faith (chapter 11).

Special features: Although Hebrews is called a "letter" (13:22), it has the form and the content of a sermon.

OUTLINE

I. THE SUPERIORITY OF CHRIST (1:1–10:18)

- A. Christ is greater than the angels
- B. Christ is greater than Moses
- C. Christ is greater than the Old Testament priesthood
- D. The new covenant is greater than the old

II. THE SUPERIORITY OF FAITH (10:19–13:25)

HEBREWS 1

JESUS CHRIST IS GOD'S SON / 1:1-3

Hebrews tells us that God spoke through many prophets at many times and in various ways. But all the messages, through the variety of God's spokespersons, simply set the stage for the unveiling of God's Son, who is the "radiance of God's glory" (1:3 NIV).

The relationship between Christianity and Judaism became a critical issue in the early church. Hebrews 1:1–10:18 presents a series of sections showing how Christ is superior to key aspects of Judaism. The book of Hebrews carefully explains how Christ is superior to angels (who gave the Old Testament law), Moses, and high priests. The new covenant is shown to be far superior to the old. In chapter 1, Christ is presented as the ultimate and superior revelation of God. This can greatly encourage us and help us avoid drifting away from our faith in Christ.

1:1-2 **In the past God spoke to our forefathers through the prophets at many times and in various ways, but in these last days he has spoken to us by his Son.**NIV The writer divides history into two segments or ages: before Christ and after Christ. He calls the time before Christ *the past.* During that time, God used prophets to reveal his message to the people. These messages are recorded in the Old Testament (because they were part of the "old covenant"). But Jesus initiated a new era (a "new covenant") between God and people. The author describes this new era as *these last days.* Translators of the Septuagint (the Greek translation of the Hebrew Old Testament) used this phrase, "last days," to describe the messianic era. The Jews of Jesus' day believed that the Messiah would usher in God's kingdom. They were hoping for political and military power that would free them from Roman rule and bring back the days of glory under David and Solomon. They believed that the Messiah would bring peace to the world. The writer of Hebrews reported that Jesus Christ, the Messiah, initiated this new, long-awaited age. But Jesus brought spiritual peace and a spiritual kingdom. Jesus, the Messiah, has already begun his kingdom on earth in the hearts of his followers.

In the past, God spoke through the *forefathers*—the readers'

Jewish ancestors, the patriarchs, and all the people who lived before Christ who had put their faith in the one true God. The *prophets* include special spokespersons for God who wrote many Old Testament books, as well as key people who did not write (such as Abraham, Isaac, and Jacob). These prophets revealed what they learned about God. Second Peter 1:20-21 explains that believers today can trust the prophets' words: "First of all you must understand this, that no prophecy of scripture is a matter of one's own interpretation, because no prophecy ever came by human will, but men and women moved by the Holy Spirit spoke from God" (NRSV). God used these prophets as his mouthpiece to deliver his message.

The original Jewish readers of the book would have remembered that God had used many approaches to send his messages *at many times and in various ways* to people during Old Testament times. God had spoken to Isaiah in visions (Isaiah 6), to Jacob in a dream (Genesis 28:10-22), and to Abraham and Moses personally (Genesis 18; Exodus 31:18). God had taught Jeremiah through object lessons (Jeremiah 13) and had taught the people through a prophet's marriage (Hosea 1–3). Elsewhere, God had revealed his direction to the people through a pillar of cloud and a pillar of fire (Exodus 13:21) and had guided them in decision making through the Urim and Thummim (see Exodus 28:30; Numbers 27:21).

The Jews who lived during the time of Christ would not find it difficult to believe that God was still revealing his will; however, many could not believe that God would speak *by his Son.* The same God who spoke through the forefathers had now *spoken* through Christ. Thus, there is continuity between old and new times. In the Old Testament, the revelation of God's nature was intermittent. It created an expectation that God was still going to reveal himself more fully. The prophets spoke of the coming Messiah and his kingdom; Jesus is that Messiah and he initiated God's kingdom. The Jews accepted the Old Testament, but most rejected Jesus as the long-awaited Messiah.

The recipients of this letter were Jewish Christians. They were well versed in Scripture and had professed faith in Christ. Through doubt, persecution, or false teaching, however, many were in danger of giving up their Christian faith and returning to Judaism. This letter to the Hebrews shows that going back to an inferior system would be foolish. Jesus Christ not only fulfills the promises and prophecies of the Old Testament, but he also is better than everything in the Jewish system. Jesus completed and fulfilled the message that was originally brought by the prophets and forefathers. When we know Christ, we have all we need to be saved from our sin and to have a perfect relationship with God. Jesus is not just another prophet; he is the perfect expression of God. God will never need to send another divine messenger because Jesus faithfully revealed everything about God that we need to know for salvation.

THE ULTIMATE AUTHORITY
God revealed himself by speaking through his Son. In our day, when tolerance is the cry from every corner, any claim for religious authority meets stubborn resistance. Hebrews claims that God spoke through his Son as the complete revelation of himself. When Jesus was revealed in his true glory at the Transfiguration (see Matthew 17:1-13), Moses and Elijah appeared with him. Jews regarded Moses and Elijah as the two greatest prophets. Moses represented the law, and Elijah represented the prophets. These two men had performed many miracles and were great leaders. Yet, God's voice from heaven said, "You are My beloved Son, in whom I am well pleased" (Mark 1:11 NKJV). Jesus Christ should be your highest authority for faith and daily living. Don't allow any religious leader or teaching to diminish the words of Christ.

God promised everything to the Son as an inheritance, and through the Son he created the universe.[NLT] The phrase "God promised everything to the Son as an inheritance" (literally, "heir of all things") refers to Jesus as an heir who will take his position as ruler of the new kingdom. Referring to Christ as the heir gives him the highest honor and position. This passage alludes to the royal Son of Psalm 2:8. In Psalm 2, the Son asks God for the nations to be given to him as an inheritance. Here Christ receives not only the nations, but all creation. Although God controls the world, he allows Satan to work. Satan, called the ruler of this world (John 12:31; 2 Corinthians 4:4; Ephesians 2:2), will continue his evil until the final day when Christ will throw him into the lake of fire (Revelation 20:10).

The poetical descriptions of the Son in 1:2 and 1:3 may have come from an early church hymn. The hymn celebrates Christ as our mediator who speaks to us from God and about God. In these two verses, Hebrews presents seven affirmations of Christ's deity:

1. Christ as heir of all things (1:2)
2. Christ as creator of the world (1:2)
3. Christ as the radiance of God's glory (1:3)
4. Christ as the representation of God's being (1:3)
5. Christ as the sustainer of the world (1:3)

6. Christ as the purifier of people's sins (1:3)
7. Christ as King over all (1:3)

Jesus worked with God to create the world: *through the Son he made the universe and everything in it* (see also John 1:2; 1 Corinthians 8:6; Colossians 1:15-16). Early Jewish Christians interpreted the role of Wisdom in Proverbs 8:22-31 as referring to Jesus' work. Jesus was active at the beginning of time as the agent of creation, and he will act at the end of time as the heir (see Psalm 2:8; Romans 8:17; Galatians 4:7). In the end, the world will be made perfect. Jesus will destroy all the works of evil and will reign over the world that he created.

STRESSFUL TIMES
Jesus was God's agent in creating the world: "For by Him all things were created" (Colossians 1:16 NKJV). As followers of Christ, we may give easy assent to this truth but deny it in practice. We may believe that Christ knows and controls the laws of heaven (pertaining to salvation and spiritual growth), but we may act each day as though our financial, family, or medical problems are beyond his reach. If Jesus could create the universe, then no part of life is out of his control. Do not exclude Jesus' wisdom and the Bible's guidance in your complex problems of life. No expert, professor, doctor, lawyer, or financial adviser knows more about your ultimate security and well-being than Jesus does. Go first to God for advice. Talk to him in prayer and listen to him in his Word. He can sustain you in times of stress. From that perspective you can evaluate all the other wisdom and help made available to you.

1:3 **The Son is the radiance of God's glory and the exact representation of his being.**NIV The writer describes Jesus *(the Son)* as *the radiance of God's glory.* In Greek, the word "radiance" *(apaugasma)* can describe a reflection of what is external or of what is internal. With Jesus, both are true, for his radiance perfectly reveals God's glory. Underneath Jesus' human appearance as a Jewish carpenter-turned-preacher was the glory of God. Jesus had said to one of his disciples, "Don't you know me, Philip, even after I have been among you such a long time? Anyone who has seen me has seen the Father. How can you say, 'Show us the Father'? Don't you believe that I am in the Father, and that the Father is in me? The words I say to you are not just my own. Rather, it is the Father, living in me, who is doing his work" (John 14:9-10 NIV). Jesus does more than merely reflect God, he *is* God. Therefore, he makes God's essence and nature clear to us (John 1:18). Furthermore, Christ radiates divine glory

(2 Corinthians 4:4). He is not a copy, but the very embodiment of God's nature. He gives us "the light of the knowledge of the glory of God" (2 Corinthians 4:6).

Not only is Jesus the radiance of God's glory, but he is also *the exact representation of his being.* Jesus is God himself—the very God who spoke in Old Testament times. The Greek word for "being" *(hypostasis)* means the very substance of God; the Greek word for "exact representation" *(character)* was used in ancient times to express an imprint, an image. Thus, Jesus is the visible expression of God's invisible being. We get a perfect picture of God when we look at Christ (John 1:18). In other words, Jesus explains God; he came to the world and portrayed God to people by his words and actions. No one can know God apart from Christ because we know God by knowing Christ. God reveals himself through Jesus (see John 1:1; 2 Corinthians 4:4; Philippians 2:6; Colossians 1:15). The prophets could only tell God's people what they saw and heard. Jesus was God himself—his message was firsthand.

He sustains everything by the mighty power of his command.[NLT] Christ not only created the universe, he also *sustains* it (Colossians 1:17). He does this by preserving and delivering the universe until he will inherit it (see commentary on 1:1-2). Christ spoke the world into existence (Genesis 1–2), and he supports the world with his omnipotent word (see 11:3). Christ does not physically hold up the world, as was said of the mythical Atlas, but he guides the world toward its appointed future—the time when he will receive it as his inheritance (1:2). Because Christ sustains everything, nothing in creation is independent from him. All things are held together in a coherent or logical way, sustained and upheld, prevented from dissolving into chaos. In him alone and by his word, we find the unifying principle of all life. He is transcendent over all other powers.

After he had provided purification for sins, he sat down at the right hand of the Majesty in heaven.[NIV] This phrase capsulizes the author's two main themes about Christ—his sacrifice and his exaltation. Jesus cleansed his people from the ugly stain of sin. Sin destroys our ability to know or approach God, but when God purifies us from our sins, he cleanses our record. He regards us as though we had never sinned and clothes us in the righteousness of Christ himself (2 Corinthians 5:21). Jesus *provided purification for sins.* This statement reveals the central theme of the letter: Christ's superior sacrifice for sins. No sacrifice for sin could be greater than the sacrifice offered by the Creator—his death on a cross. Jesus cleansed the world from the domination of sin and took the penalty for our individual sins by dying in our place. No other penalty needs to be paid. We can be completely clean because of what Jesus has done.

After paying that penalty with his death on the cross, Christ *sat down.* This signifies that the work was complete and portrays his exalted position. Earthly priests would stand and keep offering sacrifices. Their work was never finished. Christ's sacrifice was final and complete. Quoting from Psalm 110:1, the writer combined two Old Testament thoughts expressing God's greatness *(the Majesty in heaven)* and Christ's position *(at the right hand).* To be seated at the "right hand" of a monarch was to be "second in command"—the literal "right-hand man." This gives a picture of Christ's power and authority over heaven and earth (see also Mark 16:19; Romans 8:34). Psalm 110:1 is a crucial text and provides a guiding force in this book. Psalm 110:1 is the only place in the Bible where anyone else besides God is described as enthroned in power. This verse became a main text for the early church to be used as an argument for the deity of Christ. To Jews, the description of Christ at God's right hand would be more persuasive as a symbol of Christ's authority and power than even the Resurrection. This is why Jesus spoke these words to Caiaphas just prior to his death and resurrection: "You will see the Son of Man sitting at the right hand of the Mighty One and coming on the clouds of heaven" (Matthew 26:64 NIV).

FORGIVEN
The book of Hebrews links God's saving power with his creative power. In other words, the power that brought the universe into being and that keeps it operating is the very power that removes (provides purification for) our sins. God created us, maintains us, and can forgive us. No sin is too big for the Ruler of the universe to forgive. He can and will forgive us when we come to him through his Son. Be honest with God; confess your sins to him. He will forgive and cleanse (see 1 John 1:9).

GOD'S SON COMPARED TO THE ANGELS / 1:4-14

Angels, likened to the wind or flames of fire, are servants of Christ. They play a vital role in today's world as ministering spirits sent to serve those who have accepted God's salvation. God the Father calls Jesus Christ his one and only Son, and he orders angels to worship his Son. If God, who is above all, gives such praise to Jesus Christ, how can we praise him any less?

WHAT DID JESUS DO TO OUR SINS?

When we confess a sin to God, he forgives and forgets it because of Jesus' sacrifice. We never need to remember or confess that sin again. When God forgives a sin, it remains forgiven forever.

He took them away	2:17
He forgot them	8:12; 10:17
He freed us from sin's penalty	9:15
He removed sin's power over us	9:26
He offered himself as a sacrifice	10:12
He offered himself as an offering	10:18
He forgives our sins	10:19

Christ is highly exalted. His throne will last forever and ever (1:8); the earth and heaven will perish, but he will remain (1:11); he will sit highly honored at God's right hand with his many enemies serving as his footstool (1:13).

Since Christ is far superior to all the angels who worship him, we should also give him first place in our lives.

1:4 **This shows that the Son is far greater than the angels, just as the name God gave him is greater than their names.**[NLT] The writer here begins a series of arguments proving Jesus' superiority over angels. Angels are spiritual beings created by God and are under his authority (Colossians 1:16). They help carry out God's work on earth by bringing God's messages to people (Luke 1:26; Revelation 14:6-12), protecting God's people (Daniel 6:22; Matthew 18:10), offering encouragement (Genesis 16:7ff.), giving guidance (Exodus 14:19), carrying out punishment (2 Samuel 24:16), patrolling the earth (Zechariah 1:9-14), and fighting the forces of evil (2 Kings 6:16-18; Revelation 20:1-2). Other popular Jewish teachings during New Testament times said that angels brought people's requests to God and interceded for them. Because of all these beliefs about angels, the Jews honored them highly. However, Hebrews emphasizes that Christ and his work far surpass angels and their work. Jesus created the world, sustains the world, reveals God's glory, makes God known, and provides the perfect sacrifice for sins. No angel can accomplish any of these things.

Christ is far greater than the angels because *the name God gave him is far greater than their names.* The "name" he received is contrasted with the angels' names. In that time and culture, names captured the essence of a person (see Genesis 27:36). The "name"

Jesus received was "Son." This name identified that his relationship with God, his power to forgive people's sins, and his ability to make God known were far superior to any other created being's. The name "angel" *(angelos)* simply means "messenger." And some of the angels who are actually named in Scripture have names that are inferior to Christ's name. "Gabriel" means "Man (or strength) of God" (see Daniel 8:16; 9:21; Luke 1:19, 26), and "Michael" means "Who is like God?" (see Daniel 10:13, 21; 12:1; Jude 1:9; Revelation 12:7). Both names give glory to God.

Of one thing we can be sure: Angels never draw attention to themselves but ascribe glory to God and press His message upon the heavens as a delivering and sustaining word of the highest order.
Billy Graham

1:5 **For to which of the angels did God ever say, "You are my Son; today I have become your Father"? Or again, "I will be his Father, and he will be my Son"?**NIV Beginning here in 1:5 and continuing through 1:13, the writer strings together seven quotations from the Old Testament: (1) Psalm 2:7, (2) 2 Samuel 7:14, (3) Deuteronomy 32:43 (v. 6), (4) Psalm 104:4 (v. 7), (5) Psalm 45:6-7 (vv. 8-9), (6) Psalm 102:25-27 (vv. 10-12), (7) Psalm 110:1 (v. 13). All but two are found in the Greek Psalter, the hymnbook of the synagogue and early church. The writer introduces two quotations from the Psalms by asking the rhetorical question, *For to which of the angels did God ever say. . . .* The answer is, of course, he never said this to any angel.

The first quote, *You are my Son; today I have become your Father,* comes from a coronation psalm. Psalm 2:7 was also quoted at Jesus' baptism (Mark 1:11) and transfiguration (Mark 9:7), as well as in 2 Peter 1:17. The psalm was originally sung at the crowning of a new king (perhaps originally of David or Solomon). This psalm was used for centuries of Jewish history as a song of worship. Jewish rabbis attached a deeper meaning to the song—one that looked forward to the coming Messiah. Because the Messiah fulfilled the promises of the Old Testament, the writer understands that these Old Testament verses apply to Christ. The present tense, "you are" *(ei su),* describes a continuing relationship. Jesus did not become God's Son but was always God's Son. The Father acknowledged him as his Son in a special way when Jesus was enthroned on high. The Bible calls angels "sons of God" (Job 1:6; 2:1), but not *the* Son of God. No angel or person other than Christ could ever receive that honor. There are two common interpretations for the word "today": Either it could refer to Christ's glorification (he has been elevated, honored, and seated at the right hand of God), or this honor was based on Jesus' death and resurrection. The first choice is preferable because it continues the thought that Jesus is at the right hand of the Father.

God spoke the words, *I will be his Father, and he will be my Son,* to David with respect to Solomon (2 Samuel 7:14; 1 Chronicles 17:13). Although Solomon fulfilled these words, Hebrews illustrates that Christ ultimately and completely fulfilled them. In John 7:42, the religious leaders discussed Jesus' authority, and they alluded to this passage in Samuel, which said that the Messiah must come from David's family. The titles of "Father" and "Son" reveal a distinction between these two members of the Godhead. They also reveal the unique relationship of the Son to the Father. Although a unity exists in the Trinity, a distinction between the members exists, too. The question implies that no angel can claim such a relationship.

1:6 And again, when God brings his firstborn into the world, he says, "Let all God's angels worship him."[NIV] Some interpret "again" as the time when God will bring Jesus into the world a second time, namely, the Second Coming. The intent here, however, is not to paint a picture of the end times but to show Christ's superiority over the angels in his incarnation. Christ is now exalted and worshiped by angels. Therefore, the adverb "again" is better understood as marking this as a further quotation that extols the preeminence of Christ.

The writer says that *God [brought] his firstborn into the world.* In Jewish families the firstborn son held the place of highest privilege and responsibility. As firstborn of creation, Jesus surpasses any created being. The Jewish Christians reading this message would have understood the reference to God's firstborn. He had the title and rights that came with being the Son of God; thus, he was greater than any other created being. Jesus has all of the priority and authority of the firstborn prince in a king's household. (See discussion on "assembly of God's firstborn" in 12:23.)

Christ is greater than any created being. While in English the word "firstborn" conveys nothing more than the eldest child, this title in Greek *(prototokos)* signifies that Christ is preeminent over all creation (see Colossians 1:15-16) and therefore worthy of worship. Because of this, the writer had no problem ascribing the quote *"Let all God's angels worship him"* to Christ.

This is a portion of Deuteronomy 32:43, from the "Hymn of Moses," found in the Septuagint (the ancient Greek version of the Old Testament). It is not found in the Hebrew version or English translations based on the Hebrew. All quotes in Hebrews are from the Septuagint. The original Old Testament text "him" refers to the Father. Because only God should be worshiped, this verse is further proof that Jesus has a greater position than the angels—he is God. No angel can claim this status either. Rather, "all" of the angels will bow in worship—not a few, not just the underlings, but every one.

GREATER THAN ANGELS
The name Jesus inherited that is superior is "Son of God." This name, given to him by his Father, is greater than the names and titles of the angels. In many of the early churches false teachers taught that God could be approached only through angels. Instead of worshiping God directly, followers of these heretics revered angels. Hebrews clearly denounces such teaching as false. (Some thought of Jesus as the highest angel of God, but Jesus is not a superior angel.) In any case, angels are not to be worshiped (see Colossians 2:18; Revelation 19:1-10). We should not regard any spiritual beings, spiritual guides, intermediaries, or authorities as greater than Christ. Jesus is God. He alone deserves our worship. He alone should be our ultimate leader.

1:7 **In speaking of the angels he says, "He makes his angels winds, his servants flames of fire."**[NIV] This quote from Psalm 104:4 depicts the angels as "messengers." Describing angels as winds and flames of fire continues to show Jesus' superiority by contrasting his everlasting glory with the temporality of the angels. Angels are like the wind and fire in that they are not eternal; they change and they are subject to God. "Wind" and "fire" serve as metaphors to illustrate the angels' status as created beings and also their potentially destructive power. Properly utilized, wind and fire provide useful service.

1:8-9 **But about the Son he says, "Your throne, O God, will last for ever and ever, and righteousness will be the scepter of your kingdom. You have loved righteousness and hated wickedness; therefore God, your God, has set you above your companions by anointing you with the oil of joy."**[NIV] These words celebrate the Son's status. Again, the writer quoted a psalm (45:6-7) that had its origin in the Jewish court. This psalm would be sung at a Jewish king's wedding. In celebrating the high office of king, the people referred to the king as "a god." This title was used out of respect for the king's position as God's representative. The title that the people imperfectly placed on the Jewish king was perfectly true of Christ.

That his *throne . . . will last for ever and ever* stresses Jesus' exaltation. Christ has an eternal throne, and his reign is characterized by *righteousness* because he has *loved righteousness and hated wickedness.* A Jewish king needed these attributes and emotions in order to maintain the throne. But only Christ has such perfect love for righteousness and hatred for evil. Since a throne symbolizes an enduring kingdom or dynasty, these verses look forward to a time when God's enemies will be made into his footstool (see commentary on 1:13).

The full flood of my life is not in bodily health, not in external happenings, not in seeing God's work succeed, but in the perfect understanding of God, and in the communion with him that Jesus himself had. Be rightly related to God, find your joy there, and out of you will flow rivers of living water.

Oswald Chambers

PROPHET, PRIEST, AND KING

So far Hebrews has presented three offices of Jesus: prophet, priest, and king. These offices show his leadership and his superiority over all created beings.

- Jesus as Prophet—He reveals the exact nature of God (1:2-3).
- Jesus as Priest—He purified us by his atoning work (1:3).
- Jesus as King—He reigns over all creation (1:3, 8-9).

Jesus deserves honor as our ultimate authority. We can give him our highest regard by:

- Obeying his Word (2:1).
- Persevering in our faith (12:1-6).
- Enduring hardship (12:7).
- Loving fellow believers (13:1).
- Imitating solid Christian leaders (13:7).
- Worshiping him with devotion (13:15).

God has set Jesus *above* his *companions* in two ways: (1) Jesus was set above human messengers because only he was the Anointed One, the greatest mouthpiece of God (see 1:1). No prophet, priest, or king could claim the authority that Jesus possessed. (2) Jesus was set above angelic messengers. Christ is superior to any other spiritual being. These qualities allowed Jesus to be anointed with *the oil of joy.* The Jews would anoint their kings and their priests with holy oil. This description, therefore, carries a double meaning, revealing that Jesus had been anointed king *and* priest. He was able to be a sacrifice for sins because he was perfect and hated all wickedness. God expressed joy in anointing the perfect king and priest.

1:10-12 **And: "You, Lord, in the beginning laid the foundation of the earth, and the heavens are the work of Your hands. They will perish, but You remain; and they will all grow old like a garment; like a cloak You will fold them up, and they will be changed. But You are the same, and Your years will not fail."**NKJV These words of Psalm 102:25-27 were originally used of God the Father, but are used here to describe God the Son. Jesus is both the Son and Creator. He is eternal and sovereign and therefore worthy of praise.

Angels were created and can change. Jesus, on the other hand, is the Creator who cannot change. Jesus existed before creation and time, and God created the world through him (as seen in 1:2). Hebrews celebrates the permanence of Christ by contrasting him with the temporary nature of the world. The world seems permanent to us, but it will one day *grow old like a garment.* Every piece of clothing wears out, grows old, and needs to be changed or replaced. The world, like the clothing, will be folded up and *changed.* Christ, however, will never wear out. His place is permanent, and he will replace this fading world with a new heaven and new earth (see Hebrews 12:26-28; Revelation 21).

> The longest time man has to live on earth has no more proportion to eternity than a drop of dew has to the ocean.
> *D. L. Moody*

What does it mean that Christ is changeless *(You are the same)*? It means that Christ's character will never change. He persistently shows his love to us. He is always fair, just, and merciful. Be thankful that Christ is changeless, because he will always help you when you need it and offer forgiveness when you fall.

ROLLED UP

That the earth and the heavens will be "folded up" reveals that the earth is not permanent or indestructible (a position held by many Greek and Roman philosophies). God placed Jesus in authority over all of creation, so we dare not treat any created object or earthly resource as more important than he is. When we spend more time on ourselves than on serving Christ, we treat ourselves (his creation) as being more important than our Creator. When we regard our finances, rather than our faith in Christ, as the basis for security, we give higher status to an earthly resource than we do to God. Rather than trusting in changeable and temporary resources, trust in God, who is eternal.

Because the readers of Hebrews (Jews who had become Christians) had experienced the rejection of their fellow Jews, they often felt isolated. Many were tempted to exchange the changeless Christ for their familiar old faith. The book of Hebrews warns them not to do this. Christ is our only security in a changing world. If we trust him, we are absolutely secure because we stand on the firmest foundation in the universe. The famous hymn "My Hope Is Built on Nothing Less," written by Edward Mote, captures this truth: "On Christ, the solid Rock, I stand—all other ground is sinking sand."

1:13 But to which of the angels has He ever said: "Sit at My right hand, till I make Your enemies Your footstool"?[NKJV] Hebrews continues to show how the high position of Christ makes him superior to the angels. Here we see the same rhetorical style as in 1:5. Although we don't know the original occasion of this statement (quoted from Psalm 110:1), popular teaching in Jesus' day held that the psalm was messianic. Jesus will triumph over all his enemies because he is instructed to *sit at My [God's] right hand.* This victory belongs to Christ and not to any created being. The greatest archangels stand before God (Luke 1:19; Revelation 8:2), but none are allowed to sit, for sitting next to God indicates equality.

God promised to make Jesus' enemies a *footstool*—they are under his feet. This is a picture showing Christ as completely victorious over his enemies. Does God place Jesus' enemies under Jesus' feet because Jesus is not capable of doing it himself? No. This action shows that God approved of Jesus' work. The two work together for a common purpose. Jesus' honor cannot be superseded, and no angel comes close to this honor. The angels, as seen in 1:14, serve God and Jesus.

> The angels are the dispensers and administrators of the divine beneficence toward us; they regard our safety, undertake our defense, direct our ways, and exercise a constant solicitude that no evil befall us. *John Calvin*

1:14 Therefore, angels are only servants—spirits sent to care for people who will inherit salvation.[NLT] Christ possesses the right to sit at God's right hand (1:13), while the angels are his *servants.* Jesus is much greater than the angels, who serve him. The angels are ministering *spirits* who are *sent from God to care for those who will receive salvation.* The angels' purpose is to serve; Christ's purpose is to reign. Angels are higher than people in creation's hierarchy (see Psalm 8:4), being created first and with higher function. But God has reversed the order and instructed the angels to serve his people. The fact that angels serve us should encourage us when we feel unloved or forgotten. Because God loves us, he dispatches his angels to help us.

CHRIST AND THE ANGELS

Hebrews quotes from the Old Testament repeatedly to demonstrate Christ's greatness in comparison to the angels. This audience of first-century Jewish Christians had developed an unbalanced belief in angels. Christ's lordship is affirmed without showing disrespect to God's valued angelic messengers.

Hebrews	*Old Testament*	*How Christ is superior to angels*
1:5-6	Psalm 2:7	Christ is called "Son" of God, a title never given to an angel.
1:7, 14	Psalm 104:4	Angels are important but are still only servants under God.
1:8-9	Psalm 45:6	Christ's kingdom is forever.
1:10	Psalm 102:25	Christ is the Creator of the world.
1:13	Psalm 110:1	Christ is given unique honor by God.

Salvation has both present and future meaning. Hebrews stresses the role of salvation in the future sense when referring to "those who will receive salvation." Salvation extends beyond the act at the cross or at our conversion. "Salvation" as used here describes what will happen when salvation culminates in eternal life in the new heaven and new earth. Jesus' victory over all his enemies will be shared by the coheirs, namely those who put their faith in Jesus and his work and follow him (Romans 13:11; 1 Peter 1:5).

HEBREWS 2

WARNING AGAINST DRIFTING AWAY / 2:1-4

Highway travelers dislike the sudden appearance of warning signs, but travel could be dangerous without the warnings. The author of Hebrews presents a series of warning signs throughout the book. They aren't flashing lights, but they shout "danger!" If we do not heed the warning, we will not escape. Christ announced salvation, his followers confirmed it, and God testified to it.

2:1 **We must pay more careful attention, therefore, to what we have heard, so that we do not drift away.**[NIV] The author's purpose for writing Hebrews was not primarily to provide true theology or proper doctrine, although those are included. Instead, the purpose was to encourage Jewish Christians not to turn away from the faith. If these Christians were not careful, pressure from nonbelieving Jews or other influences could lead them away from Christ. Because Christ surpasses angels and other messengers of the Old Testament (1:1-3), the writer challenged the Hebrew Christians to remember Christ's teachings and the Christian message—*what we have heard.*

A boat might drift and be carried downstream past safe harbor if the crew members neglect to watch their position. Just as a boat can drift away, so a Christian can *drift away* from Christ. These words encouraged the readers to *pay more careful attention* so as not to lose their bearings. To what were they to pay attention? "To what we have heard," referring to the message of salvation through Jesus Christ alone. The Greek word for "pay careful attention" *(prosechein)* encourages readers to consider their ways and also to act on what they have heard.

Such careful attention requires work, but this labor keeps believers from drifting away from Christ. Too many people have a casual attitude toward Christian truth today. Do we pay as close attention to Christian truth as we do to our stocks or the sports results?

Drifting is always easier than maintaining the same position. Christians today also have subtle influences that could cause us to drift from Christ. We must pay careful attention to our faith and be prepared against temptations. We might think we are well anchored in our faith, but a hidden, slow-moving current of temptation or harmful attitudes could carry us away from shore without our even noticing it. Such change happens gradually and undetected. This message of Hebrews is appropriate for Christians today: Pay attention!

DRIFTERS

The book of Hebrews calls readers to pay attention to the truth they have heard so that they won't drift away into false teachings. How do Christians drift away?

- We may become careless or complacent in our devotion to Christ.
- We may backslide into sin we formerly had rejected.
- We may compromise our morals and disobey Christ's teaching.
- We may neglect Christian service and thus become inactive Christians.

The currents of temptation pull strongly at Christians. In order to resist, they must pay attention to Christ. Listening to him means not merely hearing, but also obeying and taking action on what God calls us to do (see James 1:22-25). We must listen carefully and be ready to carry out his instructions. Don't become a drifter.

2:2 **For if the message spoken by angels was binding, and every violation and disobedience received its just punishment.**NIV
Verses 2-4 explain why Christians should pay careful attention to their faith. If disregard of Moses' law brought punishment, then disregard of the gospel would bring even far greater punishment.

"The message spoken by angels" refers to the Old Testament law. The account of angels delivering God's law and putting it into effect was part of Jewish and early-Christian dogma (see Galatians 3:19). Although the book of Exodus does not mention angels, the Jews believed that God worked through angels to give Moses the Ten Commandments. Stephen, in his speech before his death, said, "You who have received the law that was put into effect through angels . . . have not obeyed it" (Acts 7:53 NIV). Angels, servants of God (see 1:14), brought God's message to the people who lived during Old Testament times. This message did not originate with angels, but with God—the one for whom the angels exist. God gave the law to govern the lives of Old Testament believers.

The Jews understood that the law *was binding,* meaning it was valid and should be obeyed. The word "if" does not indicate doubt, but means "because." Those who believed God and obeyed his instructions received his blessing, while those who rebelled discovered that *every violation and disobedience received its just punishment* (see Leviticus 26). Throughout the Old Testament, God enforced these laws by blessing people who followed him and condemning people who rejected him.

2:3-4 So what makes us think we can escape if we ignore this great salvation?[NLT] The warnings against drifting away from the faith must be heeded. The writer urged these Jewish Christians not to turn away from their faith. If they did, God's judgment on them would be as real as the judgment that had come to Old Testament believers who had drifted from God's way.

The argument in verses 2-4 goes as follows:

- The Old Testament law spoken by angels was binding on God's people.
- Those who rejected the law received just punishment.
- Christ, God's Son, is far above the angels (explained in chapter 1).
- The message of salvation that Christ brought came from God and surpasses the message of the law, for it fulfills the law and brings true forgiveness.
- Those who reject the gospel *ignore this great salvation,* and therefore will receive even greater punishment. They have rejected the only way of salvation.
- Those who are indifferent to the message of salvation will not *escape* punishment.

As Christ surpasses angels, so Christ's message surpasses their message (see 1:1-3). Old Testament believers who followed God received blessings, and those who disobeyed God received punishment. If that was true for the promise brought by angels, then no one who is indifferent to the salvation Christ offers will escape God's punishment. How can people be indifferent to God's message? They might ignore it; they might hear but fail to listen and understand it; or they might listen and accept, but then fall away. Jesus warned of such attitudes toward the Good News in his parable about the sower (Matthew 13:18-22).

This salvation, which was first announced by the Lord, was confirmed to us by those who heard him. God also testified to it by signs, wonders and various miracles, and gifts of the Holy Spirit distributed according to his will.[NIV] Three witnesses prove the authenticity of *this salvation* and why the readers should not be indifferent to it:

1. *The Lord* (see also 1:2)—The Lord Jesus himself, not angels or people, *announced* this salvation (see Luke 19:9; John 4:22).

2. *Those who heard him*—Eyewitnesses to Jesus' ministry

confirmed the value of Jesus' message of salvation by handing down his teachings to other Christians. These readers (and apparently the author) had not seen Christ in the flesh. They are like us; we have not seen Jesus personally. We base our belief in Jesus on the eyewitness accounts recorded in the Bible (see John 20:29). Jesus had told his apostles, "You also must testify, for you have been with me from the beginning" (John 15:27 NIV).

3. *God . . . by signs, wonders and various miracles, and gifts of the Holy Spirit*—God himself *testified* to our great salvation. Jesus said, "For the very work that the Father has given me to finish, and which I am doing, testifies that the Father has sent me. And the Father who sent me has himself testified concerning me" (John 5:36-37 NIV). To those who had heard Jesus speak and who confirmed the gospel message, God gave the ability to do "signs, wonders and various miracles." Just as the apostles did not invent the message of the gospel, so they could not invent the accompanying miraculous signs. "Signs, wonders and various miracles" are probably used synonymously and no differentiation should be made between them (see also Acts 2:22; 2 Corinthians 12:12). These were not given by God to glorify the apostles or to awe the people. Rather, God demonstrated his power through the apostles with these extraordinary events, thereby testifying to the truth of the great salvation that the apostles proclaimed. In the book of Acts, miracles and gifts of the Spirit authenticated the gospel wherever it was preached (see Acts 9:31-42; 14:1-20). The phrase "gifts of the Holy Spirit" reveals that the gifts given to the church are meant to testify to the truth of the gospel message.

The Holy Spirit empowers every believer with one or more gifts. These gifts are *distributed according to his will.* God decides which gifts each believer should have. To use gifts effectively, we must realize that all gifts and abilities come from God and that not everyone has the same gifts nor all the gifts. We are responsible to use and sharpen our gifts, but we can take no credit for what God has freely given us. God uses these gifts to encourage and build up the church so that the church can testify of him. Paul taught that gifts build up the church, making it strong and mature (Romans 12; 1 Corinthians 12–14; Ephesians 4). When we humbly recognize our partnership in the body of Christ, we can effectively use the gifts God has given us so that we can help his kingdom grow.

In addition, when we see the gifts of the Spirit in an individual or congregation, we know that God is truly present. These gifts serve as continuing reminders to believers across the ages that the gospel of salvation is true. It has been announced and confirmed, and many testify to its truth and power even today. To drift away from this truth (2:1) would be both foolish and disastrous.

NO SURRENDER
These members of the early Christian congregation were in danger of falling away from following Jesus. They had heard the words of the gospel, but those words had not sunk in. People raised in believing churches risk the same danger today. They hear the words and more or less agree, but mental assent to Christ's leadership is insufficient to be Christ's disciple. Are you a Sunday school teacher, a small-group leader, or a club leader? Don't assume that people who comply and conform are truly committed to Christ. Get to know each person who attends your group and challenge them with the truth and implications of commitment to Christ. Don't surrender anyone to casual belief.

CHRIST CAME AS A HUMAN BEING / 2:5-18

"You can't understand a person until you've walked in his shoes," a once-popular slogan, hints at the truth of this passage. Jesus came as a human being so that we could see, in human form, what God was like. In turn, Jesus as a human being experienced the same temptations that all people experience, but he did not sin. Then, as a human being, he experienced death. Through his life on earth and sacrifice on the cross, Jesus became a brother to all mankind and a High Priest who suffered on behalf of sinful people. Through his resurrection, he has been exalted to God's right hand. We must live now by his example.

2:5 **And furthermore, it is not angels who will control the future world we are talking about.**[NLT] The phrase "the future world we are talking about" refers to the future kingdom that Christ initiated and will fully inherit at his second coming. The writer has alluded to this future world in 1:2, 8; 2:3. The future world will not be controlled by *angels,* but by Christ. Angels will continue to serve as God's servants. These words further emphasize the superiority of the Son over the angels (1:13-14). Many Jews believed that angels ruled this present world—alluding to Old Testament passages such as Deuteronomy 32:8 and Daniel 10:13; 12:1. The future world will be different, however. Believers were encouraged to place their allegiance with Christ, not with his angelic servants.

2:6-8 **But someone has testified somewhere, "What are human beings that you are mindful of them, or mortals, that you care for them? You have made them for a little while lower than the angels; you have crowned them with glory and**

honor, subjecting all things under their feet.”NRSV The writer substantiates the words of 2:5 by here quoting Psalm 8:4-6, but does not tell readers the origin of the quote. There is just the single statement: *But someone has testified somewhere.* This is a Greek idiom, and the original readers would understand that the writer was referring to the word of God. For the writer, the exact location and author were not important in order to make the point.

This psalm tells of human beings' unimportance as well as their greatness. The psalm begins, “When I look at your heavens, the work of your fingers, the moon and the stars that you have established; *what are human beings that you are mindful of them?”* (Psalm 8:3-4 NRSV). Compared to God's power and the majesty of his creation, people are insignificant. The psalm continues, however, to tell the special place of humanity: *You have crowned them with glory and honor, subjecting all things under their feet.* God crowned people with glory and honor when he created them in his image (Genesis 1:27). God also gave people the responsibility and tremendous authority of taking care of the world (Genesis 1:28). In addition, God has been *subjecting all things under their feet.* Angels are not given this authority or responsibility; God intended this key role for people. The phrase “you have made them for a little while lower than the angels” shows human superiority over all other creation, except the angels. Due to their sin, however, people failed to live up to their potential, correctly fulfill this responsibility, or wisely use their authority. We see evidence of this failure in the worldwide damage to the ecology and in the chaos in many governments.

Some commentators believe these verses do not refer to human beings, but to Christ. The NIV and NKJV translate verse 6, “What is man that you are mindful of him, [or] the son of man, that you care for him?” Jesus used the title “Son of Man” for himself (see, for example, Matthew 8:20; 9:6; 12:8, 32, 40; John 1:51). Was the writer referring to Jesus or to humans here? The NRSV above answers that question by using the term “mortals” and the pronoun “them.” But other versions leave this question open to discussion.

Although Christ ultimately rules over all things (see 1:13), the author of Hebrews probably had mankind rather than Christ in mind at this point. Four reasons support this interpretation: (1) 2:6-8 tells that people were given dominion over the world, but Satan and sin restricted that dominion—this could not be true of Christ. (2) The focus here is on humanity's superiority over creation. Christ was created “for a little while lower than the angels," but that theme is not addressed until 2:10, when the writer shows how Christ became the perfect human. (3) The phrase "son of man" is simply Hebrew parallelism reiterating the theme of the previous line, "What is man?" The title "Son of Man" is not used in the Epistles as a name for Christ. In Daniel 7:13, the "son of man" represents humanity. (4) The original meaning of the psalm clearly referred to humans. The writer was focusing on the role of humanity in order to drive home another point about the exalted Christ. The context in 2:9 makes more sense if 2:6-8 refers primarily to humanity.

We need not completely discount Jesus' role in this verse, however. The psalm quoted here originally referred to humanity and its role in creation, and the psalm was regarded as messianic. The author may have been thinking about the double meaning included in the words "son of man," showing that Jesus fulfilled the role and destiny originally commissioned to people. What humans could not do, Jesus will do.

Now in subjecting all things to them, God left nothing outside their control. As it is, we do not yet see everything in subjection to them.[NRSV] Although God gave humans the authority and responsibility to rule the world (Genesis 1:28), sin entered the world and inhibited them from fulfilling this command (Genesis 3:17-19). Since people could not live up to their God-given commission, Jesus fulfilled this commission (see 2:9).

In the Garden of Eden, God assigned Adam and Eve to rule over all the earth (Genesis 1:28-30). But they sinned, and God took away their authority over all the creation. Today everything is obviously *not* under our control. Political institutions, marriages, families, workplaces, and the environment portray the destruction and imperfection caused by sin.

> Jesus did "stoop" when He became man. And as a man He was a little lower than the angels in His humanity—although without losing in any sense His divine nature. *Billy Graham*

Romans 8 says that "the creation was subjected to frustration" (verse 20 NIV) and that "the whole creation has been groaning" (verse 22 NIV). We will not experience perfection in this life. Here we will have problems. We do not yet see Jesus reigning on earth, but we can picture him in his heavenly glory. When you are confused by present events and anxious about the future, remember Jesus' true position and authority. He is Lord of all, and one day he will rule on earth as he does now in heaven. This truth can give you stability as you face problems and temptations each day.

2:9 What we do see is Jesus, who was given a position "a little lower than the angels"; and because he suffered death for us, he is now "crowned with glory and honor." Yes, by God's grace, Jesus tasted death for everyone.[NLT] Humanity, created *lower than the angels* and "set . . . over the works of [God's] hands" (2:7 NKJV), did not fulfill its commission because of sin. While we have not seen fulfilled what the psalm writer wrote in Psalm 8, *what we do see is Jesus.* God commissioned human beings to rule over creation. Sin halted that plan but did not change it. The writer used the name "Jesus" (instead of his title, "Christ") for the first time in this verse, stressing Jesus' humanity (see also 3:1; 4:14; 6:20; 7:22; 10:19; 12:2; 12:24; 13:12). The words from the psalm previously applied only to humans are here applied to the Messiah. Jesus became human, *"lower than the angels."* He was the only one who lived the human life as intended: sinless and in perfect fellowship with God. Before Christ, the words of Psalm 8 had not been fully realized, but the words were completely fulfilled in Christ. Jesus was not made lower than the angels in his rank or position, but he is described this way because he became part of the physical world; that is, he became human.

Because of Christ's perfect life and sacrifice for sins, he is now *"crowned with glory and honor"* (see the commentary on 1:3, 13). Christ not only received these rewards for himself, but through his death, men and women can be restored to a personal relationship with God. Christ was worthy to receive these rewards *because he suffered death for us.* By way of further explanation of this death, the writer elaborated: *By God's grace, Jesus tasted death for everyone.* "God's grace" refers to the fact that God sent his Son to die for undeserving sinners (John 3:16). "Tasted" means to "come to know, to experience." Jesus lived and died physically. He did not experience a "lesser" death than any other human. Only Jesus lived a perfect life and was the necessary sacrifice for sin so that sinful humanity could fulfill the words of Psalm 8, to finally fulfill God's plan. Jesus died "for everyone in all the world," but not everyone will be saved. The only way for people to be saved and to receive God's rewards is to "believe in the Lord Jesus" (Acts 16:31 NIV).

2:10 It was fitting that God, for whom and through whom all things exist, in bringing many children to glory, should make the pioneer of their salvation perfect through sufferings.[NRSV] Christ, the perfect human, was able to fulfill what no other human was able to fulfill. "Many children" refers back to the "mortals" in 2:6-8. Although people were commissioned to rule the earth, their sin kept them from the task. Jesus' sacrifice brings his human brothers and sisters *to glory*—the glory that will one day be restored to people in the future kingdom.

Earlier the writer of Hebrews explained that creation exists through and for Christ (1:3). The same reasons given there now give God the Father this position, calling him the one *for whom and through whom all things exist.* Because everything belongs to God, he determines what sacrifice is necessary for sin. He, the creator of the world, determined what was needed for salvation.

"The pioneer of their salvation" refers to Jesus. He was the pioneer, showing the way for the rest of us. The Greek word for "pioneer" is *archegon* and can mean "founder or champion." In the Hellenistic world, the hero figure, Hercules, was called *archegon*, for he entered the world, wrestled with evil forces, and saved his people. The author may have been using the connotation of Jesus as "champion."

That God *should make [Jesus] perfect through sufferings* does not refer to Jesus' sinless state. Jesus was already perfect before he faced suffering. Instead, it refers to Jesus' perfect position before God. In God's eyes, Jesus was the perfect sacrifice for God's people, pioneering their salvation through his suffering and death. Because humans experience suffering and death, Christ became fully human and experienced these aspects of being human as well. That Christ both lived and died gives us confidence that we have a High Priest who is able to sympathize with our weakness (4:15). We have confidence that because Christ conquered death, he also can save us from death. In the Greek version of the Pentateuch, the same verb is used for "to perfect" in describing the consecration of the priests (Exodus 29:33, 35), indicating the qualifying of a person for priestly service. So here, Jesus qualifies as High Priest because he has completely fulfilled his role as Messiah.

> The perfect surrender and humiliation were undergone by Christ: perfect because He was God, surrender and humiliation because He was man. *C. S. Lewis*

2:11 **So now Jesus and the ones he makes holy have the same Father. That is why Jesus is not ashamed to call them his brothers and sisters.**[NLT] Christians are *the ones he [Jesus] makes holy.* In 2 Corinthians 5:21, the apostle Paul wrote: "God made him who had no sin to be sin for us, so that in him we might become the righteousness of God" (NIV). This action is once and for all. We have been made holy—set apart for

God's service. When we trust in Christ, we make an exchange—our sin for his righteousness. Our sin was poured into Christ at his crucifixion; his righteousness is poured into us at our conversion. This is what Christians mean by Christ's atonement for sin. God offers to trade his righteousness for our sin—something of immeasurable worth for something completely worthless. How grateful we should be for his great mercy to us (2:10). While God sees us as completely holy through the sacrifice of his Son, we must grow in our holiness as we live for God throughout our lives.

PERFECT THROUGH SUFFERING?
Jesus' suffering made him a perfect leader, or pioneer, of our salvation (see 5:8-9). Jesus did not need to suffer for his own salvation because he was God. His perfect obedience (which led him down the road of suffering) demonstrates that he was the complete sacrifice for us. Through suffering, Jesus completed the work necessary for our salvation. And through suffering, Jesus understands our weaknesses.

Our suffering can make us more sensitive servants of God. People who have known pain are able to reach out with compassion to others who hurt. "Blessed be the God . . . of all comfort, who comforts us in all our tribulation, that we may be able to comfort those who are in any trouble, with the comfort with which we ourselves are comforted by God" (2 Corinthians 1:3-4 NKJV). If you have suffered, ask God how your experience can be used to help others.

We who have been set apart for God's service, cleansed, and made holy (sanctified) by Jesus now *have the same Father* as he does because he has made us his brothers and sisters. Various psalms look forward to Christ and his work in the world. Here the writer quotes a portion of Psalm 22, a messianic psalm. Because God has adopted all believers as his children, *Jesus is not ashamed to call [us] his brothers and sisters.* The word "ashamed" may allude to Jesus' warning, "If anyone is ashamed of me and my words, the Son of Man will be ashamed of him when he comes in his glory and in the glory of the Father and of the holy angels" (Luke 9:26 NIV). Those who are not ashamed of Jesus, gladly accepting him as Savior and Lord, will find that Jesus is not ashamed to call them members of his family.

Jesus identified with us through his humanity. Now those who have been made holy by accepting Christ's sacrifice can be Christ's spiritual brothers and sisters.

2:12 For he said to God, "I will proclaim your name to my brothers and sisters. I will praise you among your assembled people."[NLT]

The next two verses give three quotations from the Old Testament to show the relationship between Jesus and believers. Jesus readily identified himself with God's people.

While on the cross, Jesus quoted from the opening words of Psalm 22 (see Matthew 27:46). These words of abandonment at the beginning of this psalm give way to words of praise at the end, quoted here. Jesus' death and humiliation on earth ended in victory, declaring *[God's] name* to those who believed, his *brothers and sisters* (2:11). To "proclaim a name" means to reveal the character of that person. Attributing these words to Jesus from this messianic psalm means that Jesus, through his humanity, revealed God's character. The phrase "among your assembled people," quoted here from the Septuagint (the Greek version of the Old Testament), has the word *ekklesia* (meaning "congregation"), the same word the New Testament translated as "church." Praise to God comes from both the Son and from those who love the Son.

FAMILY ASSURANCE

What assurance do you have that Jesus is not ashamed to call you his brother or sister?

- Jesus died in your place, as your substitute (2:9).
- Jesus faced suffering in order to provide your salvation (2:10).
- Jesus makes you holy and accepts you into his family (2:11).

You are loved. Trust Christ, take him at his word, and be assured that you are a loved and valuable part of God's family.

2:13 And again: "I will put My trust in Him." And again: "Here am I and the children whom God has given Me."NKJV These verses, originally recorded in Isaiah 8:17-18, are applied here to Christ, further showing Christ's identification with humanity. Isaiah was persecuted and his message rejected by the people. While others around him stumbled and fell away, Isaiah, his children, and his disciples remained faithful. Isaiah encouraged the people not to listen to false advice, but to God alone. Like Isaiah, Christ put his *trust* in God the Father. Christ readily accepts his relationship with *the children whom God has given* to him. These are his spiritual "children," those who are called his brothers and sisters (2:11), God's people (2:12). While he was on earth, Jesus explained his relationship to his followers, "I give them eternal life, and they shall never perish; no one can snatch them out of my hand. My Father, who has given them to me, is greater than all; no one can snatch them out of my Father's hand" (John 10:28-29 NIV). Like those faithful to God in Isaiah's day, we should stay true to Christ and ignore the advice that would distract us from following him.

LESSONS FROM CHRIST'S HUMANITY

God, in Christ, became a living, breathing human being. Hebrews presents many reasons why this is so important.

Christ is the perfect human leader	He wants to lead you.
model	He is worth imitating.
sacrifice	He died for you.
conqueror	He conquered death to give you eternal life.
High Priest	He is merciful, loving, understanding, and is intereceding for you.

2:14 **Because God's children are human beings—made of flesh and blood—the Son also became flesh and blood. For only as a human being could he die, and only by dying could he break the power of the devil, who had the power of death.**[NLT] After building his case that Christ had become a human being, the writer explained why such association and identity were important. Death is the common fear and final experience of all people, and only as a human being, *made of flesh and blood,* could Christ *die.* Ironically, to defeat death, Christ had to die—*only by dying could he break the power of the devil, who had the power of death.* His death and his return to life showed that death had been defeated: "For we know that since Christ was raised from the dead, he cannot die again; death no longer has mastery over him" (Romans 6:9 NIV).

How does the devil have "the power of death"? Why do people still die if Jesus has defeated death? Paul explained it this way: "Therefore, just as sin came into the world through one man, and death came through sin, . . . so death spread to all because all have sinned" (Romans 5:12 NRSV). Sin and death are interconnected: Sin results in death. Only by first breaking the power of sin could Christ then break the power of death. He accomplished both through his death and resurrection. In those acts, Christ dealt the final blow to both Satan and death. First John 3:8 explains, "He who does what is sinful is of the

When God's Son took on flesh, he truly and bodily took on, out of pure grace, our being, our nature, ourselves. This was the eternal counsel of the triune God. Now we are in him. Where he is, there we are too, in the Incarnation, on the Cross, and in his resurrection. We belong to him because we are in him. *Dietrich Bonhoeffer* devil, because the devil has been sinning from the beginning. The reason the Son of God appeared was to destroy the devil's work" (NIV). Although Satan still holds great power over this world, he is mortally wounded. God allows Satan to work, but limits him (see Job 1:12; 2:6; Ephesians 4:27; 6:11; 1 Timothy 3:7; James 4:7; 1 Peter 5:8-9). Just as salvation is partly realized now and will be fully realized later, in God's kingdom, so Satan is still at work but will one day be destroyed (Revelation 20:10).

2:15 **Only in this way could he set free all who have lived their lives as slaves to the fear of dying.**[NLT] People have always feared death. This fear has motivated them to exercise, to eat right, to seek medical attention, and to try to look and feel younger. This preoccupation is so prevalent that the writer describes people as being *slaves to the fear of dying.* Eventually, however, death strikes everyone; it is unavoidable. Through Christ, however, we no longer need to fear dying and death. Christ died and rose again and *only in this way could he set free* humanity. Because Jesus died and arose, we no longer need to be enslaved to the fear of dying. We know that because Jesus rose from the dead, we will also. Jesus also promised eternal life in paradise with him, and we know we will receive it. We will die physically, but we are promised new bodies and a new life in eternity with God. Thus, death becomes the gateway to a new life. To be absent from the body will mean being present with the Lord (2 Corinthians 5:8). "Where, O death, is your victory? Where, O death, is your sting? But thanks be to God! He gives us the victory through our Lord Jesus Christ" (1 Corinthians 15:55, 57 NIV).

THE GREATEST HELP

Jesus frees and delivers us, providing the greatest help of all. The powerful results of his death and resurrection give us two assurances:

1. *Christ destroys the author of death, the devil.* Satan's power has been broken and one day will be completely removed.
2. *Christ destroys the fear of death.* Christ's death and resurrection set us free from the fear of death because death has been defeated.

Every person must die, but death is not the end; instead, it is the doorway to a new life. We have assurance that we will be resurrected from the dead. All who dread death should trust Christ to bring victory. Remember that Christ will not fail you. Live without fear. Trust the Savior.

2:16 **For surely it is not angels he helps, but Abraham's descendants.**[NIV] Angels were not the objects of God's grace.

God sent Jesus to die for people, *Abraham's descendants,* who were lost in their sin (Romans 5:8). Some believe that this phrase refers only to the Jews, but Jesus had explained that it was through faith in him that people became Abraham's true descendants (John 8:37-39). Jesus was born as a Jew, a descendant of Abraham. His death and resurrection offered salvation to all of humanity—both Jews and Gentiles. The apostle Paul wrote to the Galatian believers, most of whom were Gentiles, "If you belong to Christ, then you are Abraham's offspring, heirs according to the promise" (Galatians 3:29 NRSV). "Abraham's descendants" are all who share Abraham's faith. Christ did not become an angel; he became a human in order to help humans.

2:17 **Therefore, it was necessary for him to be made in every respect like us, his brothers and sisters, so that he could be our merciful and faithful High Priest before God. Then he could offer a sacrifice that would take away the sins of the people.**NLT Jesus Christ became *like us, his brothers and sisters,* so that he could become *our merciful and faithful High Priest.* In the Old Testament, the high priest was the mediator between God and the people. The high priest's job was to regularly offer animal sacrifices according to the law and to intercede with God for forgiveness for the people's sins. The Jews understood the high priest as the one who had special duties that no other priests had. He alone could enter the Most Holy Place in the tabernacle or temple on the yearly Day of Atonement to pray to God about the sins of the nation. But Jesus' death and resurrection inaugurated a new covenant. Under the old covenant, the high priests had to go before God once a year; Jesus' death accomplished forgiveness once and for all for those who believe in him. Christ performed perfectly and completely the duties of a high priest. Thus the writer calls him our High Priest, our representative before God.

Jesus became like us *in every respect* except for the sinful nature—Jesus never shared in that part of humanity (4:15; 7:26). Only in this way could he *offer a sacrifice that would take away the sins of the people.* That sacrifice was his life. Jesus' death on the cross wiped out our sin and the grip it had on our lives. When we commit ourselves fully to Christ, we are released from sin's domination over us.

How did Jesus' sacrifice "take away" our sins? A holy God cannot overlook sin; thus, the sinfulness of humanity had to be punished. In the Old Testament, God required his people to sacrifice animals ("perfect" animals, healthy and whole) to atone for their sins. The costly sacrifice of an animal's life impressed upon the sinner the seriousness of his or her sin before God. When

JESUS, OUR HIGH PRIEST

The book of Hebrews is the only place in the New Testament where Jesus is referred to as a High Priest. The role was understood by the Hebrews reading this book because of their religious background.

Jesus is our merciful and faithful High Priest in the service of God	2:17
We are to focus our thoughts on Jesus, the High Priest, whom we confess	3:1
Jesus is our great High Priest who has gone through the heavens	4:14
Jesus, our High Priest, is able to sympathize with our weaknesses because he has been tempted as we are, but he is without sin.	4:15
Jesus did not glorify himself, but he became our High Priest by God's will.	5:5
Jesus is the author of eternal salvation, called by God as High Priest.	5:9-10
Our hope in eternity is sure, for Jesus went before us, having become a High Priest forever.	6:18-20
Jesus is the High Priest who meets our needs; he is holy, blameless, pure, set apart from sinners, and exalted above the heavens	7:26
Jesus, as our High Priest, sits at the right hand of God's throne in heaven	8:1
Jesus came as High Priest of the good things to come.	9:11

animals' blood was shed, God regarded the people's faith and obedience, cleansed them, and took away their sins. At the right time, God dealt once and for all with sin and its ultimate consequence—death and eternal separation from God. Instead of sending all humanity to eternal punishment, God took the punishment himself (Romans 8:3). Sin had to be punished, but Jesus shed his blood—gave his life—to take away our sins so that we wouldn't have to experience spiritual death. His sacrifice transforms our lives and hearts and makes us clean on the inside.

2:18 **Because he himself was tested by what he suffered, he is able to help those who are being tested.**[NRSV] As the mediator between God and humans, Jesus offers a suitable sacrifice to God in order to take away people's sin (2:17). But this verse also tells us that he is able to bring hope to people in need. Jesus came to earth as a human being; therefore, he understands our weaknesses and shows mercy to us. Because he was fully human, Jesus *himself was tested by what he suffered.* "Testing" refers to Jesus' exposure to conflicts, tensions, and suffering. The testing was not to show that he might fail, but to show his real power and strength under fire. This suffering refers not only to the Cross, but also to the testing Jesus experienced throughout his life—from Satan's temptations in the wilderness to the drops of blood he shed in prayer before his crucifixion. Having undergone all the tests and temptations of human life, Jesus *is able to help those who are being tested.*

HELP!
Knowing that Christ suffered pain and faced temptation helps us face our trials. Jesus understands our struggles because he faced them as a human being. We can trust Christ to help us survive suffering and overcome temptation. What are you facing that you need Christ to face with you? When you face trials, go to the Lord for strength and patience. Jesus understands your needs and is able to help (see 4:14-16).

HEBREWS 3

JESUS COMPARED TO MOSES / 3:1-6

Moses has always been highly revered by Jewish people, by the Christian church, and even in Hollywood movies. But Jesus should receive much more honor and glory than Moses. "The Lawgiver," Moses, served God faithfully. But Christ was much more than a servant—he was God's Son. He was put in complete charge of God's house, the church. As Christians, we are part of God's house, and Christ is in charge of us. We must recognize him as our highest authority.

3:1 Therefore, holy brothers, who share in the heavenly calling, fix your thoughts on Jesus, the apostle and high priest whom we confess.[NIV] Because Jesus was the perfect sacrifice and high priest (2:14-18), those who are Christians should remain focused on their perfect leader; that is, they should emulate his example, obey his teachings, and follow his lead. Chapter 2 tells that we are brothers and sisters along with Christ. We are *holy,* meaning we are set apart by Jesus for service to God. Because of this relationship, we *share in the heavenly calling* given to us by God (2:10). Salvation, the "heavenly calling," refers to both a present and future reality. Just as God brought the Jewish people into their promised land, so he promises to bring Christians into their promised land: heaven, which is the eternal rest (a theme discussed further in chapter 4).

> The spiritual battle, the loss of victory, is always in the thought-world.
> *Francis Schaeffer*

In 2:1, the writer warned Christians not to "drift away" from their faith. This verse gives a command that will help believers keep from drifting: *Fix your thoughts on Jesus.* This command reminds us that living for Christ takes effort. The command "fix your thoughts" comes from a strong Greek verb *(katanoesate)* meaning "to give thoughtful and diligent reflection." To avoid drifting away from Christ, we must fix our eyes on the goal. When we keep our eyes on him, we will be secure against falling into temptation or drifting into false teaching. One day, because of our heavenly calling, we will leave this world and live with Christ. Until then, we must carefully fix our thoughts on Christ—who he is and what he has done for us. The writer repeats this theme in 12:2-3, "Let us fix our eyes on Jesus, the author and perfecter of our faith, who for the joy set before him endured the cross, scorning its shame, and sat down at the right hand of the throne of God. Consider him who endured such opposition from sinful men, so that you will not grow weary and lose heart" (NIV).

Hebrews calls Jesus *apostle* and *high priest.* The term "apostle," which means "sent one," demonstrates that Jesus was sent as God's representative. Although there were many apostles, Jesus was the greatest. Although Jesus is named an apostle here, the idea that Jesus was sent from God occurs in other places in the New Testament (see, for example, John 3:13, 17; 5:36; 14:24). God sent Jesus to earth as an apostle; Jesus returned to heaven as our high priest (a role introduced in 2:17-18). He came delivering God's message to people; he returned bringing people back to God. Jesus now serves as the mediator between people and God (a theme developed in 8:6; 9:15; 12:24). These words would have been especially meaningful to Jewish Christians. For Jews, the highest human religious authority was the high priest. For Christians, the highest human religious authorities were the apostles. Jesus, God's apostle and high priest, is the ultimate authority in the church. Both of these titles demonstrate how Jesus fulfilled the Old Testament revelation to people.

TAKING THE TIME

How much do we think about Jesus? Hebrews tells us to fix our minds, ponder carefully, and focus on the true significance of Jesus. In our age of sound bites, fast food, and quick-fix solutions, very few people take time to think about anything or anyone. In Jesus we have one to whom we should listen (God's messenger), through whom we come to the Father (High Priest), and to whom we give obedience (the ruler of God's house). When you think about the significance and superiority of Jesus, how does it affect your life today? your decisions? your actions?

The word "confess" (literally "our confession") refers to our outward acknowledgement of our love for Jesus. This requires both a once-for-all decision and a daily commitment to live for Jesus, willingly showing our allegiance to him (see also 4:14). Some scholars think this refers to an early baptismal confession. Either way, it forms a binding obligation.

3:2 For he was faithful to God, who appointed him, just as Moses served faithfully and was entrusted with God's entire house.NLT Few people in Scripture have these three roles: prophet, priest, and leader. Moses was one such man, honored by the Jews. Moses *served faithfully and was entrusted with God's entire house* (see also Numbers 12:7). Moses' life and writings attest to his faithfulness. To the Jewish people, Moses was a great hero; he had led their ancestors, the Israelites, from Egyptian bondage to the border of the Promised Land. He was the prophet through whom God had given the law, and he had written the first five books of the Old Testament. "God's entire house" most likely refers to God's chosen people, among whom Moses exercised his ministry. Moses had served God faithfully, and the writer of Hebrews honored Moses by comparing him to Jesus, who *was faithful to God, who appointed him.*

> A man were better to say there is no God than say that God is unfaithful.
> *Thomas Brooks*

Jesus was "faithful" to God in that he dutifully obeyed God's will, even to death. In his humanity, Jesus struggled against the horror of death and separation from God. In the garden he prayed, "Father, if it is Your will, take this cup away from Me; nevertheless not My will, but Yours, be done" (Luke 22:42 NKJV). Jesus served God on earth, and he serves now in heaven as our "merciful and faithful High Priest" (2:17).

Jesus also was "appointed" by God. Since the Greek word for "appoint" *(poieo)* can be translated "make" or "create," Jehovah's Witnesses and other cults use this translation to support their beliefs that God created Jesus. But the verb can also mean "to make someone something"—i.e., "create a position for someone." The word should be translated "appointed" for three reasons: (1) the word was commonly used to mean appointing a person to a position (see Mark 3:14—Jesus appointed the Twelve); (2) the book of Hebrews explicitly tells about the deity of Christ, who created everything (1:2, 8-12); (3) the context compares Jesus' ministry with Moses' ministry. Just as Moses was appointed to his position, so Jesus was appointed to his position as Savior of the world. Moses led the people of Israel out of Egyptian bondage; Christ leads us out of bondage to sin. Both were faithful to the work God gave them to do.

3:3 But Jesus deserves far more glory than Moses, just as a person who builds a house deserves more praise than the house itself.NLT Moses was a human servant; Jesus is worthy of greater honor as the central figure of faith because Jesus is God himself.

HOW DOES MOSES COMPARE TO JESUS?

For further study on the Holy Spirit in Matthew, study the following passages:

Moses:	*Jesus:*
served as a prophet	served as the greatest of prophets
honored God as a servant	remains honored as God's Son
led God's people out of bondage from Egypt	leads people out of bondage to sin
administered the law	fulfills the law
received the law from angels	receives worship from angels
sinned	never sinned
died and was buried	died but rose from the dead
had a ministry that could only condemn, not save	had a ministry that brought righteousness and eternal salvation
had a fading glory	has glory that is eternal

Although Moses faithfully served in God's house (among God's people) and deserved credit for his work, Jesus *deserves far more glory* because he created that house and possesses the glory of God himself (1:3). Moses worked within the house, but Christ oversees the house.

The Jewish Christians respected Moses as one of God's greatest messengers. In order to show that Christ was superior to the old covenant, the writer both compared and contrasted Jesus and Moses. Because of Moses' faithfulness, he is worthy of great honor. But Jesus is worthy of greater honor. As human leaders go, there was no greater leader in the Old Testament than Moses. Yet Jesus has greater superiority. No human leader alive or dead deserves greater veneration than Jesus. In the Christian world today, it seems so natural for Christians to esteem great authors, preachers, pastors of huge churches, and great influential leaders, but the Bible teaches that their allegiance and ours should be to Christ, first and foremost. No amount of success, notoriety, or education can elevate a person over Christ.

Even the great leader Moses is nowhere near being Christ's equal. Moses merely followed the instructions he was given. Jesus, the Son of God, ruled over the house, yet submitted for a time in order to accomplish salvation. Through Moses, lawgiver and leader, God gave the old covenant. But it was merely a shadow of what was coming (10:1). Moses was an intermediary, the people's leader and intercessor (see Exodus 32:11; Numbers 14:13); he could not save the people's souls. Jesus enacted the new covenant, whereby salvation could be offered to all who believe. The book of Hebrews reminded the Jewish believers (to whom this letter was written) that *just as a person who builds a house deserves more praise than the house itself,* so they should honor Jesus Christ far above their greatest prophet—Moses.

GIVING GLORY

Giving Jesus glory is not as complicated or old-fashioned as it sounds. Try this:

- When blue sky breaks in the east and you feel the rush of a great day ahead, pray, "Thank you, God, because Jesus came."
- When at bedtime you realize how much your family means to you, pray, "Thank you, God, because Jesus cares for each one of them."
- When you have opportunity to help others, open your purse or wallet, because Jesus gives generously to you.
- When your church needs help but no one volunteers because the job is thankless and carries no prestige at all, step forward—because Jesus came forward for you.

3:4 **For every house is built by someone, but He who built all things is God.**[NKJV] If the builder deserves more praise than the house (3:3), how much more does God deserve praise, for he *built all things*—referring not just to the Jewish nation or to the Christian church, but to all of creation. The switch from calling Jesus the builder (3:3) to calling God the builder affirms Christ's deity. The idea in the Greek is that the one who builds all things could be none other than God. These first readers, who were considering abandoning Christianity and returning to their Jewish roots and Jewish laws, were in danger of praising the "house" more than the builder. Such action would effectively turn them away from the one who is God, Jesus Christ.

3:5-6 **Moses was faithful as a servant in all God's house, testifying to what would be said in the future. But Christ is faithful as a son over God's house.**[NIV] This repeats the thought from 3:2—that *Moses was faithful as a servant in all God's house* (see commentary there). Moses was faithful to God's appointment not only to deliver Israel, but also to prepare the way for the Messiah by *testifying to what would be said in the future.* Moses wrote the Pentateuch, the first five books of the Old Testament, recording Israel's history. But that history was not complete; Moses' words point forward to what was to come—fulfillment through God's Son.

Christ is superior to Moses as a son is superior to a servant. While both had been appointed (3:2), and while both were faithful, Moses was "faithful as a servant" while Christ is *faithful as a son over God's house.* Moses served, but Jesus rules. This illustrates 1:1-2: "In the past God spoke . . . through the prophets . . . but in these last days he has spoken to us by his Son" (NIV). Moses' service prepared the way for Christ. "God's house" refers here to the believers, the church. God's Son himself cares for his people.

So what exactly is Christ doing right now? The Bible tells us

- Christ presides at God's right hand, a place of distinction, uniqueness, and power (1:3; 8:1).
- Christ intercedes for us before God (7:25; 9:24).
- Christ stands as our mediator (John 14:6; 1 Timothy 2:5).
- Christ functions as the head of the church (Ephesians 4:15).
- Christ, through the Holy Spirit, leads and guides us (John 14:26; 16:13).

BOTH OLD AND NEW

The Old Testament prepared the way for the future coming of the Messiah. Thus, knowing the Old Testament provides the best foundation for understanding the New Testament. In reading the Old Testament, we see

- how God used people to accomplish his purposes,
- how God used events and personalities to illustrate important truths,
- how, through prophets, God announced the Messiah,
- how, through the system of sacrifices, God prepared people to understand the Messiah's work.

If you include the Old Testament in your regular Bible reading, the New Testament will grow clearer and more meaningful to you.

We are his house if we hold firm the confidence and the pride that belong to hope.[NRSV] Christ is the son placed in charge of God's house—and *we are his house,* part of God's family, under God's care. "House" refers to the church, the believers. Those who are part of God's household became so through faith in Christ. Christ makes our salvation secure, but that salvation comes with a solemn responsibility to hold firm, to persevere. John 8:31 says, "To the Jews who had believed him, Jesus said, 'If you hold to my teaching, you are really my disciples'" (NIV). "Confidence" can also mean "boldness," referring to the free access to God given to believers through Christ. Christians can freely approach God's throne with full confidence of his welcome (4:16). The phrase "pride that belong to hope" is also translated, "hope of which we boast." This pride or boast is similar to Paul's in Galatians 6:14, "May I never boast of anything except the Cross of our Lord Jesus Christ" (NRSV). Paul could boast about the cross because of what it had accomplished in his life. In the same way, believers can take pride in their hope, because that hope is secure and changeless. God's promises will never disappoint us by being unfulfilled. When we place our hope in God, we have absolute assurance that he will fulfill all that he has promised—we will be resurrected to eternal life and will be with him in glory (Romans 5:5).

These remarks certainly encouraged the readers to *hold firm* and to keep their hope in Christ and not in Jewish tradition or ritual. Perseverance becomes the reality test for faith. Those who profess Christ ought to demonstrate true faith. God had required faithfulness from the great leader Moses and even from the Son himself. All of God's people, his household, the brothers and sisters of Christ, must remain faithful. Only those who "hold firm" to their faith are part of God's house (see 3:14). Christ lives in believers; he will help us remain courageous and hopeful to the end. We are not saved by being steadfast and firm in our faith, but our courage and hope do reveal that our faith is real. Without this enduring faithfulness, we could easily be blown away by the winds of temptation, false teaching, or persecution.

KEEPING COURAGE

Members of God's household are to hold firm and be courageous. The virtue of courage has an ancient history. Aristotle called courage the "golden mean" between foolhardiness and cowardice.

Sometimes Christians think true faith requires people to be foolhardy: to withhold normal medical treatment in favor of prayer alone, or to try physically impossible tasks in the face of contrary advice.

Sometimes Christians are cowards. When a secular society regards evangelism as "religious harassment," we keep quiet about God's Good News.

Being courageous means that we continually seek God in prayer, Bible study, and worship, despite appealing distractions; that we live for God each day, despite attractive alternatives; that we trust God in all things, despite prevailing modern doubts about God's existence and character.

NOW IS THE TIME TO LISTEN TO GOD / 3:7-19

Moses led the Israelites out of long years of bondage in Egypt toward the Promised Land. Because of hardened hearts and a lack of faith, however, an entire generation wandered in the wilderness. Only two faithful men of that generation, Joshua and Caleb, entered "God's rest." After exhorting the believers to hold on to their faith (3:6), the writer reminded the Hebrew readers of how their ancestors had failed to do so. This central warning—repeated as a refrain throughout this section of Hebrews (3:7, 15; 4:3, 5, 7)—needs to ring in the ears of today's generation: trust *and* obey, for the disobedient will never experience God's rest because of their hardened hearts or lack of faith.

3:7-9 Therefore, as the Holy Spirit says: "Today, if you will hear His voice, do not harden your hearts as in the rebellion, in the day of trial in the wilderness, where your fathers tested Me, tried Me, and saw My works forty years."NKJV God, through the *Holy Spirit,* is the true author of the Old Testament (see also 10:15). The Holy Spirit inspired the prophets and forefathers (1:1). This guarantees that all of Scripture was given by God. Peter wrote, "Above all, you must understand that no prophecy of Scripture came about by the prophet's own interpretation. For prophecy never had its origin in the will of man, but men spoke from God as they were carried along by the Holy Spirit" (2 Peter 1:20-21 NIV). The Holy Spirit's words applied to believers who lived in the past, and the Holy Spirit continues to speak. The Holy Spirit used the quote from Psalm 95 (described in the following paragraphs) to speak to the Hebrew believers of the first century, and it applies to believers today as well.

GOOD FOR NOTHING

Hebrews 3:9 refers to the Israelites who had "hardened" their hearts. A hardened heart is as useless as a hardened lump of clay or a hardened loaf of bread. Nothing can restore it and make it useful. The writer of Psalm 95 warns against hardening our hearts as Israel did in the wilderness by continuing to resist God's will (Exodus 17:7). The people were so convinced that God couldn't deliver them that they simply lost their faith in him. People with hardened hearts are so stubbornly set in their ways that they cannot turn to God. This does not happen suddenly or all at once; it is the result of a series of choices to disregard God's will. Let people know that those who resist God long enough, God will toss aside like hardened bread, useless and worthless.

The quotation comes from a psalm of worship used as an opening to synagogue worship on Friday evening and Sabbath morning. The first part of the psalm calls God's people to worship him. The second part of this psalm (the part that is quoted here) warns the people that worshipers can only worship God if they are not rebelling against him. These words encourage us to learn from the Israelites' mistakes. While there are many Old Testament examples to follow (see chapter 11), this example of rebellion and hard-heartedness is not one we should emulate.

"Do not harden your hearts" means "do not rebel and persist in your stubbornness." The Hebrew readers knew the story well. The generation who left Egypt had witnessed astounding miracles, yet they had lost faith in God. They were poised to enter the Promised Land, but they became afraid of the spies' report of walled cities and giant men. At that point they rebelled, hardening their hearts, refusing to trust that God would help them take the land he had promised them (Numbers 13:26–14:38). Their unbelief kept them from receiving the rewards and blessings God had for them. Although God had miraculously rescued them from Egypt and had demonstrated his power and care over his people, the people disobeyed God, complained against him, and refused to take possession of the land God had given them. They *tested* him, *tried* him, and saw him work both for and against them during their *forty years* of wandering. They tested his patience and challenged his authority. Despite seeing God's works for forty years, the people continually rebelled against him. The books of Exodus and Numbers tell the sad story. Rather than encouraging the people to move on in faith, most of the spies encouraged the people to give up hope for the land. That's when the people revolted against God, Moses, and Aaron. God punished their lack of faith by sending them back into the wilderness for forty years. God said, "None of the people who have seen my glory and the signs that I did in Egypt and in the wilderness, and yet have tested me these ten times and have not obeyed my voice, shall see the land that I swore to give to their ancestors; none of those who despised me shall see it" (Numbers 14:22-23 NRSV). Not only at that point, but throughout the wanderings in the wilderness, the people constantly hardened their hearts against God.

The original readers of this letter were on the verge of abandoning Christ and returning to Judaism. This passage reminded them of the consequences of hardening their hearts against God by using the example of their ancestors. Hopefully, these Christians would learn from their ancestors' mistakes. Believers are warned, *do not harden your hearts.* Hard hearts can be the result of disobedience, rebellion, lack of trust, neglect of worship, refusal to submit, and ungratefulness for what God has done for us. Rather than rebelling, we must endure. We must seek maturity, not taking Christ, his work, or his kindness for granted.

HARD HEARTS
In many places, the Bible warns people not to "harden" their hearts (Proverbs 28:14; Ezekiel 3:7; Mark 8:17; Hebrews 3:13). Hardening our hearts means stubbornly setting ourselves against God so that we are no longer able to turn to him for forgiveness. We harden our hearts when we habitually disobey the word of God and choose our own desires instead.

What causes hardening of the heart? The deceitfulness of sin (3:13) seduces us away from taking pleasure in the goodness of God to finding pleasures outside of God's will. Lack of gratitude for God's grace makes us callous and indifferent. Doubt and fear can make us lax and unresponsive to God's leadership. Any time we close our minds to the word of God and shut out the influence of his Holy Spirit, we are in danger of hardening our hearts. Look for signs of hardening, and turn back to God. Ask him to keep you "soft" and receptive.

3:10-11 "Therefore I was angry with that generation, and said, 'They always go astray in their heart, and they have not known My ways.' So I swore in My wrath, 'They shall not enter My rest.'"NKJV Many people would like to believe that God does not get angry. They believe that God is only loving, compassionate, and kind. While God does have these characteristics, he also has many others. One of these is anger, as expressed in these words from Psalm 95: *Therefore I was angry with that generation. . . . I swore in my wrath.* Rebellion makes God angry. God does not look away from sin; he acts against it and punishes it.

God grew angry because the people went *astray in their heart.* The Greek word for "heart" *(kardia)* denotes the center of physical, spiritual, and mental life. Every thought, emotion, and desire comes from this "heart." The people continually turned away from God in their actions, attitudes, thoughts, and beliefs. If the heart of the people had honored God, they would have trusted God and entered the Promised Land. However, Psalm 95 continues: *they do not know My ways* (NKJV). The people had seen God's mighty miracles; they knew what God expected of them, for he had given them his law. Yet they did not seek to truly "know" him and love him. The people could have known God better and made the effort to trust him; instead, they chose to depend on themselves—the very danger that the original readers of Hebrews were urged to avoid.

Rebellion led to punishment. The Israelites lost their chance to enter the Promised Land when God said, *'They shall not enter My rest.'* God's "rest" has several meanings in Scripture: (1) the seventh day of Creation and the weekly Sabbath commemorating it (Genesis 2:2; Hebrews 4:4-9); (2) the promised land of Canaan (Deuteronomy 12:8-12; Psalm 95); (3) peace with God now because of our relationship with Christ through faith (Matthew 12:28; Hebrews 4:1, 3, 8-11); and (4) our future eternal life with Christ (Hebrews 4:8-11). All of these meanings were probably familiar to the Jewish Christian readers of this book.

The verse in the psalm seems directly addressed to the generation of Hebrews who left Egypt but died during the wilderness wanderings and thus did not enter Canaan. Since that whole experience is frequently used as a metaphor for disobedience resulting in loss of reward, we can apply the verses as a warning about God's anger in the face of human rebellion against his kingdom. By rejecting God's provision (Christ) and not enduring in our faith, we miss the opportunity for spiritual rest.

GOD'S WRATH

The Bible talks about God's wrath in many places. For example, "Whoever believes in the Son has eternal life; whoever disobeys the Son will not see life, but must endure God's wrath" (John 3:36 NRSV); and "For the wrath of God is revealed from heaven against all ungodliness and wickedness of those who by their wickedness suppress the truth" (Romans 1:18 NRSV).

But God's wrath must not be thought of as uncontrolled fury or personal animosity. His response to sin could better be described as righteous indignation. God hates sin, but he is not the enemy of anyone. He loves everyone (see Romans 5:8), yet his perfect moral nature automatically rejects sin; he cannot ignore or condone willful rebellion. God is not out of control; he is patient and long-suffering. His anger is very real, but the full force of it, with manifested action, will be revealed later. He wants to remove the sin and restore the sinner—if the sinner does not reject the truth. But his wrath erupts against those who persist in sin. God's love is as real as his wrath. Do not overstate one in favor of the other.

3:12 **Be careful then, dear brothers and sisters. Make sure that your own hearts are not evil and unbelieving, turning you away from the living God.**NLT The lesson from Israel's experience applies to all believers. By calling his readers *dear brothers and sisters,* the writer clues us in that the readers had not yet revolted against Christ or drifted away from him. But they were in danger of emulating Israel's rebellion. The writer saw the potential danger, however, and reminded the readers that Christians must *be careful.* The Israelites, who, with their own eyes, had seen great miracles from God's hand, had fallen away from God. Christians must be careful not to fall into the same snare. No Christian is immune from turning away from

> Unbelief is at the bottom of all our staggerings at God's promises.
> *Matthew Henry*

or rejecting God. Sometimes people gradually drift (as in 2:1-4); sometimes they rebel. We believers should carefully watch our Christian lives so that our *hearts are not evil and unbelieving.*

An evil or unbelieving heart leads to dire consequences; it causes a person to turn *away from the living God.* As illustrated by the Israelites, complacency in the Christian life can cause us to drift away from or rebel against God. Turning away from Christianity implies more than turning away from a system of beliefs or a set of doctrines; it means turning away from God. God lives, so he sees whether people follow him or rebel against him. Because God lives, he will judge and punish those who reject him and will reward those who hold firm. The writer warned these Hebrew believers against going back to Judaism. How could that be considered "turning away from the living God" when Judaism worships the same God? This entire letter to the Hebrews focuses on the superiority of Jesus Christ over everything in Judaism because nothing in Judaism can provide ultimate salvation and eternal rest. To reject Christ for Judaism is to miss out on God's eternal rest.

MAKE SURE

"Make sure that your own hearts are not evil and unbelieving" (3:12 NLT). Our hearts turn away from the living God when we stubbornly refuse to believe him. If we persist in our unbelief, God will eventually leave us alone in our sin. But God can give us new hearts, new desires, and new spirits (Ezekiel 36:22-27). To prevent developing an unbelieving heart, stay in fellowship with other believers, talk daily about your mutual faith, be aware of the deceitfulness of sin (it attracts but also destroys), and encourage other believers with love and concern.

3:13 But encourage one another daily, as long as it is called Today, so that none of you may be hardened by sin's deceitfulness.[NIV] A safeguard against believers turning away from God is for them to *encourage one another daily.* Believers should continually remind each other to turn away from sin and to stay focused on Christ. The writer urged Christians to be alert themselves and to encourage others. A person cannot encourage or be encouraged apart from fellowship; thus, believers are urged not to give up meeting together (10:24-25). People cannot live as Christians in a vacuum. They need more than individual vigilance. They need encouragement and correction from their brothers and sisters in Christ. Allow fellow Christians to encourage you, and also see that you do not refuse to listen to a fellow

> The fundamental deception of Satan is the lie that obedience can never bring happiness.
> *R. C. Sproul*

HOW DOES SIN DECEIVE US?

Satan's goal is to deceive us

Genesis 3:1-2	Satan is crafty—he sought to trick Eve
Genesis 3:13	Eve knew that the serpent had deceived her
John 8:44	Satan is a liar, the father of lies
2 Corinthians 2:11	Satan schemes in order to outwit us
2 Corinthians 4:4	Satan blinds the eyes of unbelievers to keep them from the truth
2 Corinthians 11:13	Satan masquerades as an angel of light
2 Thessalonians 2:9	Satan will deceive many in the end times through counterfeit miracles, signs, and wonders
Revelation 12:9	Satan is the deceiver of the whoe world

Wealth can deceive us

Deuteronomy 8:11-14	Wealth can cause us to become proud and forget the Lord
Proverbs 11:28	Whoever trusts in riches will be disappointed
Matthew 13:22	The deceitfulness of weath can choke out the gospel message
1 Timothy 6:9-10	Wealth is a trap that can lead to destruction; the love of money is a root of all kinds of evils

Our desires can deceive us

Ephesians 4:22	Our old nature is corrupted by its deceitful desires
Titus 3:3	Before believing we were enslaved to and deceived by passions and pleasures
James 1:14-15	Evil desires lead to sin, which leads to death

Because deceitfulness is Satan's weapon, we must arm ourselves against him. We must encourage one another, assemble for worship, clearly warn against those dangers, and constantly show the benefit of faithfully following Christ.

Christian who may see sin or a problem in your life. Don't just wait for a pastor or leader to encourage someone else; each person, you included, has the responsibility (see Galatians 6:1-2).

Unfortunately, however, many Christians end up discouraged, rather than encouraged, by other Christians. Be careful that you take opportunity to actively encourage others. Without constant self-evaluation and encouragement, a person's sin can become a deceived mind, a hardened heart, leading to unbelief and rejection of Christ.

Sin is subtle, and often enjoyable, so we are easily drawn to it. Christians need each other so that they don't become *hardened by sin's deceitfulness*. Satan, the author of sin, could never be described as stupid. In fact, Satan is so intelligent that he can and does deceive people, even intelligent and normally faithful people. We protect against sin's deceitfulness by checking our private intentions and desires against those of a group of trusted Christian friends, and by checking our group's intentions and desires against the teachings of the word of God.

3:14 For we have become partners of Christ, if only we hold our first confidence firm to the end.NRSV True Christians, as mentioned in 3:6, must hold firm. Believers *have become partners of Christ,* meaning we have a great privilege in our relationship with him. The business terminology provides a metaphor: the believers can rely on Christ; he is the senior partner managing the firm. Christ, in turn, can trust that his partners will carry out his directions and pursue the best interests of the firm. Again we see the paradox of "now" and "not yet" in the Christian life. While believers have already become partners, we must still *hold our first confidence firm to the end.* That "first confidence" in Christ and all he has done brought us to belief; as time goes by, we must not let doubts or fears draw us away from that first confidence. The writer was concerned that the faith of some of these Hebrew Christians was faltering. He urged them to hold on to that first confidence until the end.

Faith is a journey, not just a state of mind. Many Christians today imagine faith to be like a pill to be ingested or like a pillow to be embraced. But Hebrews pictures faith as what Norwegians call a *joggetur*—a brisk walk or run along a wilderness path. Christians should be able to say with Paul: "I have finished the race, I have kept the faith" (2 Timothy 4:7).

Jewish readers of Hebrews would understand this picture of faith because it was the actual experience of the generation that had fled Egypt in the Exodus. Through unfaithfulness and rebellion, the Israelites had lost God's blessings. The writer turns to this theme in the following verses.

3:15 As has just been said: "Today, if you hear his voice, do not harden your hearts as you did in the rebellion." NIV By repeating a quote used in 3:7, the writer continues to remind the people not to harden their hearts. The Israelites did not trust God, nor were they faithful to the end. Christians must be. The repeated (from 3:13) word "today" shows the urgency of this message.

Today we can act; we don't know what will happen tomorrow. (For more on hard hearts, see the commentary on 3:7-9.)

3:16-17 **And who was it who rebelled against God, even though they heard his voice? Wasn't it the people Moses led out of Egypt? And who made God angry for forty years? Wasn't it the people who sinned, whose corpses lay in the wilderness?**[NLT] The writer's illustration points out that a good beginning does not guarantee a victorious end. If people could rebel against God even after they had actually *heard his voice,* the danger for falling away is real for any Christian. Not only did the Israelites hear God's voice (Exodus 20), they also saw the plagues God sent on Egypt before Moses led the people out. They saw those amazing miracles, yet they rebelled. The rebellious Israelites failed to enter the Promised Land because they did not believe in God's protection, and they did not believe that God would help them conquer the giants in the land (see Numbers 13–14). So God sent them into *the wilderness* to wander *for forty years.* This was an unhappy alternative to the wonderful gift God had planned for them. In the wilderness for forty years, God continued to care for them: They received water from a rock and ate manna from heaven. Yet even though they had seen, heard, touched, and tasted of God's care and love for them, they hardened their hearts against him. Those who rebelled died in the wilderness without ever experiencing the Promised Land. Open defiance of God leads to catastrophic results, barring entrance to God's rest. We must not take God's wrath lightly.

3:18-19 **And to whom did God swear that they would never enter his rest if not to those who disobeyed? So we see that they were not able to enter, because of their unbelief.**[NIV] The rebellious generation of Israelites could not *enter his rest* (the Promised Land) *because of their unbelief.* But this "unbelief" was more than just a mental process; their unbelief caused them to disobey. There is a strong connection between unbelief (the underlying attitude) and disobedience (the resulting action). Both their actions and their beliefs condemned them.

The nation had been rescued from Egypt, had seen God's salvation, and had been given the hope of a new land. Yet the people had *disobeyed.* Christians have been rescued from sin, have seen God's salvation, and have

> Men would understand, they do not care to *obey.* They try to understand where it is impossible they should understand except by obeying. There is no salvation in correct opinions. A man's real *belief* is that by which he lives.
>
> *George MacDonald*

been given the hope of eternal life. For those who reject Christ, the penalty is greater than it was for the Israelites. The penalty is God's rejection.

RECOVERING LOST FAITH

Can adults recover the joy of the faith they had when they were young?

On the one hand, no. Adults cannot become innocent children again. The faith of an adult must face up to hard questions and live up to concrete realities. An adult's faith is mature, intelligent, and steady. It accepts consequences and losses without cynicism.

On the other hand, yes. Adults can be young again, in the New Testament sense. Adults are wholeheartedly invited to depend on God and to pray to him as their loving Father. With childlike faith, adults should put their trust in Jesus, their Savior and Lord, today. Then the hardening process can be reversed. Begin now to recover your faith. Let Christ soften your heart.

HEBREWS 4:1–5:10

A REST FOR GOD'S PEOPLE / 4:1-13

People have always attempted to earn their way into heaven. Some have been zealous in religious efforts of all kinds to earn approval from their gods. Others have thought that they could comprehend the ultimate reality through philosophy. In our day, many people piece together a religious faith with parts of a variety of religious viewpoints.

These verses state that only those who believe the word of God will enter God's rest and receive his approval. The word of God—sharp, living, active—cuts through all human endeavors, laying everything bare before the eyes of God.

4:1 **Therefore, since the promise of entering his rest still stands, let us be careful that none of you be found to have fallen short of it.**[NIV] The word "therefore" ties this verse to the preceding verses. The end of chapter 3 explains that the Israelites who rebelled against God never entered "his rest" (referring to the Promised Land in 3:18-19). Having shown that Jesus is superior to the great leader Moses, the author turned to another great Israelite leader, Joshua. God's servant Joshua led Israel into the Promised Land, yet he did not provide God's true "rest" (see 4:8). One greater than Joshua accomplished that.

In this chapter, the word "rest" is used in three different ways: (1) the rest Israel had been promised in Canaan; (2) God's rest after creating the world (see 4:4); and (3) the rest experienced by Christians—both now and in the future.

Deuteronomy 12:9-11 describes the "rest" that Israel had been promised in Canaan:

- the land itself
- security and protection because they were God's people
- rest from fighting (peace)
- God's presence through the tabernacle (and later the temple)

While the next generation of Israelites did enter and possess the land, this was still only a shadow of the final "rest" that was to come. The Jewish people refused God's plan and rejected their

Savior; thus, *the promise of entering his rest still stands*—God has made this rest available to Christians. Since God had barred the rebellious Israelites from the Promised Land, the promise stands for those who remain obedient to him. The promise has not been fulfilled, but neither has it been revoked.

For those who have come to trust in Jesus, he gives rest. They first find rest from trying to fulfill all the requirements of the law (see Matthew 11:28). Unshackled from this yoke, they can experience salvation and God's "rest" today. This rest will be fully culminated in heaven. While Christians presently enjoy "rest" with God, at the same time, we look forward to that day when our final rest will be in face-to-face fellowship with the Father. Christians are promised the full extent of God's rest:

- heaven
- security and protection because we are God's people
- relief from earthly struggles and sin
- God's perfect presence in our lives through the Spirit and eventually face-to-face

Christians must learn from the tragic mistake of the Israelites. The writer of Hebrews warned readers how serious it would be to turn away from Christ by saying *let us be careful that none of you be found to have fallen short of it.* This is not a mere encouragement, but a warning sign: Danger ahead! Just as God rejected the rebellious Israelites on the basis of their unbelief (3:19), so he will reject those who turn away from Christ, refuse to believe him, or refuse to follow him.

NO COMPLACENCY

Some of the Jewish Christians may have been on the verge of "falling short" of their promised rest in Christ, just as many of their ancestors had "fallen short" of true rest in the Promised Land. In both cases, the difficulties of the present moment overshadowed the reality of God's promise, and the people doubted that God would fulfill his promises. For many today the problem takes the form of complacency toward Christ's demands, rather than doubt. Do not take Christ's words for granted or take lightly his promises. Those who do so may end up falling short.

4:2 **For we also have had the gospel preached to us, just as they did; but the message they heard was of no value to them, because those who heard did not combine it with faith.**[NIV]
The Jewish believers to whom this letter was written were in danger of turning away from their faith, just as their ancestors

had turned away from the Promised Land. The word for "gospel" is *logos,* meaning God's word or message communicated from him or demonstrated through his acts of love. The Old Testament Jews received God's message in the great deliverance from Egypt and the covenant given to Moses at Mount Sinai. These New Testament believers received God's message in the person of Jesus Christ, his death on the cross, and his resurrection. Jews from both the Old Testament era and the New Testament era had received communication from God. But for many of the Old Testament Jews, *the message they heard was of no value to them.* Why not? *Because those who heard did not combine it with faith.* Not only must God's message be heard, it must also be combined with faith before it will be effective. Hearing must lead to believing. Implicit in these words is the warning to these New Testament Jewish believers not to make the same mistake.

MORE THAN HEARING

The Israelites of Moses' and Joshua's day heard great messages from God, but they still did not respond in faith. Many people in our churches today reflect the same problem. They have heard many messages, they may have even read the Bible, but they have not responded in faith. People know a great deal about Christ, but they do not know him personally—they don't combine their hearing with faith. They are not real believers who take God at his word and obey him. Religion without obedience to God has no value. Hearing many sermons and not responding only makes us indifferent to the word of God. Believe in Christ and then act on what you know. Are you just hearing the word? Or are you hearing and obeying?

4:3 **For we who have believed enter that rest, just as God has said, "As in my anger I swore, 'They shall not enter my rest.'"**NRSV The point has already been made that the Old Testament Jews had failed to enter God's "rest" (see commentary on 3:10-11, 18-19), yet this promise of rest still stands (4:1). The promise is fulfilled for those *who have believed.* Those who have placed their faith in Jesus Christ as Savior *enter that rest.*

What does it mean to "believe"? Believing in Jesus may seem easy, almost effortless, just a nod, a quick

To all of us Christ offers "rest," not in the other life only, but in this. Rest from the weight of sin, from care and worry, from the load of daily anxiety and foreboding. The rest that arrives from handing all worries over to Christ and receiving from Christ all we need. Have we entered into that experience? *F. B. Meyer* prayer, or a walk forward at a church service. While making a profession of faith in Christ is simple, truly believing in Jesus leads to a life of commitment and discipleship that will put the believer at odds with the greedy, self-centered, cruel, and power-grabbing world. People who believe in Jesus find that each day requires a full effort. Those who believe in this way enter God's place of rest. The phrase "they shall not enter my rest" describes realities both present and future. When we believe, God's "rest" becomes ours as we live in this present evil world. The "rest" also remains in the future as we look forward to heaven.

For those who fail to believe, there is a stern warning (see also 3:11, 18-19; 4:5). Because the Israelites lacked the faith to receive God's rest when he offered it, God, in his *anger,* vowed that they would never enter it. God's anger is not spiteful or reactionary. Rather, his anger emerges from the perfection of his character. Since God is perfect, he becomes angry at sin. The Israelites' unbelief caused them to forfeit God's promised rest; Christians' belief causes them to enter into that rest.

Even though this rest has been ready since he made the world.[NLT] When God finished creation, his *rest [was] ready* (4:4). Did God sit back and do nothing more, letting the world go? No. God chose his people and developed them into a great nation. He engineered the Exodus. He became a human being to save the world. And he will act mightily in the world in the last days, as the book of Revelation attests. Yet God's work has been ready in the sense that, at creation, the plan was in place. God's "rest" refers not to inactivity, but to completion of the plan. Everything God will do had already been planned and foreseen. The point is that God's rest has been available to his people since the dawn of time. The "rest" offered in the Promised Land merely pictured the true and final rest for those who believe.

4:4 For He has spoken in a certain place of the seventh day in this way: "And God rested on the seventh day from all His works."[NKJV] The *certain place* where God spoke these words is Genesis 2:2. *God rested on the seventh day* after creating the universe, not because he was tired, but to indicate the completion of creation. The world was perfect, and God was satisfied with it, so he rested. This does not mean that God became idle; Jesus taught that God still works (John 5:17). God was able to rest because creation was good, exactly as it should be, with nothing that needed to be added. God's rest is both present peace with God and future eternal joy when creation will be renewed, every mark of sin removed, and the world made perfect again. Those who believe will join God in his rest and one day be restored to a perfect condition. Our rest in Christ begins when we trust him to complete his good and perfect work in us.

4:5 **And again in the passage above he says, "They shall never enter my rest."**[NIV] But to those who don't believe, the author repeats his warning taken from Psalm 95 (see also commentary on 3:10-11, 18-19; 4:3). God's people who had seen great miracles in the Exodus from Egypt never entered God's rest. Having great leaders like Moses, Joshua, and Caleb did not cover for the people's unbelief and rebellion. Not only did the people's sin keep them from possessing the land, it kept them from close fellowship with God. We must be careful that we don't believe we are Christians just because we belong to a good church or have a good Christian family. How do we know if we have entered God's rest? The answer comes in the next verse.

4:6 **It still remains that some will enter that rest, and those who formerly had the gospel preached to them did not go in, because of their disobedience.**[NIV] The Israelites had failed to enter, but there must remain some who will enter if God's promise is to be fulfilled. There will be *some* who will enter, but it will be only those who obey God. This obedience is linked to faith in his Son.

4:7-8 **Therefore God again set a certain day, calling it Today, when a long time later he spoke through David, as was said before: "Today, if you hear his voice, do not harden your hearts." For if Joshua had given them rest, God would not have spoken later about another day.**[NIV] As in 3:15, the writer used the word "today" to show that salvation was still possible and that rest from the sins and troubles of this world was still available. Humanity did not lose its chance for salvation with Israel's failure, but the writer again warned his readers not to *harden* their hearts (see commentary on 3:7-9).

The phrase "God again set a certain day" means that the time of rest will come, indeed it has come, for the time is "today." We cannot understand God's relationship to time. God is above time and apart from time, yet he relates to a creation where people measure time. God lives always in the now, and each moment is important. Who can imagine God ever being casual about what's happening right now? Thus, the word of God to us, "today," is the most important word we have ever received. The use of the word "today" has two functions. First, it is a warning saying that the time for decision is now. There may be no tomorrow. Second, "today" conveys the time of opportunity. Because it is the word of God, we should give it preeminent attention. *Today* the word of God is active and true; *today* is the time of redemptive history—the "last days" between Christ's resurrection and his second coming. Someday God's word will be judgment, and his offer of forgiveness and reconciliation will become an awesome declaration that time is over. Believe God *today!*

At the time of the writing of Psalm 95, partially quoted in this verse, no one had entered God's complete rest. Many Jewish people may have believed that they had already received God's rest by inhabiting the Promised Land. But the writer argues that it cannot be so. *Joshua* and the Israelites did settle Canaan and did achieve periods of peace and prosperity. Yet, if this had been God's promised rest, *God would not have spoken later about another day.* In other words, there would have been no need for this renewal of the promise recorded here from the psalm. If God only intended an earthly kingdom, God would not have promised "another day." Therefore the rest was not in the land, but in God's eternal kingdom.

The King James Version translates the name Joshua as "Jesus" here in 4:8. Both names have the same Greek spelling, and the writer may have had a play on words in mind. However, since this verse refers to Israel's history, the word is better understood as referring to the Israelite leader Joshua.

WHY SO URGENT?

This passage emphasizes *today.* Is God's offer of salvation just another example of the hustle we face every day? Rush to the store before the sale ends. Rush through the light before it changes red. Rush through homework to watch TV.

No. God isn't rushing you. God's offer is no blue-light special that leaves you panting for breath, racing for bargains before prices return to normal. Every day is "today" for God. Every day God offers you salvation. On the other hand, God has a plan for the world and for your life in particular. This great salvation God offers is a real thing that's coming soon. Today is the best time, the most important time, you've got. Before God's plan for history reaches its climax and before your own life plan reaches its last day, God beckons you to faith in his word. When we put faith on hold, we in effect say to God, "It's not really that important." Today God offers his best to you. Today, in faith, trust God fully.

4:9 **So then, a sabbath rest still remains for the people of God.**[NRSV] The phrase "so then" indicates that the following is a logical conclusion from what has preceded. In 4:6, we read the words, "It still remains that some will enter that rest" (NIV). In the final conclusion to the matter recorded in this verse, the writer describes the "some" as *the people of God,* and the "rest" as *a sabbath rest.* The words "sabbath rest" are one word in the Greek, occurring only here in the entire Greek Bible. This "rest" provided by God didn't even have a word descriptive enough for the writer, so he coined a new one, calling it "a sabbath rest." The kind of rest the author described is different from what the Israelites expected. This rest refers to what God did when he completed creation (see commentary on 4:4, 10). It pictures the rest of the Sabbath—not the legalistic inactivity demanded by the Jewish Pharisees, but the joyful, festive adoration and praise for God characterized by the early church. God's promised rest includes perfect fellowship and harmony with him.

This rest *still remains;* it has not been fulfilled, as the author has explained above. Why would this rest have been so important to the readers of this book? The readers, Jewish Christians, had two important reasons to look forward to rest. (1) Jewish history was filled with wanderings and political turmoil. On rare occasions, the people could relax from worries about foreign armies or internal political corruption. But to finally rest in the full and realized promises of God would be great comfort. (2) Christians in the first century often faced deprivation and hardships, the animosity of Satan's agents, and the carrying of one's "cross"—identifying with Jesus. Those who turned from the Jewish faith to Christianity often incurred the wrath of other Jews (facing excommunication) and of their families (being disowned). To enter God's promised rest was a great promise—struggle will be done and pain will be over.

Yet this rest remains only *for the people of God.* Although the Jewish people who were originally offered the rest had refused it, God's plan could not be thwarted; God offered it to others—both Jews and Gentiles who believe in Jesus Christ as Savior. (This teaching is similar to Jesus' parable of the great banquet recorded in Luke 14:15-24.)

COME AND REST

God wants us to enter his rest. The Israelites of Moses' time experienced a foretaste of this rest in the Promised Land. Even though Christians will experience everlasting life on a new earth in the future, they can enjoy this rest now by knowing God's peace. We do not need to wait for the next life to enjoy God's rest and peace; we may have it now! Our daily rest in the Lord will not end with death, but will become an eternal rest in the place that Christ is preparing for us (John 14:1-4). Have you fully trusted Christ and entered his rest?

4:10 **For all who have entered into God's rest have rested from their labors, just as God did after creating the world.**[NLT] The author has shown that the rest remains for the people of God—the Christians (4:6, 9). That rest remains and people will enter it, and *all who have entered into God's rest have rested from their labors.* The author combined two Old Testament references from Genesis 2:2 and Psalm 95:11. (Combining two similar verses was a popular method of Jewish teaching called a midrash.)

Does this "rest from labors" begin now, or do believers have to wait for heaven? Some suggest that it begins after death, citing Revelation 14:13. Most likely, however, believers do experience God's rest in this present life, but will receive it completely and fully after death when they arrive in heaven. The "labors" from which believers can rest does not mean inactivity. After all, believers have much work to do in this world in order to advance God's kingdom. "Labors," therefore, may refer to ceasing from trying to work for salvation. Many of these Jewish readers had been brought up under the Pharisees' system of strict laws and rule keeping. These Jewish Christians could rest from those labors, resting instead on what Christ has done. The promised rest for believers is the same as God's rest, and just as certain; it will be *just as God [rested] after creating the world* (see 4:4).

MOTIVATED BY A PROMISE

Busy people often work especially hard the week before vacation, tying up loose ends so they can relax. Students usually have their final exams right before semester breaks. When we know a rest is coming, we put extra effort into finishing our work.

Healthy Christians love the work God has given them, doing it with passion and gusto, putting all their strength and care into it. But Christians love God's promise of heaven's rest even more and look forward to God's rest with great joy. Today, renew your effort to work hard for God. Rest is coming. Relish the thought.

The Bible is filled with examples of hard workers, but here God himself becomes the example. That should tell us something. When, in the corporate world, a middle manager suggests that you take a holiday, you may have reason to wonder whether it's really appropriate. But if the CEO awards a holiday, then you know you really have one.

God is awarding a holiday to all who belong to him, to all who trust his word and believe in his Son, Jesus.

4:11 **Let us, therefore, make every effort to enter that rest, so that no one will fall by following their example of disobedience.**[NIV]

Drawing from his conclusion in 4:10, the writer includes himself with the statement, "Let us . . . make every effort to enter that rest." This statement is an intentional paradox: labor so that you can rest. We need to strive to obtain what is ours by promise but not yet ours by experience. The children of Israel had been promised the good land, but it wasn't theirs until they possessed it.

Jesus saves us, but we "work out [our] own salvation with fear and trembling" (Philippians 2:12 NKJV). All believers must diligently work out their faith, seeking to obey Jesus day by day, drawing closer to God through experiences in life. There is no time while living on earth at which a Christian "arrives" at spirituality. Each day God's people are making a choice either to grow closer to him or to drift away.

Nevertheless, the message here is a warning to people who would be lazy in their spiritual life. Laziness can cause a person to fall into disobedience. "So that no one will fall by following their example of disobedience" refers back to that generation of Israelites in the wilderness who turned away from the Promised Land (see 3:7-11, 15-19; 4:1-6). Paul describes their disobedience in 1 Corinthians 10:1-12. Today's pressures make it easy to ignore or forget the lessons of the past. But the author cautions readers to remember the lessons the Israelites learned about God so they will avoid repeating the Israelites' errors. The key to "making every effort" is to study the Bible regularly so that these lessons remind us of how God wants us to live. We need not repeat the mistakes of the past.

4:12 For the word of God is living and powerful, and sharper than any two-edged sword, piercing even to the division of soul and spirit, and of joints and marrow, and is a discerner of the thoughts and intents of the heart.[NKJV] God will discern whether or not we make every effort (4:11) and whether or not we have truly come to faith in Christ; nothing can be hidden from God. We may fool ourselves or other Christians with our spiritual lives, but we cannot deceive God. He knows who we really are because *the word of God is living and powerful.* Does this "word" refer to Jesus or to Scripture? While Jesus Christ is called "the Word" (John 1:1) who came as God's ultimate communication to humanity, the comparison with a sharp sword indicates that "the word of God" here more likely refers to God's revelation in the Bible. Only in the Gospel of John (1:1) and in Revelation (19:13) is Jesus called "the Word."

> The Scriptures were not given to increase our knowledge but to change our lives.
> *D. L. Moody*

THE WORD OF GOD

The word of God, the Bible, describes itself and its work in many ways:

Isaiah 55:11.	God's word will not return to him empty, but willl do what God desires and achieve the purpose for which he sent it.
Jeremiah 23:29 . .	God's word is like fire and like a hammer that can break a rock into pieces.
John 6:63.	God's word is spirit and life.
Acts 7:38	God's word is living.
Ephesians 6:17 . .	God's word is part of the believer's armor—the sword of the Spirit.
Heberws 4:12 . . .	God's word is living, powerful, sharper than a two-edged sword, judging people's thoughts and intentions.
1 Peter 1:23.	God's word is living and enduring, through which people are born again.

How is this word of God, the Bible, "living and powerful"? The word of God is not simply a collection of God's words, a vehicle for communicating ideas; it is living, life changing, and dynamic as it works in us. The demands of the word of God require decisions. We not only listen to it, we let it shape our lives. Because the word of God is living, it applied to these first-century Jewish Christians, and it applies as well as to Christians today. The word of God lives, and it gives life to those who believe—energizing this present life and promising eternal life. Most books may appear to be dusty artifacts just sitting on a shelf, but the word of God collected in Scripture vibrates with life. The Pharisees imagined that the word of God was a set of static rules, and modern critics have argued that the word of God is nothing more than an archival record of a nation. Both groups have erred. The word of God—living and powerful—breathes life for people today. God reaches out to those who look into its pages, calling them to life, meeting their needs, expressing their deepest emotions, offering answers to their greatest questions.

The word of God cannot to be taken for granted or disobeyed. The Israelites who rebelled (described at length in previous verses) learned the hard way that when God speaks, they must listen. Going against God means facing judgment and death.

The word of God penetrates through our outer facade and reveals what lies deep inside. The metaphor of a *two-edged sword* pictures the word of God, like a knife, revealing who we really are on the inside. It discerns what is within us, both good and evil. It penetrates the core of our moral and spiritual lives. This "two-edged sword" pictures the sharp, short sword that the Roman soldiers used in close combat. The sword's double edges made it ideal for "cut and thrust" warfare. The word of God, sharper than a two-edged sword, pierces *even to the division of soul and spirit, and of joints and marrow.* These words develop the metaphor; they are not a commentary on people's physiological or spiritual makeup. Nothing can be hidden from God; neither can we hide from ourselves if we sincerely study the word of God. It reaches deep past our outer life as a knife passes through skin. It delves deep into our inner lives, and *is a discerner of the thoughts and intents of the heart.* The word translated "is a discerner" can also be translated "judges" (NIV). At this point, our thoughts, motives, attitudes, and intentions are shown to us as being good or evil; we cannot escape God's judgment on them and we dare not ignore God's warning to us. We cannot keep secrets from God.

THE SECRET YOU
Who really knows you?

Maybe you think your best friend knows the real you. But does this person know how jealous you are of his or her talents, career, or good looks? Does he or she hear your bickering and your put-downs that try to equalize your popularity with his or hers?

Maybe your spouse knows you. But does your spouse know all about your past, your moral weakness, your caving in to crowd pressure? Can he or she read your thoughts about all the other handsome men or pretty women who cross your path and divert your fancy?

Maybe no human knows you that well. But God does. God's way of talking to you about your secret thoughts—and helping you confront them—is his word, the Bible. The Bible, opened to you through the work of the Holy Spirit, is your clearest mirror and strongest counsel. Read the Bible and see for yourself. Study the Bible and learn about yourself and God. Apply the Bible and change your life.

4:13 **Nothing in all creation is hidden from God's sight. Everything is uncovered and laid bare before the eyes of him to whom we must give account.**[NIV] This verse reiterates the truth expressed in 4:12. God sees everything. *Nothing in all creation* (literally "no creature") *is hidden from God's sight.* No one can hide anything from God. He sees every thought, intention, and attitude—no matter how secretly these are held; he sees every deed—no matter how secretly it was accomplished. Two thoughts are presented by the phrase "everything is uncovered and laid bare." (1) We are naked before God. We cannot give excuses, justifications, or reasons—everything is seen for exactly what it is. No one can deceive God. (2) We are exposed, powerless, and defenseless before God. The word refers to the paralyzing grip of a wrestler in a choke hold.

The word of God penetrates like a sword (4:12), exposing us to God himself, *to whom we must give account.* All people must give an account to God, but without trappings and rationalizations. The Bible speaks about this fact in many places. For example, see the following verses (quoted from the NRSV):

- Psalm 62:12—"And steadfast love belongs to you, O LORD. For you repay to all according to their work."
- Matthew 16:27—"For the Son of Man is to come with his angels in the glory of his Father, and then he will repay everyone for what has been done."
- Acts 17:31—"Because he has fixed a day on which he will have the world judged in righteousness by a man whom he has appointed, and of this he has given assurance to all by raising him from the dead."
- Romans 2:16—"On the day when, according to my gospel, God, through Jesus Christ, will judge the secret thoughts of all."
- 1 Corinthians 4:4—"I am not aware of anything against myself, but I am not thereby acquitted. It is the Lord who judges me."

These words give warning that believers must be careful not to drift away, but to obey God wholeheartedly. God is the final Judge. This verse paves the way for the following section describing Jesus Christ as our High Priest. With our lives laid bare before God, we would be hopelessly lost without Christ. Because he took our judgment and serves as our advocate with God, we can rest secure with God.

HIDE AND SEEK

Nothing can be hidden from God. He knows about everyone everywhere, and everything about us is wide open to his all-seeing eyes. God sees all we do and knows all we think. Even when we are unaware of his presence, he is there. When we try to hide from him, he sees us. We can have no secrets from God. Can your Christian life stand the test? Is your faith living and real?

JESUS CHRIST IS OUR HIGH PRIEST / 4:14–5:10

Under the old covenant, the worship of God involved sacrifices. The first high priest, Melchizedek, also served as the ruler of Salem (Jerusalem). He offered sacrifices to God and also ruled the people. After Melchizedek, the priesthood from Aaron's line performed priestly duties only—no ruling powers. This stayed in place from the giving of the law to Moses on Mount Sinai until the first advent of Christ. During those centuries, the Jewish priests operated as emissaries between God and his people.

When Jesus became our High Priest, he also became our spiritual king, combining both duties as high priest and ruler, as Melchizedek had done. Furthermore, Jesus offered himself as the supreme sacrifice, a service no other person could ever perform.

4:14 Therefore, since we have a great high priest who has gone through the heavens, Jesus the Son of God, let us hold firmly to the faith we profess.NIV These verses logically follow from 2:17–3:1, "For this reason he had to be made like his brothers in every way, in order that he might become a merciful and faithful high priest in service to God, and that he might make atonement for the sins of the people. . . . Therefore . . . fix your thoughts on Jesus, the apostle and high priest whom we confess" (NIV). The intervening section explains how Jesus is greater than Moses and Joshua, two of Israel's greatest leaders. Jesus is greater than the law Moses gave; he gives a rest greater than Joshua gave in conquering the Promised Land. The writer moved on to show how Jesus is also greater than anyone in the Jewish priesthood, another important part of the Jewish heritage.

The word "therefore" ties in with the description of Jesus in 2:17–3:1 quoted in the previous paragraph. Our merciful and faithful high priest, Jesus, became like us in order to die for us, offering the once-and-for-all sacrifice for sin. *Since we have a great high priest* would have portrayed a vivid picture to the Jewish Christian readers. The high priest had been their highest religious authority. The priesthood began with Aaron, Moses' brother (Exodus 28:41). Only the high priest could enter the Holy of Holies in the temple, and then only once a year to make atonement for the sins of the whole nation (Leviticus 16).

Jesus is the "great" High Priest, better than all the high priests of Israel. Here is why:

- The high priests were humans who could offer sacrifices but could do nothing to take away sin. Jesus gave his life and died as the final sacrifice for sin.

- The high priests could enter the Holy of Holies only once a year to atone for the sins of the nation. Jesus *has gone through the heavens* and has unrestricted access to God the Father. "Gone through the heavens" is a critical concept in Hebrews. In 7:26, Christ is referred to as exalted above the heavens, and 9:24 states that Christ entered heaven itself. "Gone through the heavens" refers to Christ's transcending nature as our high priest and to his work for us in the highest of all sanctuaries, heaven itself.
- The high priests interceded between God and the people, but they were human and sinful themselves. Jesus intercedes between God and people as the sinless *Son of God,* human yet divine. He had been tempted in every way humans are, so he can mercifully intercede for us and assure us of God's forgiveness.
- The high priests were the highest religious authorities for the Jews. Jesus has more authority than the Jewish high priests because he is both God and man.
- People could not approach God except through a high priest. When Jesus died, the veil that separated the Most Holy Place in the temple was torn in two, indicating that Jesus' death had opened the way for sinful people to reach a holy God.

Because of all that Christ has done and is doing for us, *let us hold firmly to the faith we profess.* Do not drift away (2:1), but cling to this faith. "The faith we profess" most likely refers to a formulation or confession of faith they had once publicly accepted (see 3:1). The writer explains to the Jewish audience that they should not go back to an inferior system because they can have all that the system promised and longed after—access to and acceptability by God. "Jesus fulfilled those desires," says the writer, "hold on to that faith!" Allow Jesus to be your High Priest; only he can protect you from inevitable judgment (described in 4:12-13).

This is good news to people who wonder, "How can I approach God?" or "Will God listen to me?" Because Jesus is the High Priest, Christians can approach God and God will hear them when they pray. No sin is too great to keep God from hearing you, no background is too severe to cause your great High Priest to refuse to represent you. No matter what your family background, job history, ethnic roots, or past behavior, Christ is a faithful High Priest who represents all who trust in him.

> Jesus Christ is not only the Son of God mighty to save, but the Son of Man able to feel.
>
> *J. C. Ryle*

4:15 For we do not have a High Priest who cannot sympathize with our weaknesses, but was in all points tempted as we are, yet without sin.[NKJV] Because Jesus, our *High Priest* (4:14), was made like us, he experienced life completely. He grew tired, became hungry, and faced normal human limitations. Thus Jesus can *sympathize with our weaknesses.* Not only that, but he also *was in all points tempted as we are.* Jesus, in his humanity, felt the struggle and reality of temptation. Matthew 4:1-11 describes a specific series of temptations from the devil, but Jesus probably faced temptation throughout his entire earthly life, just as we do (see 1 John 2:16). He experienced the full pressure of temptation—all its power, tricks, and enticements. Temptation often ends for people when they give in to it, but Jesus was different. Being God, Jesus could never have given into sin. Although he was a human being, he was unlike us in that he was *without sin.* From our limited perspective it is difficult to understand this great mystery. What we can say is that Jesus *could* have sinned (which makes temptation real), but we know that he *didn't* sin (which means he never yielded to temptation).

We can find comfort in knowing that as Jesus faced temptation, he knows how difficult it is to resist. We can be encouraged in knowing that Jesus faced temptation without giving in to sin and that he gives us the power to do so as well. For more on Jesus' sinlessness, see 2 Corinthians 5:21; 1 Peter 2:22; 1 John 3:5.

4:16 Let us therefore come boldly to the throne of grace, that we may obtain mercy and find grace to help in time of need.[NKJV] Through his death on the cross, our great High Priest, Jesus, opened access to God. Now people can approach God directly because of Jesus' sacrifice for sins. Because Jesus gave his life to do this for us, *let us therefore come boldly to the throne of grace.* This verse is an open invitation to regard God as a great ally and true friend. Yes, God occupies a throne, a seat of power and authority, but it is a throne of grace, not a throne of greed or domination. The term "throne of grace" describes the constant care and love offered to God's undeserving children. God's grace is a characteristic of his reign. "Grace" means undeserved favor. Our ability to approach God does not come from any merit of our own but depends entirely on him.

> Faith enables us so to rejoice in the Lord that our infirmities become platforms for the display of his grace.
>
> *C. H. Spurgeon*

Believers can "come boldly" and confidently to this throne, for the king is our Father, who loves us as his children. At God's throne, we will not receive anger or be ignored; instead, we will *obtain mercy and find grace to help in time of need.* God is not only concerned with converting people and collecting disciples; he also cares and nurtures those children who are his own. He listens to our needs. No request is insignificant, and no problem is too small for the one who sits on the throne of grace. God will never reject a Christian's plea or ignore one who brings requests before God. When we come to God, we are promised "mercy," God's loving-kindness and forgiveness. When we come to God, we will receive "grace," God's undeserved favor, that will help in time of need. No matter what the problem, no matter what sin caused the need, God promises to help us at just the right time—his time. This doesn't mean that God promises to solve every need the moment we come to him. Nor does it mean that God will erase the natural consequences of any sin that was committed. It does mean, however, that God listens, cares, and will answer in his perfect way, in his perfect timing.

BOLDLY

Prayer is our approach to God, and we are to come "boldly." Some Christians approach God meekly with heads hung low, afraid to ask him to meet their needs. Others pray flippantly, giving little thought to what they say. Come with reverence because he is your King. But also come with bold assurance because he is your Father, Friend, and Counselor.

5:1 **Every high priest is a man chosen to represent other people in their dealings with God. He presents their gifts to God and offers sacrifices for their sins.**NLT The Hebrew readers would have known that *every high priest is a man chosen to represent other people in their dealings with God.* A high priest had two primary jobs: representing God to the people by teaching the word of God, and representing the people to God in making atonement for their sins (Leviticus 1–4; 16). The annual Day of Atonement was the only time a person could enter the Most Holy Place where the ark of the covenant rested and where God himself resided among his people. On that day, it was the high priest who entered the Most Holy Place, bringing the blood of slain animals to atone for the sins of the entire nation: "No one is to be in the Tent of Meeting from the time Aaron goes in to make atonement in the Most Holy Place until he comes out, having made atonement for himself, his household and the whole community of Israel" (Leviticus 16:17 NIV).

The high priest served as the "boss" over all the other priests. Priests had other functions, as well: diagnosing disease (Leviticus

13; 14), purifying people after they were cured from their disease (Leviticus 14), examining property that was dedicated to God's service (Leviticus 27), and inspecting sacrificial animals (Leviticus 22). Priests also oversaw temple worship and introduced religious holidays (Leviticus 25:9). Sometimes priests served as judges (1 Samuel 7:16; 2 Chronicles 19:8); sometimes they delivered God's guidance to the people (Numbers 27:21). Priests represented human beings in their dealings with God, but the chief mediator was the high priest, who symbolized all the people in his approach to God. Yet the high priest was only a man, himself subject to sin, himself needing atonement for sin. This atonement came through the sacrifices. Therefore, the high priest *presents [the people's] gifts to God and offers sacrifices for their sins.* In addition to the sacrifices on the Day of Atonement, God designated five different kinds of "gifts and sacrifices" (also called "offerings") that the people could bring to the priests:

1. A burnt offering was a voluntary offering by someone who wanted to demonstrate commitment to God (Leviticus 1; 6:8-13).
2. A grain offering was a voluntary offering that accompanied other sacrifices (Leviticus 2; 6:14-23).
3. A fellowship offering was a voluntary offering demonstrating a person's thankfulness for fellowship with God (Leviticus 3; 7:11-21).
4. A sin offering was a mandatory offering that paid for unintentional sins or helped cleanse an unclean person (Leviticus 4:1–5:13; 6:24-30; 12:6-8; 14:12-14).
5. A guilt offering was made to atone for unintentional sins against another person (Leviticus 5:14–6:7; 7:1-10; 14:12-18).

Every sin required a penalty and a sacrifice in order for the worshiper to receive forgiveness. No person could offer a sacrifice without the aid of a priest as a mediator. The idea of mediator is central to the Bible. Humans subject to sin and by nature inclined to sin need mediation in order for them to establish any relationship with a holy God.

> The awful majesty of the Godhead was mercifully sheathed in the soft envelope of human nature to protect mankind. *A. W. Tozer*

5:2 **He can have compassion on those who are ignorant and going astray, since he himself is also subject to weakness.**[NKJV] The Jewish high priest was only a human, subject to the same faults as other people. In actual practice, the high priest was also subject to delusions of grandeur and political power brokering (as seen in the example of Caiaphas, high priest at the time of Jesus' death; see John 11:49-50). This verse, however, pictures a high priest who, fully alert to his own sinfulness and mortality, empathizes and identifies with the people he represents: *He can have compassion on those who are ignorant and going astray, since he himself is also subject to weakness.* The priest's knowledge of the people is intense, personal, and empathetic. The high priest is not a student of the people (a sociologist of religion), but a normal participant of the human drama who knows full well his own need for mediation, and who earnestly cares for the others under his care (much like a public defender arguing bail before a judge).

5:3 **That is why he must offer sacrifices for his own sins as well as theirs.**[NLT] The high priest, while holding an honorable and prestigious position as mediator between God and the people, was not absolved from penalty for his own sin. Neither was he in a special category of human beings or exempt from the law himself. Rather, he had to face, more directly and personally than all others, the immense gulf between sin and holiness, between people and God. Of all people, the high priest should understand how humbling a job he had—and how vital a role he played. Without his mediation, the people would perish. In a specific ceremony each year, on the Day of Atonement, a priest was required to *offer sacrifices for his own sins as well as theirs.* Once a year the priest would enter the Most Holy Place (Leviticus 16) to offer sacrifices for all the people's sins. Before he could enter, however, the priest was required to purify himself with sacrifices:

> *"This is to be a lasting ordinance for you . . . because on this day atonement will be made for you, to cleanse you. Then, before the LORD, you will be clean from all your sins. It is a sabbath of rest, and you must deny yourselves; it is a lasting ordinance. The priest who is anointed and ordained to succeed his father as high priest is to make atonement. He is to put on the sacred linen garments and make atonement for the Most Holy Place, for the Tent of Meeting and the altar, and for the priests and all the people of the community. This is to be a lasting ordinance for you: Atonement is to be made once a year for all the sins of the Israelites." And it was done, as the LORD commanded Moses.* (Leviticus 16:29-34 *NIV*)

5:4 **No one takes this honor upon himself; he must be called by God, just as Aaron was.**[NIV] The position of high priest carried special honor; however, *no one takes this honor upon himself.* The NLT translates this verse: "No one can become a high priest simply because he wants such an honor." God himself appointed the high priest. Scripture records the disaster that came upon men who tried to take the honor upon themselves: Korah (Numbers 16), Saul (1 Samuel 13:8-14), and Uzziah (2 Chronicles 26:16-21).

The high priest *must be called by God, just as Aaron was* (Exodus 28:1-3). Aaron, brother to Moses, served as Israel's first high priest. He had gone with Moses into Egypt, acting as Moses' spokesman with Pharaoh (Exodus 4:13-16). In the wilderness, he sinned against God by making a golden calf for the people to worship (Exodus 32). Yet God "called" Aaron to serve him as high priest in the tabernacle during the time of Israel's wanderings. Leviticus 8 and 9 describe the ordination ceremony for Aaron and his sons. They were washed with water (Leviticus 8:6), clothed with special garments (Leviticus 8:7-9), and anointed with oil (Leviticus 8:12). They placed their hands on a young bull as it was killed (Leviticus 8:14-15) and on two rams as they were killed (Leviticus 8:18-19, 22-23). This showed that holiness came from God alone, not from the priestly role.

TAKING THE HONORS

In sports, honor falls to the toughest competitor. The same happens in business, war, politics, and school. Sometimes that notion creeps into spiritual matters when honor goes to the man or woman "who earned it."

Real spiritual work is not subject to those rules. It is bestowed by God as a matter of calling, not of competition. Do you want to be a pastor or teacher? The honor is given, not earned. Do you want to be an evangelist or counselor, helping people hear and live in God's truth? God's call opens those opportunities.

When you find an evangelist who has scrambled to the top of the heap, fought for and won the presidency of his organization—turn to another person. If you want to do significant spiritual work, concentrate on spiritual disciplines and leave competition to someone else.

5:5 **So Christ also did not take upon himself the glory of becoming a high priest. But God said to him, "You are my Son; today I have become your Father."**NIV After having reminded his Jewish Christian readers of the original intent for the role of their high priest, the writer returned to his explanation of Jesus as our "great high priest" (4:14). As the Old Testament high priests did not take upon themselves the honor but were honored by God's selection, *so Christ also did not take upon himself the glory of becoming a high priest.* Jesus said, "If I glorify myself, my glory is nothing. It is my Father who glorifies me, he of whom you say, 'He is our God'" (John 8:54 NRSV). Christ also was appointed by God, as demonstrated by the quotation from Psalm 2:7, *You are my Son; today I have become your Father.* Christ became the high priest and perfectly fulfilled the requirements. He fulfilled them more perfectly in that he did not have to offer sacrifices for his own sins. He was sympathetic toward the people he represented because he "was in all points tempted as we are, yet without sin" (4:15 NKJV). In 1:5, the writer also quoted this verse from Psalm 2:7 to show that God never said these words to an angel; this passage explains that God never said these words to any of the high priests either. Only Jesus is God's Son. (See also commentary on 1:5.)

The "today" spoken of in this passage is the day of Christ's enthronement—the day when God exalted the crucified Jesus and simultaneously declared his divine priesthood and sonship.

OUR HUMBLE SAVIOR

One of the Bible's greatest and most perplexing themes is the humility of Jesus. Fully worthy of glory, he does not claim it. Fully a participant in divine glory, he does not exercise it or even talk much about it. Jesus' humility is weakness in the sight of competitors, but meekness in the sight of God. The world, hungry for power and success, wonders at an all-powerful being who does not play all his cards, who instead takes on human sin in order to die for undeserving sinners. In every worldly sense, a humble Savior makes little sense at all. But in God's eyes, the humbled Son is the world's Savior, the one who brings the once-for-all sacrifice to God. The one who brings us into God's loving arms.

5:6 **As He also says in another place: "You are a priest forever according to the order of Melchizedek."**[NKJV] Although Christ fulfilled the above requirements for becoming the perfect high priest, he did not have one significant requirement: he was not born into the tribe of Levi and had not descended from Aaron. Jesus was of the tribe of Judah (see Genesis 49:10; Matthew 2:6; Revelation 5:5). Only Levites could be priests, and only descendants of Aaron could be high priests in the Jewish system. The book of Hebrews, however, tells how Christ's priesthood was greater than the Aaronic priesthood by quoting Psalm 110:4: *"You are a priest forever according to the order of Melchizedek."* These words, coming from the inspired psalmist David predicted that the Messiah would come from a line of priests not traced back to Aaron. This theme is discussed extensively in chapter 7 (see the commentary there). By quoting Psalm 110:4, the writer shows that God called Jesus to the office of priest; Jesus did not take it upon himself. This passage is quoted and alluded to many times in Hebrews. It forms a key argument to support the writer's view of Christ as the heavenly High Priest (thus, the most authoritative). The priests in the line of Aaron were not priests forever.

Jesus, however, is "a priest forever." In addition, Aaron's descendants were priests but not kings. Israel's kings could not serve the functions of the priests (those who tried faced dire consequences, such as Saul in 1 Samuel 13:8-14 and Uzziah in 2 Chronicles 26:16-21).

5:7 **In the days of his flesh, Jesus offered up prayers and supplications, with loud cries and tears, to the one who was able to save him from death, and he was heard because of his reverent submission.**[NRSV] High priests had to be human (and thus able to sympathize with those they represented), and they had to be called by God. Christ fulfilled both of these requirements (4:15; 5:5-6). Jesus' humanity allowed him to sympathize with us. His humanity, the time when he lived on this earth in a human body, is described as "in the days of his flesh."

SUBMITTING TO GOD

Jesus is our model for true submission to God. To resist or to submit is a choice made hundreds of times each week. Through practice we build resistance to advertising messages, and through moral training we learn to resist overt sin.

In response to God, resistance is always wrong and submission is always right. Our problem is to determine when the word of God is clear and when a human voice has subverted it. We may need to resist a minister's message if he twists the word of God or misrepresents it. A "guilt trip" needs resistance when it is borne by a frail human psyche or the need to control others.

We must follow Christ's example and submit to God. We must learn to hear only the word of God when there are so many other messages to distract us.

During these days, Jesus agonized as he prepared to face death (Luke 22:41-44). Although Jesus cried out to God, asking to be delivered, he was prepared to suffer humiliation, separation from his Father, and death in order to do God's will. He *offered up prayers and supplications, with loud cries and tears.* Jesus did not seek his own glorification; rather, he wanted to bring glory to God. He knew he had been sent to die, but in his humanity, he faced great fear and sorrow over what he knew would happen. He prayed to God, *the one who was able to save him from death.* Only God could change the plan. In the garden, Jesus prayed, "Father, if it is Your will, take this cup away from Me; nevertheless not My will, but Yours, be done" (Luke 22:42 NKJV). In his humanity, he did not want to die, but he submitted himself to the Father's will *and he was heard because of his reverent submission.* Did God hear Jesus? Yes. Did God change the plan? No.

Jesus suffered extreme agony and death in submission to God. But his prayer was answered in that he was saved from the power of death. He overcame death through his resurrection.

5:8 **Though He was a Son, yet He learned obedience by the things which He suffered.**NKJV In the kingdoms of any ancient regime, no prince suffers; the crown prince especially is pampered and prepared for kingship. But Jesus, *though He was a Son . . . learned obedience by the things which He suffered.* The bewildering lesson of this verse is that God himself, born of human parentage, actually learned something in the suffering he underwent. Was the all-knowing God in need of learning? Jesus learned about the human condition. That knowledge brought more empathy than intelligence, more personal identification than measurable data.

> In the creation, the Lord made man like himself; but in the redemption he made himself like man.
> *John Brys*

Jesus is a model for us in our suffering. Jesus' human life was not a script that he passively followed. It was a life that he chose freely (John 10:17-18). In his humanity, Jesus continuously made the choice to follow the will of God. Jesus chose to obey, even though obedience led to suffering and death. Because Jesus obeyed perfectly, even under great trial, he can help us obey, no matter how difficult obedience may be. (For more on this, see Life Application Bible Commentary on 1 Peter 2:20-24; 3:12-14.) Like Jesus, believers often learn obedience through their suffering (see 12:2-11). This example from Christ encouraged the readers to remain firm and not drift away from the faith in times of suffering. Just as Christ was perfected through his suffering, so Christians will be, too.

5:9 **And, once made perfect, he became the source of eternal salvation for all who obey him.**NIV The author of our salvation was *made perfect* through suffering (2:10). No human high priest became "perfect." The words "once made perfect" do not refer to Jesus' sinless state. Jesus was already perfect before he faced suffering; his perfection was put to the test and came out with flying colors. Because humans experience suffering and death, Christ became fully human and experienced these parts of humanity as well. Christ was always morally perfect. By obeying, he demonstrated his perfection to us, not to God or to himself. In the Bible, "perfection" usually means completeness or maturity. By sharing our experience of suffering, Christ shared our human experience completely. Because Christ lived, died, and rose again, he became *the souce of eternal salvation for all who obey him.* Christ alone is the only source of salvation. These last words warned those who would turn away from Christ and turn back to an inferior system. Salvation comes only to those who obey as Christ obeyed—with complete submission to God and his will, even in the face of suffering.

WHAT IS SALVATION?
Jesus provides it.
God offers it.
We are supposed to want it.
What is it?

Salvation is the elimination of a verdict on human sin, the setting aside of judgment, the award of undeserved membership in God's family. It is a change in destiny, an awakening of hope, an overcoming of death. Salvation turns a person toward heaven and inaugurates a life of discipleship with the living Christ. It is God's vote for you, God's invitation to you, God's energy invested in you.

Salvation is the reason you can smile in the morning and rest in the evening. God loves you, and you belong to him.

5:10 **And God designated him to be a High Priest in the order of Melchizedek.**[NLT] Going back to the theme in 5:6, Jesus was *designated . . . to be a High Priest in the order of Melchizedek.* All priests in Aaron's family line needed mediation for their own sins. All human priests died and were succeeded by others. But Jesus was fundamentally different. Jesus did not need mediation for personal moral flaws. Jesus died, but rose again to die no more. No one succeeded Jesus; he is a priest forever. He is both human and divine, made perfect through suffering, able to understand our weaknesses. That's quite unlike the Aaronic priesthood, so the writer compares Christ's priesthood with "the order of Melchizedek."

The theme of Melchizedek is postponed until chapter 7 so that the writer can give a parenthetical remark addressing the spiritual state of the readers.

HEBREWS 5:11–6:20

GO BEYOND ELEMENTARY PRINCIPLES / 5:11–6:12

Young parents become excited to see the development of their first child. Jars of baby food quickly augment milk, and garbled "mama-dada" soon gives way to counting to ten, repeating some of the alphabet, and uttering a few emphatic *no*s. Parents would feel devastated if the child never progressed beyond one-syllable words or if the child remained on a milk diet until puberty.

The writer of Hebrews exhorted his readers to become spiritually mature by learning to distinguish between good and evil. Mature Christians move from the elementary teachings of the gospel (milk) to the substantial biblical teaching of righteous living (solid food).

A child learns to walk by falling down, then getting up and trying again. Christians learn to know the difference between good and evil by prayerfully examining the word of God and putting it into practice in their lives.

5:11 **There is much more we would like to say about this, but it is difficult to explain, especially since you are spiritually dull and don't seem to listen.**[NLT] Regarding Christ's role as High Priest, there is *much more* that the writer *would like to say about this.* The writer will further explore Christ's priesthood (chapter 7), but here pauses the argument to give readers a wake-up call. The concepts that follow in this letter will be understood by growing Christians, not stagnant ones. Christians must not be casual about the word of God; people must listen attentively. Hebrews continually challenges Christians to persevere in their faith. Instead of working hard in their faith, these Christians were choosing the easier road. The writer illustrates this by saying, *you are spiritually dull and don't seem to listen.* The readers were "hard of hearing" (see 6:12 for the same concept, there translated "sluggish" or "lazy"). Apparently the writer was personally acquainted with many Jewish believers who fit this description or had heard about their unwillingness to apply some of these important concepts about their faith.

5:12 **In fact, though by this time you ought to be teachers, you need someone to teach you the elementary truths of God's word**

all over again. You need milk, not solid food![NIV] Apparently, these Christians had been in the Christian faith for some time; so long, *in fact,* that *though by this time you ought to be teachers, you need someone to teach you the elementary truths of God's word all over again.* These Christians should have grown, but they had been lazy in their faith—no wonder they were in danger of drifting (2:1)! Rather than explore and deepen their knowledge of Christ, rather than trying to please God with their actions, they considered abandoning Christ when they faced opposition. Sufficient time had elapsed for these Christians to be grounded in the "elementary truths of God's word" so that they could teach them to others, passing on their faith. These Christians, however, were not doing so. "Elementary truths" refers to the simple message of the gospel and the basic beliefs of the faith. Instead of teaching them to others, these believers needed to be taught all over again. They were like young children, still drinking *milk* instead of growing up into eating *solid food*—the more difficult teachings of God's word, such as the significance of Christ's position as High Priest (which the writer had just begun to discuss and will continue to discuss in chapter 7).

NEED FOR TEACHERS
Many of the Jewish Christians to whom this letter was written were immature. They should have been teaching others, but they had not even applied the basics to their own lives. They were reluctant to move beyond the basic doctrines of Christianity. They wouldn't be able to understand the high-priestly role of Christ unless they moved out of their comfortable position, cut some of their Jewish ties, and stopped trying to blend in with their culture. Commitment to Christ moves people out of their comfort zones into roles where they can teach others.

Perhaps you should consider how you can teach others. Can you volunteer for helping in Sunday school? Are there homebound people to whom you could read Scripture? Teaching others will help you grow as well.

5:13 Anyone who lives on milk, being still an infant, is not acquainted with the teaching about righteousness.[NIV] These Christians, described as immature, were *not acquainted with the teaching about righteousness.* They lived *on milk,* that is, they had not grown in their faith. They remained inexperienced and unskilled in applying their knowledge to their lives. They had received enough instruction and should have been able to teach others the elementary truths of the faith, but they were still acting like infants, not moving ahead, not digging deeper, not applying what they learned to enhance a life of righteousness.

CHRISTIAN MATURITY

Christian maturity is greatly discussed throughout the New Testament. Here are some of the descriptions:

Description	*References*
Complete	1 Corinthians 2:6; 3:1; Ephesians 4:13; Colossians 1:28; Hebrews 5:14; 6:1
Blameless	Luke 1:6; Philippians 2:15; 3:6; 1 Thessalonians 3:13, 5:23
Whole	2 Corinthians 13:9-11; Galatians 6:1; 1 Thessalonians 3:10; Hebrews 13:21; 1 Peter 5:10
Disciplined	Hebrews 2:10; 5:9; 12:10
Love for God and others	1 Corinthians 13:1-13; 14:20; 1 Peter 4:8; 1 John 4:12, 17-21
Christlike	Matthew 5:48; Luke 6:36; Romans 12:2; Colossians 3:10

Part of the writer's persuasive strategy may have been to "deflate the ego" of obstinate readers. "You may think you're smart," the writer could be saying, "but you're no smarter than a baby." Yet even babies naturally grow and want to learn more and try new things. These "baby believers" had stymied their own growth. Growth, while fraught with bumps and bruises, is the most natural process in the world. Likewise, growth in God's truth makes such perfect sense that no one should be stunted!

5:14 But solid food is for the mature, who by constant use have trained themselves to distinguish good from evil.[NIV] This verse contrasts the spiritual babies (5:13) with the spiritually mature. Interestingly, those who are called *the mature* (or those who are now complete) are mature because they have disciplined themselves: *who by constant use have trained themselves.* They have disciplined themselves on *solid food,* that is, they have learned about and appropriated the high-priestly role of Christ. Spiritually mature Christians constantly examine themselves, turn away from sin, and learn what actions, thoughts, and attitudes will please God. These people "have trained themselves" to *distinguish good from evil.* The Greek word for "trained" *(gumnazo)* gives the athletic imagery of training through much practice.

Had these believers been mature, they would have recognized that the temptation to abandon Christ was "evil." They were not mature, however, because they didn't understand the significance

THE CHOICES OF MATURITY

One way to evaluate spiritual maturity is by looking at the choices we make. The writer of Hebrews notes many of the ways those choices change with personal growth.

Mature choices	*Versus*	*Immature choices*
Teaching others	rather than . . .	just being taught.
Developing depth of understanding	rather than . . .	struggling with the basics.
Evaluating self	rather than . . .	criticizing self.
Seeking unity	rather than . . .	promoting disunity.
Desiring spiritual challenges	rather than . . .	desiring entertainment.
Studying and observing carefully	rather than . . .	accepting opinions and halfhearted efforts.
Having an active faith	rather than . . .	cautious apathy and doubt.
Living with confidence	rather than . . .	fear.
Evaluating feelings and experiences in the light of God's Word	rather than . . .	evaluating experiences according to feelings.

of Christ's position. Therefore, they were ready to drift away from him (2:1).

In order to grow from infancy to maturity, we must learn discernment. We must train our consciences, senses, and minds to distinguish good from evil. We must incorporate from the word of God principles of right thinking and right action whereby we can correctly judge moral situations that occur. Can you recognize temptation before it traps you? Can you tell the difference between a correct use of Scripture and a mistaken one? How much time do you spend reading the word of God? Do you spend greater amounts of time watching TV or reading the newspaper?

6:1-3 Therefore let us leave the elementary teachings about Christ and go on to maturity.[NIV] Just after admonishing readers for baby-food spirituality, the writer indicated that "real food" would be coming. The writer would not give in to their immaturity and provide them with only milk, because rehashing the basic doctrines would not help them resist the temptation to drift away from Christ. They must gain a deeper understanding, moving beyond the basics, *the elementary teachings about Christ.* The phrase "elementary teachings" might also refer to the Old

Testament or the Jewish system. If this is so, the writer was not calling his people to abandon their roots to the Old Testament but to advance beyond them to *maturity.*

MOVING ON

Hebrews 5:14 discusses discerning good from evil. Psychologists Jean Piaget and Lawrence Kohlberg are famous for research on how people move through stages of moral growth. (Admittedly, their ideas are hotly disputed by scholars.) The abbreviated version goes like this:

- Stages 1-2: Do good in order to add to your pleasure and reduce your pain.
- Stages 3-4: Do good in compliance with established rules, including religious rules.
- Stages 5-6: Do good as an expression of your informed conscience and your empathetic care for others.

Are you pleasure-oriented and therefore obey God to avoid punishment on Judgment Day?

Are you rule-oriented and therefore obey God through mechanistic obedience to rules, including the many religious rules that are really human inventions?

Are you God-oriented and therefore obey God because he loves you and you love him? All the Christian martyrs faced their death from this orientation. They had learned to distinguish good from evil. They had moved from infancy to maturity.

Of course, believers don't "leave" these teachings as if they didn't need them anymore; the elementary teachings are essential for all believers to understand. Everyone needs to first learn the ABCs before being able to read complex books. The elementary teachings about Christ include the importance of faith, the foolishness of trying to be saved by good deeds, the meaning of baptism and spiritual gifts, and the facts of resurrection and eternal life. To have a mature understanding, we need to move beyond (but not away from) the elementary teachings to a more complete knowledge of the faith. This is what the author intended for these believers to do (see 6:1). Mature Christians should be teaching new Christians the basics.

Not laying again the foundation of repentance from acts that lead to death, and of faith in God, instruction about baptisms, the laying on of hands, the resurrection of the dead, and eternal judgment. And God permitting, we will do so.[NIV] These Christians needed to move beyond these basics of their faith to an understanding of Christ as the perfect high priest and the fulfillment of all the Old Testament prophecies. Rather than arguing about the respective merits of Judaism and Christianity, they needed to depend on Christ and live effectively for him. These verses list three pairs of elementary teachings that Christians should move beyond.

GROWING CHRISTIANS

In one important sense, the entire Bible follows this theme of maturity (6:1-3). Everything in the Bible leads us toward mature faith, which is always characterized by

- *a sense of becoming, not arriving.* The growing Christian is reaching forward, not resting on what has already happened.
- *a sense of wonder, not complacency.* The growing Christian is more likely to know how difficult the questions are, rather than how easy the answers are.
- *a sense of commitment, not lethargy.* The world's people need the peace God offers; our social systems need God's justice; our bodies need God's healing. The growing Christian acts in faith to become God's servant to the world, even under stress.

Paul wrote in Philippians 3:13-14, "Beloved, I do not consider that I have made it my own; but this one thing I do: forgetting what lies behind and straining forward to what lies ahead, I press on toward the goal for the prize of the heavenly call of God in Christ Jesus" (NRSV).

All Christians, including you, should be growing, maturing, and pressing on!

The first two elementary teachings *(foundation of repentance* and *faith in God)* represent basic teachings of salvation. The gospel calls Christians to die to themselves, to turn away from their sinfulness, and to obediently follow Jesus Christ. The gospel calls people to redirect their lives from self-gratification to God's pleasure. Self-gratification leads to *acts that lead to death* (see notes on 9:14), but faith in God brings life. The phrase "acts that lead to death" may have a complex meaning. For Gentiles, these acts may have included idolatry and immorality, while for the Jews they may have included external efforts at salvation and a self-righteous attitude concerning the law.

The next two elementary teachings represent ordinances of the Christian community: *baptisms* and *the laying on of hands.* The word "baptisms" is plural because the Christian sacrament was often contrasted with the Jewish or pagan baptisms. Often those who were baptized would come out of the water and receive the "laying on of hands" at the completion of their baptism. This rite concluded the new Christian's initiation into the church. It might also refer to the ordination of pastors (1 Timothy 4:14; 2 Timothy 1:6).

The last two elementary teachings *(the resurrection of the dead* and *eternal judgment)* represent teachings about the end times.

While all the teachings are important, these last two are basic to becoming a believer. After believing, Christians should live out these words in daily life, and they should seek deeper understanding of God by studying the more difficult concepts in his Word. The author is saying, "You've talked plenty about the sacraments, church ordinances, and our future hope—and that's good. But Christians must grow beyond those teachings." If the readers never moved beyond these teachings, they might revert to their previous faith in Judaism. If, however, they would move on to study deeper doctrines about Jesus Christ, their study would keep them from drifting away from Christ. It is interesting that often these basics are what pass for deep teaching in some churches today, and disagreements over these basics have caused painful splits.

Choosing to press on and become spiritually mature requires dedication and work, but it cannot happen without God's help. Before the writer moves on to more "solid food," he acknowledges the need for God's help: *God permitting, we will do so.*

6:4-6 For it is impossible for those who were once enlightened, and have tasted the heavenly gift, and have become partakers of the Holy Spirit, and have tasted the good word of God and the powers of the age to come, if they fall away, to renew them again to repentance, since they crucify again for themselves the Son of God, and put Him to an open shame.[NKJV] Let us first consider the subject of these verses. The writer described certain people with four phrases: (1) *once enlightened,* (2) *tasted the heavenly gift,* (3) *partakers of the Holy Spirit,* and (4) *tasted the good word of God and the powers of the age to come.* We will discuss each of these phrases in turn. The writer was saying that *it is impossible* for such people, *if they fall away, to renew them again to repentance.* There are four main interpretations of this passage.

1. One interpretation states that this passage means Christians can lose their salvation. According to this interpretation, the four phrases describe believers. Those who are in Christ are "enlightened"; that is, Christ has opened their eyes, making them children of light (Ephesians 1:18; 3:9; 5:8). This salvation allows them to "taste the heavenly gift"; that is, they have come to know Christ, the one who came from heaven, so they experience salvation and the gifts that the Spirit gives (see also notes on 1:14). Through this taste, Christians become "partakers of the Holy Spirit"; that is, these people have truly been brought into union

with Christ and they have been given the gifts (discussed in 2:4). This Holy Spirit also allows them to taste "the good word of God and the powers of the age to come"; that is, they have seen Christ work supernaturally in their lives, changing them from an old creation to a new. While we can agree that the phrases may describe believers, we cannot accept this interpretation that Christians can lose their salvation. This idea is dismissed by other portions of Scripture (for example, see John 10:27-29; Romans 8:38-39).

2. Some interpret this passage as hypothetical: "if it were possible." This interpretation, however, is unnatural and does not fit into the greater context of 6:7-8. If this passage were only hypothetical, then the warning would be unnecessary. Because the warning is urgent and real, we dismiss this interpretation.

3. Another interpretation is that the writer may have intended to illustrate someone who seemed to be a Christian but really never was a true follower of Christ. All of the descriptive phrases could describe someone who is not really in the faith. That person could be "enlightened," for the word was used by the early church to describe Christians who had been baptized and had professed Christ. The person could have "tasted the heavenly gift," if this phrase refers to the sacrament of the Lord's Supper. The person could have been a "partaker of the Holy Spirit," if that phrase means that they fellowshipped alongside true believers and witnessed the Spirit's work. Nonbelievers (even Judas Iscariot) saw the Holy Spirit work, heard the "good word of God," and saw the "powers of the age to come." Yet Judas was not a true disciple of Christ. This interpretation is acceptable when considered in the greater context. Hebrews 3:16-19 reviews how each Jew living in the wilderness had seen God's great power, had eaten manna, had accompanied God, and had looked like God's people, yet they never entered the Promised Land. The writer did not want the Christians to fall into the same category and experience the same fate.

4. Another reasonable interpretation arises by linking this portion of Scripture with 10:25-31 (another severe warning). The writer of Hebrews was warning against a specific kind of apostasy: forsaking Jesus as the perfect sacrifice for sins and returning to animal sacrifices as a means of atoning for sins. Thus, the severe warning is for those Jewish Christians who had originally accepted Christ's redemption through his shed blood and then reverted to offering up the blood of bulls and goats as a means of cleansing their sins.

In the first century, a pagan who investigated Christianity and then went back to paganism would make a clean break with the church. But for Jewish Christians who decided to return to Judaism, the break was less obvious. Their lifestyle remained relatively unchanged. But by deliberately turning away from Christ, they were cutting themselves off from God's forgiveness. Those who truly believe are glorious saints; those who reject Christ are unbelievers, no matter how well they behave—thus, this warning not to "fall away" (2:1; 3:12).

It is impossible for people who have professed to be Christians and have experienced all of the beautiful gifts described in these verses, then have turned away from Christ to turn around and repent again *since they crucify again for themselves the Son of God, and put Him to an open shame.* It is impossible because these people show contempt for Christ through their deliberate actions. It would be like personally crucifying Christ again. Many have argued whether someone who turns away from Christ can be restored to Christ. Some point to this passage to prove that a backslider cannot be restored. But "backsliders" are not the subject here. This passage refers to people who walk with Christ for a while and then deliberately turn around and walk the other direction, rejecting Christ. Hebrews 10:26 says, "For if we willfully persist in sin after having received the knowledge of the truth, there no longer remains a sacrifice for sins" (NRSV). These people can never be restored because they will not *want* to be restored. They have chosen to harden their hearts against Christ. It is not impossible for God to forgive them; rather, it is impossible for them to be forgiven because they won't repent of their sins.

In the final analysis, having a debate about the meaning of these verses should not be a priority for churches today. What matters most is the warning against apostasy, and the warning must be taken seriously. The passage describes people in our churches who act like and seem to be Christians, but who have not truly believed. When those assumed to be believers turn away, the debate may take place afterward, "Were they originally believers or not?" But people reading these words must heed the warning, not just debate the issue.

To the Hebrew Christians, these verses revealed the danger of returning to Judaism and thus committing apostasy. Some apply this verse today to superficial believers who renounce their Christianity, or to unbelievers who come close to salvation and then turn away. Either way, those who reject Christ will not be saved. Christ died once for all who believe. He will not be crucified again. Apart from his cross, there is no other possible way of salvation. The author had already denounced readers for their unwillingness to grow in the faith (6:1-3). Such unwillingness can lead to hardness of heart and to eventually turning away from the faith.

CAN'T GOD DO IT?

Hebrews 6:4-6 says that it is impossible for some to turn to Christ. But is it impossible for a really bad sinner to be forgiven? Even a bad sinner who stumbles again and again?

Some alcoholics are like that. The best of intentions cannot overcome the strongest of temptations, and they're back on the bottle. When weak faith is like alcoholism, can God forgive and restore?

The word "impossible" is not used here to restrict God or to describe a divine stubborn streak. It is simply a recognition that onetime believers who have quit following Christ rarely recover the joy and peace of a strong relationship with God. Normally, to quit faith means spiritual life is over. Christians who are trying to follow the Lord should not worry whether they have committed the unpardonable sin. That one is concerned about his or her spiritual condition proves that the unpardonable sin has not been committed.

In the twentieth century, a host of ideologies have swept Western civilization away from faith toward materialism, scientism, and egoism. Don't let it be your story. Pray every day, grow in faith, learn about God, renew your devotion, and "move on" toward maturity.

6:7-8 When the ground soaks up the falling rain and bears a good crop for the farmer, it has God's blessing. But if a field bears thorns and thistles, it is useless. The farmer will soon condemn that field and burn it.[NLT] In these verses, a farming illustration further describes the argument of 6:4-6. Someone who abandons Christ can be compared with a field that *bears thorns and thistles.* Such land refuses to yield a good crop no matter what attention it gets; *it is useless.* So with those who do not persevere to the end (6:11); their punishment is real and guaranteed—*the farmer will soon condemn that field and burn it.* (See also Matthew 3:10; John 15:1-6.)

However, believers who stay close to God, seeking to grow closer to him, can be described as those who bear *a good crop* and receive *God's blessing.* Just as both fields receive *rain,* so both groups receive God's concern and care. Only one group is genuine, however. Genuine faith results in "a good crop"; that is, it perseveres and produces fruit. Often you cannot tell from looking at the fields which one is good and which one is bad. Only time reveals the good fields. Jesus told a parable with the same principle (Matthew 13:24-30).

The cure for being ineffective, unfruitful, and "useless" is to grow in one's experiential knowledge of Jesus Christ. The apostle Peter wrote:

> *For this very reason, you must make every effort to support your faith with goodness, and goodness with knowledge, and knowledge with self-control, and self-control with endurance, and endurance with godliness, and godliness with mutual affection, and mutual affection with love. For if these things are yours and are increasing among you, they keep you from being ineffective and unfruitful in the knowledge of our Lord Jesus Christ. For anyone who lacks these things is nearsighted and blind, and is forgetful of the cleansing of past sins. Therefore, brothers and sisters, be all the more eager to confirm your call and election, for if you do this, you will never stumble. For in this way, entry into the eternal kingdom of our Lord and Savior Jesus Christ will be richly provided for you. (2 Peter 1:5-11 NRSV)*

FRUITFUL LIVES

The writer uses an analogy from agriculture to make a simple point. Real seeds (the gospel) given genuine care by the farmer (God) and planted in a fertile field (your heart and life) will produce a bountiful crop (spiritual maturity). Weeds (temptations) threaten to overwhelm the crop. If the field produces only weeds, then the seeds are lost and the field ruined.

An unproductive Christian life falls under God's condemnation. You have been watered by God's grace with clear and abundant teaching and preaching. What excuse do you have for a useless or unproductive life? Don't be a Christian in name only. Make sure your life bears fruit.

6:9 **Dear friends, even though we are talking this way, we really don't believe it applies to you. We are confident that you are meant for better things, things that come with salvation.**NLT

After arguing that it is possible for non-Christians to seem like true Christians, the writer continued that *we really don't believe it applies to you.* The stern warnings are now balanced with an encouraging note. The writer assures readers that the dire warnings of tragedy and spiritual loss are, thankfully, not going to be enacted against the Hebrew believers. This encouraging word tells readers that they are "on course" and indeed receptive to the spiritual food (or fertilizer) offered here. The criticism of 5:11 has melted away into recognition that the readers really are faithful Christians with awesome potential for growth and service. Confidence in the Farmer and a positive survey of the soil overcome the writer's earlier worry about the appearance of weeds (in this case, the Christians who felt like retreating into prior religious ritual). But these Christians must make headway in their Christian faith. They cannot be lazy, but now must move on. The time of being spiritual babies is over. The phrase "You are meant for better things, things that come with salvation" refers to the new covenant as compared to the old. The *better* things are those that *come with salvation* in the new covenant through Jesus Christ. There would be no reason to return to the old things that could not bring salvation.

6:10 For God is not unjust. He will not forget how hard you have worked for him and how you have shown your love to him by caring for other believers, as you still do.[NLT] The promise of "better things" in 6:9 is guaranteed because *God is not unjust. He will not forget how hard you have worked for him.* While we do not need to work for our salvation, our salvation ought to change our lives so that we naturally want to serve God, do good works, and advance his kingdom. The works show our love for God; however, works of service to God often go unheralded and unnoticed in this life. We can become discouraged, wondering why we work so hard for so little response or so little thanks. Yet God has not forgotten us. He never overlooks or forgets our hard work for him, done out of love. Believers must continue to do good wholeheartedly, for God remembers our efforts.

Although you may not presently be receiving rewards and acclaim, God knows your efforts of love and ministry. Let God's love for you and his intimate knowledge of your service for him bolster you as you face disappointment and rejection here on earth.

We show our love for God *by caring for other believers.* As discussed elsewhere in the New Testament, what we do to others is done to God (Matthew 25:35; Romans 12:6-18; 1 John 4:19-21). Good works do not guarantee salvation, but salvation changes the lives of God's people, leading them to perform good works.

How will God regard our hard work? Scripture speaks often of rewards awaiting God's faithful servants. God may not reward Christians in a material way, but the spiritual rewards will be great. To read more about the promised rewards, see Matthew 16:27; Romans 14:12; 1 Corinthians 3:8-15; 4:5; 9:16-27; 2 Corinthians 5:10; Ephesians 6:8; Colossians 3:24; 2 Timothy 4:8; James 1:12; 1 Peter 5:4; Revelation 2:10; 22:12.

6:11-12 And we desire that each one of you show the same diligence to the full assurance of hope until the end, that you do not become sluggish, but imitate those who through faith and patience inherit the promises.[NKJV] The service mentioned in 6:10 should be continued with *the same diligence* (renewed in both zeal and concern) by *each one* of the believers *until the end.* It pleases God when his people serve him. Believers have work to do in the world "until the end" (i.e., when we die or when Christ returns again). We must continue showing that diligence to grow and serve. Why? Because we have *full assurance of hope.* In other words, we serve, not in order to get to heaven (as in some religions of the world), but because we are assured of the full realizations of what we hope for and because we love the one who gave us that assurance. Our conviction must produce actions that show our true colors. We don't serve merely for the fun of it or for humanitarian principles, but because our hope is in our future life with Christ.

> God's promises are like the stars; the darker the night the brighter they shine. *David Nicholas*

The opposite of being diligent is to *become sluggish,* unreceptive, or lazy (see 5:11). Believers are to be diligently growing and serving, not sitting back making everyone else do the work. To keep from becoming inactive or indifferent, believers would do well to *imitate those who through faith and patience inherit the promises.* The writer anticipates the example of many Old Testament followers of God (who are discussed later in chapter 11; see also 13:7). Their example should be actively imitated, not merely learned and acknowledged. Imitating these people's examples of faith in God will help Christians of all times keep from drifting away from Christ (2:1-4) or becoming hard-hearted (3:7–4:13).

In 6:10-12, we find the trilogy of faith, hope, and love. These three words show up together often in the New Testament as a simple program for Christian living (see, for example, 1 Corinthians 13:13; Galatians 5:5-6; Ephesians 4:2-5; 1 Thessalonians 1:3; 5:8; 1 Peter 1:21-22). While we may talk much about faith and love, hope is vitally important. The key lies in the future. Why have faith in Jesus if there is no hope for a glorious future? Why love others if it doesn't matter in the end? If we have no hope in the afterlife, Paul wrote that "we are more to be pitied than anyone in the world" (1 Corinthians 15:19 NLT). For these Jewish believers suffering for their faith, hope mattered tremendously. In fact, hope makes all the difference. The Christian's hope is a confident expectation. Our hope is "stored" in heaven, where Christ returned to be with the Father. That hope will be fulfilled in the future. We look forward to a hope that is awaiting us; yet we also have that hope with us, enabling us to live our Christian lives with unhindered faith and love. Our confidence gives us stronger faith in God and deeper love for others.

FULL OF HOPE

What makes most kids excited about tomorrow? Little clusters of hope that spark a young imagination. What makes many elderly people grumpy and sad? Every hope they ever had is spent; tomorrow offers nothing.

The gospel is full of hope. Young and old, wealthy and poor, extroverted and bashful—all are invited to the great hope of heavenly peace and joy. This hope doesn't work if what you *really* want is youth, wealth, and popularity. These pass with time. But for all who set their hope in God, tomorrow offers huge possibilities.

So wipe off that sad face and live a little! God has promised you a home. Jesus is there to show you the way.

GOD'S CERTAIN PROMISE GIVES HOPE / 6:13-20

A ship's captain must know where to safely drop anchor. Too much mud or a bottom covered with small, loose rocks will keep the anchor from holding the ship secure. Just throwing out the anchor guarantees little; one of the prongs must dig into the ocean floor or lodge against a substantial rock to hold the vessel safe.

Thankfully, God provides us the firm and secure Word so that our ship of faith is securely anchored on his solid promises. Our Captain has guaranteed a safe anchorage in any storm. Trust him to see you through.

6:13-14 **When God made a promise to Abraham, because he had no one greater by whom to swear, he swore by himself, saying, "I will surely bless you and multiply you."**[NRSV] After encouraging the readers to imitate other faithful people, the writer offered one of the examples in the Old Testament whose example would be worth imitating: *Abraham.* The readers could trust in God's promises because Abraham did, and he was rewarded. *God made a promise to Abraham.* It was not really necessary for God to swear that he would keep his promise, because God cannot lie or break his word. However, *because he had no one greater by whom to swear, he swore by himself.* God made the

> I believe the promises of God enough to venture an eternity on them.
> *Isaac Watts*

promise, swearing by the greatest standard and with the highest accountability possible. Abraham could not have received greater assurance.

The concept of making a promise and swearing on a higher authority than oneself has ancient precedent. Even in the Old Testament, a sovereign assured the credibility of his word by linking it to the power of a god, implying that that god would penalize promise breakers. But if the one making a promise is God himself, to what higher authority could an appeal be made? None. "The buck stops here" was the famous slogan on the desk of President Harry Truman. And surely, the "buck" finally stops with God. There is none higher. Though God needs no surety for his promises, this verse means that divine promises are guarded by God's own character.

To what promise is the writer referring? Recorded in Genesis 22:17, God promised Abraham, *I will surely bless you and multiply you.* Abraham only needed to wait patiently.

6:15 And so after waiting patiently, Abraham received what was promised.[NIV] The author's antidote for apostasy is *waiting patiently.* Abraham waited patiently, and that patience was rewarded. Abraham's patient wait lasted for twenty-five years—from the time God had promised him a son (Genesis 17:16) to Isaac's birth (Genesis 21:1-3). Because our trials and temptations are often so intense, they seem to last for an eternity. Both the Bible and the testimony of mature Christians encourage us to wait for God to act in his timing, even when our needs seem too great to wait any longer. God's promises always come true—we can count on him. It may take a while. The answers may not come as soon as we expect or in the timing that we think is perfect, but we must trust in our sovereign God. We will receive what he has promised.

6:16 Now when people take an oath, they call on someone greater than themselves to hold them to it. And without any question that oath is binding.[NLT] This description of taking *an oath* has carried over the centuries so that today we understand the concept completely. Even in modern wedding ceremonies, the oaths (vows) that the man and woman make to each other are witnessed by other people, who are then obliged to hold the two people accountable for their promises. But even more than that, the oath is made before God—*someone greater* than the couple who holds them to those vows. It follows, then, that *without any question that oath is binding.* We call on greater authority because we know that difficulty in keeping promises may wear at our resources and efforts.

ABRAHAM IN THE NEW TESTAMENT

Abraham was an ancestor of Jesus Christ.	Matthew 1:1-2, 17; Luke 3:23-24	Jesus Christ was human; he was born into the line of Abraham, whom God had chosen to be the father of a great nation through which the whole world would be blessed.
Abraham was the father of the the Jewish nation.	Matthew 3:9; Luke 3:8; Acts 13:26; Romans 4:1; 11:1; 2 Corinthians 11:22; Hebrews 6:13-14	God wanted to set apart a nation for himself, a nation that would tell the world about him. He began with a man of faith who, though old and childless, believed God's promise of innumerable descendants. We can trust God to do the impossible when we have faith.
Abraham was honored by God.	Hebrews 7:4	God honors those who trust him. Although the world may have disdain for us if we trust in God, God promises to honor us.
Abraham, because of his faith, now sits in the kingdom with Christ.	Matthew 8:11; Luke 13:28; 16:23-31	Abraham followed God, and now he is enjoying his reward—eternity with God. We will one day meet Abraham because we have been promised eternity as well.
God is Abraham's God; thus Abraham is alive with God.	Matthew 22:32; Mark 12:26; Luke 20:37; Acts 7:32	As Abraham lives forever, we will live forever because we, like Abraham, have chosen the life of faith.
Abraham recevied great promises from God.	Luke 1:55, 72-73; Acts 3:25; 7:17-18; Galatians 3:6, 14-16; Hebrews 6:13-15	Many of the promises that God made to Abraham seemed impossible to be realized, but Abraham trusted God. The promises to believers in God's Word also seem too incredible to believe, but we can trust God to keep all his promises.
Abraham followed God.	Acts 7:2-8; Hebrews 11:8, 17-19	Abraham followed God's leading from his homeland to an unknown territory that became the Jews' Promised Land. When we follow God, even before he makes all his plans clear to us, we will never be disappointed.
God blessed Abraham because of faith.	Romans 4; Galatians 3:6-9, 14-16; Hebrews 11:8, 17-19; James 2:21-24	Abraham showed faith in times of disappointment, trial, and testing. Because of Abraham's faith, God counted him righteous and called him his friend. God accepts us because of our faith.
Abraham is father of all those who come to God by faith.	Romans 9:6-8; Galatians 3:6-9, 14-29	The Jews are Abraham's chidlren,and Christ is Abraham's descendant. Because all believers are Christ's brothers and sisters we are Abraham's children and God's children. Abraham was righeous because of his faith; we are made righteous through faith in Christ. The promises made to Abraham apply to us because of Christ.

PATIENTLY WAITING

Abraham's twenty-five years of patience is stunning! God promised, and then delivered twenty-five years later. Yet God did eventually deliver. We, by contrast, have such a hard time waiting.

Sometimes patience requires an *hour*—waiting for an important phone call, a doctor's report after surgery, a late plane to arrive.

Sometimes patience requires a *day*—tomorrow's mail brings the letter, tomorrow's recital determines the future, tomorrow's interview changes your plans.

Sometimes patience requires a *year*—for a spouse in the military to complete overseas duty, for graduation, for retirement.

Sometimes patience looks toward *eternity*.

Patience means that time doesn't dim our hope, because time has no bearing on the promise's delivery. Waiting is OK. It's easy time. Soon the promise comes.

6:17 Because God wanted to make the unchanging nature of his purpose very clear to the heirs of what was promised, he confirmed it with an oath.NIV While God didn't need to make an oath (because he cannot lie nor violate his own word), he *confirmed . . . with an oath* his promise to Abraham to multiply Abraham's descendants (6:13-14). Humans often need promises sealed with oaths, so God did this for us because he *wanted to make the unchanging nature of his purpose very clear to the heirs of what was promised.*

The writer and the original readers would also have remembered the rest of God's promise to Abraham: "In your seed all the nations of the earth shall be blessed" (Genesis 22:18 NKJV). Not only did Abraham have countless descendants (the Jewish nation), but his descendants came to include all people of faith who had been blessed through the "seed" (or descendant) of Abraham—Jesus Christ. Galatians 3:7-9 says, "Understand, then, that those who believe are children of Abraham. The Scripture foresaw that God would justify the Gentiles by faith, and announced the gospel in advance to Abraham: 'All nations will be blessed through you.' So those who have faith are blessed along with Abraham, the man of faith" (NIV). This was the "unchanging nature of his purpose." From the very beginning, God's plan was to build a people of faith—not just from one nation, but from all nations, people brought together by common trust in Jesus Christ (born into the line of Abraham) for their salvation.

6:18 So God has given us both his promise and his oath. These two things are unchangeable because it is impossible for God to lie. Therefore, we who have fled to him for refuge can have

great confidence as we hold to the hope that lies before us.NLT God confirmed his promise with an oath (6:17), because *these two things are unchangeable.* Why are they unchangeable? *Because it is impossible for God to lie.* God provides us security because of his own character. Patience is our part whereby we *hold to the hope that lies before us.*

The phrase "we who have fled to him for refuge" pictures a person who fled to one of the cities of refuge that provided protection for someone who accidentally killed another (Numbers 35). Christians also have fled for safety to the place of security and protection from the punishment against them. Christ provides the safest place, the hope we count on, the encouragement we need. We must "hold to the hope that lies before us," grasping it, refusing to let go no matter what might happen around us. For more on this promise, see commentary on 6:11-12.

> My own weakness makes me shrink, but God's promise makes me brave.
> *C. H. Spurgeon*

6:19-20 **We have this hope as an anchor for the soul, firm and secure. It enters the inner sanctuary behind the curtain, where Jesus, who went before us, has entered on our behalf. He has become a high priest forever, in the order of Melchizedek.**NIV *This hope* (referred to in 6:11-12, 18) is *an anchor for the soul,* secure and immovable, anchored in God as a ship's anchor holds firmly to the seabed. Just as an anchor keeps a ship from drifting away, so the *firm and secure* hope that believers have can keep them from drifting away from their faith (2:1). The two words "firm" and "secure" are virtually synonymous in Greek and are used to describe anything about which we have assurance.

Not only does this hope hold us secure, but *it enters the inner sanctuary behind the curtain, where Jesus, who went before us, has entered on our behalf.* The "inner sanctuary behind the curtain" refers to the Most Holy Place in the Jewish temple. A curtain hung across the entrance to this room prevented anyone from entering or even getting a fleeting glimpse of the interior of the Most Holy Place where God resided among his people (see also 9:1-8). The high priest could enter there only once a year (on the Day of Atonement) to stand before God's presence and atone for the sins of the entire nation (see 5:1-3). But Jesus "went before us," opening the way into God's presence by his death on the cross. His death *on our behalf* tore the curtain in two (Mark 15:38), allowing believers to come directly into God's presence. Jesus, "who went before us" (literally, "forerunner"), expects

Christians to follow him and enter God's presence. What only the high priest could do before, Christ did and allows us to do as well. In this way, Christ's high-priestly work was different from any other priest. Other priests took people's sacrifices and represented them in the presence of God. Now, through Christ, we can approach the throne of grace with confidence (10:19). Repeating the theme touched on in 5:5-10, the writer again describes Jesus as *a high priest forever, in the order of Melchizedek.* An explanation of this comparison follows in chapter 7.

Note Jesus' crucial role in communicating and securing God's eternal promises for us. The promises, an expression of God's holy character, are eternally valid. Jesus activates the promises, eliminating, as it were, the impediment (sin) that renders the promises ineffective. By God's promises and Jesus' intercession, believers are incorporated into the family of God.

THANKS, JESUS!

Inside a judge's chamber, an attorney pleads for a client. The judge listens, waiting to determine guilt or innocence, release or penalty. The defendant sits outside. A similar picture is presented here. Israel's high priest would "argue the case" with the righteous God once a year in a secret place where each would meet to hear the plea. Jesus is pictured here as our perpetual High Priest, always advocating judicial acquittal for all who put faith in his work. Thanks, Jesus, we need that! We indigent clients have not much of a case apart from you. Our prospects are grim, but you turn judgment into blessing. There's no fee we can pay you, but in gratitude we give our lives to you. Whatever happens from now on, we know there's nothing to fear.

HEBREWS 7

MELCHIZEDEK COMPARED TO ABRAHAM / 7:1-10

If the prolific survey-takers in our day asked you for the most respected names in the Old Testament, would Melchizedek make your list?

Although mentioned only twice in the Old Testament, Melchizedek, king of Salem (Jerusalem) and priest of God Most High, draws great praise. At one time, Abraham, the patriarch, the founder of the Jewish nation, gave 10 percent of his plunder from battle to this mysterious figure. Because there is no record of this man's birth or death, the Bible uses Melchizedek as an example of Jesus' eternal ministry. After the warnings given in 5:11–6:12, chapter 7 picks up the theme of 5:10, which says that Christ was designated High Priest in the order of Melchizedek. Jesus is superior in rank and authority to Melchizedek and any other religious authority. We should always hold forth Jesus as our highest authority.

7:1-2 **This Melchizedek was king of the city of Salem and also a priest of God Most High. When Abraham was returning home after winning a great battle against the kings, Melchizedek met him and blessed him. Then Abraham took a tenth of all he had captured in battle and gave it to Melchizedek.**[NLT] The author begins to describe the priesthood of Jesus by illustrating how Jesus was a priest in the same way that *Melchizedek* was a priest. Having already mentioned Melchizedek in passing (5:6, 10; 6:20), the author now returns to discuss him at length. In this discussion, the author shows that the Levitical priesthood, very familiar to Jewish readers, has been replaced by a new order of priests who were foreshadowed and characterized by Melchizedek.

Melchizedek *was king of the city of Salem and also a priest of God Most High.* This description of Melchizedek comes from Genesis 14:18-20. He seems to have been an extraordinary man who served his people in both the offices of priest and king. While this was not that unusual in ancient times, it *was* unusual among God's people. Not even King David served in both roles.

In fact, God punished other kings who attempted to do both. When Saul offered sacrifices, God rejected him as king (1 Samuel 13). When Uzziah offered incense at the temple, God punished him (2 Chronicles 26). "Salem" may later have become the city of Jerusalem. Melchizedek, however, served as the king and priest. The appellation "God Most High" means that Melchizedek worshiped the one true God. Genesis 14:18-20 uses the term "God Most High" three times in three verses. (For more uses of the name, see Psalm 57:2; 78:35, 56; Daniel 3:26; 4:2, 24-25, 34; 5:18, 21; 7:18, 25; Mark 5:7; Luke 8:28; Acts 16:17.)

This passage refers to the time *when Abraham was returning home after winning a great battle against the kings.* Four kings in Abraham's region had united and had conquered Sodom and other neighboring cities (Genesis 14:1-11). Abraham's nephew Lot and his family lived in Sodom. When Abraham heard that Lot and his family had been captured, Abraham mobilized 318 men for battle. With a surprise attack, Abraham and his tiny band of men liberated Lot and the others who had been captured (Genesis 14:12-16).

After defeating the four kings, Abraham became the greatest power in the land, and *Melchizedek met him and blessed him.* Then Abraham *took a tenth of all he had captured in battle and gave it to Melchizedek* because Melchizedek was a priest of God Most High. By giving the tithe to Melchizedek, Abraham was giving the gift to God's representative. Although these two men were strangers to each other, they shared a most important characteristic: Both worshiped and served the one God who made heaven and earth. This was a great moment of triumph for Abraham. He had just defeated an army and had freed a large group of captives. If he had any doubt in his mind about who had gained the victory, Melchizedek set the record straight by reminding Abraham, "Blessed be God Most High, who delivered your enemies into your hand" (Genesis 14:20 NIV). Abraham recognized that he and this man worshiped the same God.

The original readers of Hebrews would have known that Melchizedek was greater than Abraham because he was able to receive tithes and give a blessing (see 7:7). This argument may not carry the same logical forcefulness for readers today as it did then, but these early Jewish believers understood the argument.

The name Melchizedek means "king of justice," and king of Salem means "king of peace."NLT One of the reasons why Melchizedek is so significant is that his name *means "king of justice"* or righteousness. (The suffix of his name, "zedek," means righteousness.) He is also the *"king of peace"* because

Salem means "peace." In Melchizedek's name and position, righteousness and peace come together. Therefore, Melchizedek represents the same character traits as the Messiah, Jesus, who revealed God's righteousness and peace.

GOD RESPECTS COURAGE

Abraham's campaign to recover plunder and captives from the four pirate kings was an act of courage. He recruited his troops, developed strategy, and pressed to victory. Justice was done, and a lot of people breathed easier. God showed his approval by sending the great priest Melchizedek to bless Abraham. God approves of courage today. Most of us do not take up swords against marauders, but we do face constant injustice. People around us need help. Powerful bullies need to be confronted. Courage sets you apart and puts you at risk. Courage cannot be selfish and does not always win. But courage for God's sake is still approved. When your leadership is needed, God will help and bless you.

Justice and peace were extremely relevant to the readers of Hebrews. On one hand, they were eager to find God's peace as a key element in the promises to be inherited from Abraham. Justice and peace were key characteristics of the future life every Jew desired and anticipated. Also, as a Christian community, they were facing persecution and oppression. So being justly treated and experiencing peace were doubly important to them.

Who was Melchizedek? Through the years, many have believed that he was Christ himself appearing in human form to Abraham—technically called a "Christophany" (an appearance of Christ in the Old Testament). This seems unlikely because Melchizedek is said to *resemble* Christ. Ancient Jewish interpretation said he was an angelic being, but there is no evidence in Genesis, Psalm 110:4, or Hebrews to support this theory. The best interpretation is that Melchizedek was a historical priest-king who lived in ancient times and was a symbol and type of Christ. He was unrelated to the Jews because Abraham was the first Jew.

7:3 **There is no record of his father or mother or any of his ancestors—no beginning or end to his life. He remains a priest forever, resembling the Son of God.**[NLT] To bolster the argument, the author of Hebrews used what is not said in Genesis 14 as much or more as what is said. The Bible does not provide a genealogy for Melchizedek nor a record of his death. While the Bible does not supply details of Melchizedek's life, most likely Melchizedek was a human king and priest who really did have parents, and thus was born and eventually died. Jewish theology and typology, however, is built only on what the Bible text says. Because in the Bible text *there is no record of his father or mother or any of his ancestors,* it is as though he didn't have any. Because the text records *no beginning or end to his life,* it is as though Melchizedek never was born or died.

While some have taken this to mean that Melchizedek was an angel or a preincarnate appearance of Christ, the text does not support this. Rather, the contrast is being made between Melchizedek and Aaron's priestly line, which depended entirely on genealogy. Priests in Aaron's family succeeded upon the death of the prior priest, making the date of death extremely important. None of the apparatus of the Aaronic priesthood (Exodus 39) applied to Melchizedek, except God's appointment. In this way, Melchizedek foreshadows Jesus, God's special emissary.

Melchizedek did not become a priest because his father handed down the priesthood to him. The contrast with Aaron's priesthood is clear. The lineage of priests was very important. Priests who could not prove their lineage were excluded from service (see Nehemiah 7:64).

With no record of beginning or end, Melchizedek *remains a priest forever, resembling the Son of God* (see also Psalm 110:4). Hebrews doesn't say that Jesus resembled Melchizedek, but that Melchizedek resembled Jesus. Melchizedek was a real man, a servant of God, whose history is recorded in the book of Genesis in such a way as to make him resemble the one who would come and fulfill completely the offices of priest and king, and who would truly be "a priest forever."

RESEMBLING JESUS TODAY

Melchizedek resembled Jesus by way of his special priestly office. Today we are called to resemble Jesus by way of our character.

Study Jesus. Learn of his virtues, characteristics, and commitments. Ask how his life can educate yours. Build your character around the traits that he displayed. Personalities will differ. Gifts and talents will never be identical from person to person. But character can be learned. Learn from the Master.

7:4 **Now consider how great this man was, to whom even the patriarch Abraham gave a tenth of the spoils.**[NKJV] Scripture describes *the patriarch Abraham* as a great man and a friend of God, a man God considered righteous because of his faith and obedience (see James 2:23). God singled out Abraham to be the father of a nation. As great as Abraham was, Hebrews says to

GIVING A TENTH

Many ancient peoples observed the practice of tithing—that is, giving a tenth of their earnings (or produce, harvest, etc.) back to a leader or a god. God commanded the Israelites to tithe, and the first instance appears in Abraham's encounter with Melchizedek.

The Israelites were required to tithe of their crops, fruit, and herds	Leviticus 27:30-32
The tithe was received by the Levites to support them.	Numbers 18:21, 24
The Levites, in turn, gave "a tithe of the tithe" to support the priests.	Numbers 18:26-29; Nehemiah 10:39
The Israelites were to bring their tithes to Jerusalem, and offering them came in the form of a ritual meal in whch Levites were invited to share. If Jerusalem was too far for a person to transport the tithe, he could take the tithe there in the form of money. Every third year the tithe could be offered in one's local area, but the person was still to go to Jerusalem to worship.	Deuteronomy 12:5-7, 11-19; 14:22-29; 26:12-15
God promises blessings for those who faithfully tithe, and he says that refusing to tithe is like robbing him.	Malachi 3:8-12
Tithing, without love for or obedience to God, amounts to nothing more than a meaningless ritual.	Matthew 23:23; Luke 11:42

consider how great this man [Melchizedek] was, because *even the patriarch Abraham gave a tenth of the spoils* to him. The argument follows a simple logic here. The major premise: Greater beings receive donations from lesser beings. The strength of the argument hinges entirely on this premise, which is not as persuasive to today's readers as it was to the original readers. Since Melchizedek received a tithe from Abraham, Melchizedek is greater than Abraham (see 7:7). In a context where the major premise is understood as true, Melchizedek is seen as an awesome person. He is in another class altogether different from the greatest of the patriarchs.

Abraham paying tithes to Melchizedek showed that Abraham acknowledged Melchizedek's superiority. Not only did Abraham give "a tenth of the spoils," but the Greek word for "spoils" *(akrothinion)* denotes that these were the choicest spoils. Because Melchizedek was greater, the author will argue that the priesthood that comes from Melchizedek must be greater than the priesthood that comes from Abraham, who is the "patriarch" of the entire Jewish nation. In the same way, Jesus is in another class altogether different from the prophets, angels, priests, and patriarchs.

7:5-6 Now the law requires the descendants of Levi who become priests to collect a tenth from the people—that is, their brothers—even though their brothers are descended from Abraham. This man, however, did not trace his descent from Levi, yet he collected a tenth from Abraham and blessed him who had the promises.[NIV] The major premise of 7:4 is further explained by the Jewish law: *Now the law requires the descendants of Levi who become priests to collect a tenth from the people—that is, their brothers.* In the Old Testament, as God began teaching the Israelites his laws, he also was teaching his people how to worship him. To help in this, he needed ministers to oversee the operations of the tabernacle and to help the people maintain their relationship with God. The tribe of Levi (called Levites, "descendants of Levi") was set apart to be servants in God's tabernacle. The priests came from the tribe of Levi, but also had to be descended from Aaron, Israel's first high priest. The priests had more responsibilities than Levites. The priests performed the daily sacrifices, maintained the tabernacle, and counseled the people on how to follow God. They were the people's representatives before God and thus were required to live worthy of their office.

Because the "descendants of Levi" were dedicated to serving God, their jobs meant that they did not have the time to maintain land. When the tribes were allotted land in the book of Joshua, the Levites were given no particular section. Instead, God arranged for the other tribes to meet the Levites' needs through donations—thus the mention of them receiving "a tenth from the people." The Levites were supported by the tithes of the people, who gave them homes, flocks, and pasturelands. The Levites, in turn, paid a tithe of that amount ("a tithe of the tithe") to support the priests (Numbers 18:21-28). So the priests and Levites were assigned by God's law to receive a tithe, even though the Levites had the same ancestry as all the other Jews, that is, they were "brothers," all descended from Abraham. The gifts came from their "equals."

Now Melchizedek *did not trace his descent from Levi, yet he collected a tenth from Abraham.* Apparently, even the great patriarch Abraham recognized Melchizedek's greatness and superiority by giving him a "tenth of everything" that had been captured in battle. To comprehend this argument, we need to understand that Abraham represents his entire nation. Israel's first high priest, Aaron, descended from Levi (the tribe of priests), and Levi descended from Abraham. Therefore, if Abraham recognized Melchizedek as his superior, then Melchizedek is also superior to all of Abraham's descendants, including the line of priests. This makes Melchizedek's priesthood greater than the Jewish priesthood. Melchizedek "did not trace his descent from Levi" and neither did Jesus, who was born into the tribe of Judah.

The priests and Levites owed their position to their birth; they owed their receiving of tithes to provisions in God's law. Melchizedek, however, stands in history as a solitary figure. He was given the tithe, not because of provision in the law, but because Abraham recognized his greatness. Melchizedek, in turn, acknowledged his superior position as he *blessed* Abraham, the man who *had the promises* (referring to the covenant promise given to him by God; see Genesis 12:1-3).

7:7 **And without question, the person who has the power to give a blessing is greater than the one who is blessed.**NLT This is another statement of the major premise of the argument (see notes on 7:4). Today we might not grasp the forcefulness of this argument *without question,* but for the original readers, this logic secured the conclusion. Melchizedek, as a priest of God Most High, had *the power to give a blessing.* Therefore, Melchizedek must be superior to Abraham, who was *blessed.* A blessing was a significant ritual passed along from fathers to sons, as well as from prominent to less prominent people. Thus it follows that the one who has the power to bless is obviously greater than the one being blessed.

7:8-10 **The priests who collect tithes are men who die, so Melchizedek is greater than they are, because we are told that he lives on. In addition, we might even say that these Levites—the ones who collect the tithe—paid a tithe to Melchizedek when their ancestor Abraham paid a tithe to him. For although Levi wasn't born yet, the seed from which he came was in Abraham's body when Melchizedek collected the tithe from him.**NLT The strength of the argument continues with assumptions that are not as persuasive today as they were in the first century.

> The tithe prescribed by Israelite law is paid to mortal men; the tithe which Abraham gave Melchizedek was received by one who, so far as the record goes, has no "end of life."
> *F. F. Bruce*

First, Melchizedek is compared to Levitical priests, whose mortality is plainly attested to in the Old Testament: In the case of Jewish priests, tithes are paid to men who will die. Because Scripture does not record Melchizedek's death, it is as if he *lives on* (see note on 7:3). Because Melchizedek is not recorded to have died, his priesthood extends forever, in contrast to the Levites, who died and passed on their service to their sons. This is how Melchizedek resembled Christ, who really does live and serve forever. What the author asserts about Melchizedek "from the record," Jesus fulfills in person and power. Having died on the cross and risen again, Jesus lives never to die.

Second, Melchizedek is compared to Levitical priests, who, by ancestry, paid him a tithe: *these Levites . . . paid a tithe to Melchizedek* through *their ancestor Abraham.* Although gene theory was unknown to our author, the idea is that the future generations participate in (or are affected by) the life and fate of a forefather. The Levites are represented by their ancestor Abraham: *For although Levi wasn't born yet, the seed from which he came was in Abraham's body when Melchizedek collected the tithe from him.* If Abraham gave Melchizedek one-tenth of his booty, the unborn Levites also participated in the action. In this way, Melchizedek would also be greater than the Levites and the Levitical priests. This principle of corporate solidarity was very popular in Eastern and Middle Eastern customs and is often seen in the Old Testament when blessings and punishments are given to sons' sons. Even Paul used this argument when he said, "All die in Adam" (1 Corinthians 15:22 NRSV). Abraham was a great man, and his descendants served as acceptable priests. But Melchizedek was greater and therefore his priesthood was better.

CHRIST IS LIKE MELCHIZEDEK / 7:11-28

Centuries after Melchizedek, the psalmist predicted that the Messiah would be a priest in the order of Melchizedek (Psalm 110:4). More than one thousand years later, the author of Hebrews quoted the psalmist, adding that Jesus Christ had become the "guarantee of a better covenant" and was made "perfect forever." Melchizedek was not the final priest. Neither was Aaron. Christ became the perfect, final priest. He is the one who allows us to follow him as he enters God's presence.

7:11 If perfection could have been attained through the Levitical priesthood (for on the basis of it the law was given to the people), why was there still need for another priest to come—one in the order of Melchizedek, not in the order of Aaron?NIV In 7:11-19, the writer seeks to show how the Levitical priesthood and the ritual system of sacrifice were insufficient to save people. Thus, that system was merely a preparation, a picture, of what would come and fulfill it. This fulfillment was prophesied in Psalm 110:4, which says (NIV), "The Lord has sworn and will not change his mind: 'You are a priest forever, in the order of Melchizedek'" (see 7:17). If the Levitical priesthood had been sufficient, the author asks, *why was there still need for another priest to come,* as prophesied in the psalm? This priest came as a fulfillment of what had been pictured in the Old Testament, offering *perfection* that could not be attained *through the Levitical priesthood.* This priesthood could not allow people to approach God alone with their sacrifice because the animal sacrifices alone, without faith in God, really could do nothing to remove sin. Thus "perfection" could not be achieved through the Old Testament priesthood, not because there was anything wrong with it, but because all along it had been meant as a shadow of what was to come. Perfection—complete with access to God and personal relationship with him—would have to come through "another priest to come."

When this better way would come, the old way would become obsolete (see Hebrews 8:7ff.). The old systems and priesthood, on the basis of which *the law was given to the people,* would no longer be necessary. A new way would mean a new law and a new system (7:12). God could not simply provide another human priest; instead, he provided something new. The psalmist prophesied of the new priesthood *in the order of Melchizedek, not in the order of Aaron.* For an explanation of Melchizedek, see notes on 7:1-10. Aaron was Moses' brother and Israel's first high priest (see Leviticus 8–9). All future priests in Israel had to descend from his line—"in the order of Aaron."

Because Christianity provided a better way, any Christian who would consider returning to Jewish practices would be acting foolishly. The Old Testament sacrificial system could not effectively (permanently and perfectly) remove sin or help anyone draw closer to God.

THE NEW PRIEST

Jesus' high-priestly role was superior to that of any priest of Levi because the Messiah was a priest of a higher order (Psalm 110:4). If the Jewish priests and their laws had been able to save people, why would God need to send Christ as a priest, who came not from the tribe of Levi (the priestly tribe), but from the tribe of Judah? The animal sacrifices had to be repeated, and they offered only temporary forgiveness; but Christ's sacrifice was offered once, and it offers total and permanent forgiveness. Under the new covenant, the Levitical priesthood was canceled in favor of Christ's role as High Priest. Because Christ is our High Priest, we need to pay attention to him. No minister, priest, or leader can substitute for Christ's work and for his role in our salvation.

7:12 And if the priesthood is changed, the law must also be changed to permit it.[NLT] Provisions for the Levitical priesthood were given in the law—including their duties, ordination, clothing, etc. But the law could not foresee a change in priesthood, such as a new priest arising from the tribe of Judah (as did Jesus Christ, 7:13). Therefore, *if the priesthood is changed, the law must also be changed to permit it.*

Few things were as stable as the Old Testament law. Kings came and went; high priests died and made way for new high priests. But the law never changed. The Old Testament law is not God's final word, however; it was, in fact, preparatory. Christ himself became the final word. The law was not changed, but rather was fulfilled, rendering the ceremonial parts of the law (such as the system for animal sacrifice) out of date. The ceremonial laws have been superseded by Christ himself, who was the final and sufficient sacrifice.

Christ was not just another priest in the old system; rather, the entire system was changed with Christ as the High Priest in the new system. For readers who were close to lapsing into Judaism, these words would remind them that their old Jewish ways had been fulfilled and replaced by Christ.

7:13-14 He of whom these things are said belonged to a different tribe, and no one from that tribe has ever served at the altar. For it is clear that our Lord descended from Judah, and in regard to that tribe Moses said nothing about priests.[NIV] Many important people had come from the tribe of Judah, but not priests. By law, only Levites could serve as priests (see commentary on 7:5-6). "He of whom these things are said" refers to Jesus, who *belonged to a different tribe.* The Messiah high-priest was not a Levite; his lineage was *from Judah* (Luke 2:4; 3:31, 33). Judah, one of the twelve tribes of Israel, was the largest tribe (Numbers 1:20-46), and it was the tribe from which most of Israel's kings had come (see Genesis 49:8-12). Later, Judah was one of the few tribes to return to God after a century of captivity under a hostile foreign power. Also, Judah was prophesied as the tribe through which the Messiah would come (Micah 5:2).

No one from that tribe has ever served at the altar . . . and in regard to that tribe Moses [the lawgiver] said nothing about priests. Although no one from Judah had ever served as a high priest ("ever served at the altar"), Jesus was able to do so on two counts: (1) The old system was eliminated; (2) Jesus was appointed a priest on the basis of his "indestructible life" (see 7:15). This indestructible life allowed Jesus to serve at an altar greater than the one in Jerusalem, which means he serves continually in the presence of God.

This is only one example, but an undisputed one, that the Old Testament ceremonial law cannot bring salvation. The descendants of Levi were made to be the priests, but God proclaimed through prophecy that the Messiah would come through the tribe of Judah. This is further proof that the Levitical priesthood was temporary. The better High Priest was coming.

7:15-17 **And what we have said is even more clear if another priest like Melchizedek appears, one who has become a priest not on the basis of a regulation as to his ancestry but on the basis of the power of an indestructible life. For it is declared: "You are a priest forever, in the order of Melchizedek."**NIV Which of the priests of Aaron lived forever? None. Thus no priest in all of Israel's history was "a priest forever." Old Testament priests were vital to the spiritual life of Israel, but they were imperfect and temporary. Only one priest could fulfill God's plan. The writer explained that this "other priest" came from "another tribe."

- He is *like Melchizedek* and has a priesthood *in the order of Melchizedek*—as described in 7:1-10. By being in the order of Melchizedek, Jesus Christ was both priest and king. Some Jews of Jesus' day (particularly those at Qumran) were anticipating two messiahs, one priestly and one kingly. Jesus was both.
- He became a priest *not on the basis of a regulation as to his ancestry.* As Melchizedek was a Gentile priest, so Jesus did not fit the pattern. As described in 7:13-14, Jesus was not born into the tribe of Levi, but the tribe of Judah.
- He became a priest *on the basis of the power of an indestructible life.* Because there is no record in Scripture of Melchizedek's death, it is as if he never died. So with Jesus—death could not master him. He died, but he rose never to die again. As a result, he will never cease his priestly ministry.
- He fulfills the qualification of being *a priest forever.* The one who never dies has become the final High Priest, and his sacrifice has forever settled the breach that human sin created between almighty God and sinful humanity. Christ is immortal, fulfilling the prophecy of Psalm 110:4. The old priesthood was incomplete and is now abolished.

How important is the Resurrection to Christian teaching? Paul wrote that if Christ is not raised, Christian faith is useless and futile (1 Corinthians 15:14, 18). The author of Hebrews wrote that if Jesus died and is still dead, then all is lost. Aaron's priestly clan is all dead. But the good news is that Jesus was raised—he is "a priest forever," serving on our behalf. We can place our confidence in him.

GOD'S FINAL ARGUMENT

To all skeptics, God directs a final argument

- not founded on reason, as ancient Greeks would insist. Rational and coherent it is, but God does not win our allegiance through logical argument.
- not founded on rhetorical or military power, which the ancient Romans would admire. Yes, God's kingdom is powerful, but God never beats people into submission.
- not founded on written rules and regulations, as scholars and preachers might prefer. Words can be disputed and regulations misrepresented. No, God puts his final argument in the form of a . . . *life.*

Born of a virgin, raised in a carpenter's home, Jesus preached the good news of God, healed the sick, and rose from the dead. Here he is, God's final argument, a life. All who seek eternal and abundant life should follow him. Place your faith in the indestructible life of Jesus Christ.

7:18-19 **Yes, the old requirement about the priesthood was set aside because it was weak and useless. For the law never made anything perfect. But now we have confidence in a better hope, through which we draw near to God.**[NLT] The law had limitations. If the law had been the perfect path to God, all the people would have been able to enter God's Most Holy Place. As it was, only the high priest could enter God's presence—and only once a year. Even then, the sacrifices could not completely atone for sin. But God had already planned for a better way: *the old requirement about the priesthood was set aside because it was weak and useless.* There was nothing inherently wrong with the system, for God himself had created it. Rather, it was meant to foreshadow what God would do through his Son.

While the priesthood could truly accomplish nothing lasting, neither could the law—*for the law never made anything perfect.* This law was powerless to strengthen or aid the people. This does not mean, however, that the law was purposeless. The law taught the consequences of sin (see Romans 3:20; 5:20) and pointed people to Christ (see Galatians 3:24-25). Salvation comes through Christ, whose sacrifice brings forgiveness for sins. Being ethical, working diligently to help others, and giving to charitable causes are all commendable, but all of our good deeds cannot save us or make us right with God. Neither can religious systems or sacrifices.

If the old system couldn't accomplish anything for sinful

people, what could they do? The first-century readers needed to realize that *a better hope* had been made available to them. This "better hope" allowed them to draw near to God, a nearness that represents a new personal friendship and relationship with God (Romans 3:21-22, 28). In essence, these Jewish Christians could picture themselves walking right into the Most Holy Place, something that would have brought certain death under the old system. This "better hope" is not a matter of ordinances, commands, and rituals; rather, it provides a new place in which God writes his commands on the hearts of his people (Jeremiah 31:33). This "better hope" is only partially experienced now; the full experience will take place in heaven (see notes on 1:14).

Hebrews speaks often about the believers' hope (verses quoted from NIV, italics ours):

- "But Christ is faithful . . . . if we hold on to our courage and the *hope* of which we boast" (3:6). Our hope is based on Jesus' faithfulness. Hope should be the hallmark of our identity as members of God's household.
- "Show this same diligence to the very end, in order to make your *hope* sure" (6:11). We must renew our zeal in order to fully portray our confidence and hope.
- "We who have fled to take hold of the *hope* offered . . ." (6:18). The objective gift that God set before his people (present and future salvation) is not merely a subjective attitude of hopefulness.
- "We have this *hope* as an anchor for the soul, firm and secure" (6:19). Our confidence in the realities that God promised provides our soul with the utmost confidence and stability. Our total assurance in God enables us to draw near to him now.
- "A better *hope* is introduced, by which we draw near to God" (7:19). The hope Christians have is better than the hope in the Old Testament sacrificial system. Our hope is guaranteed to be effective because it is based on God's faithfulness.
- "Let us hold unswervingly to the *hope* we profess, for he who promised is faithful" (10:23). Hope embodies our confession of faith. We must hold fast to it and confess it boldly.
- "Now faith is being sure of what we *hope* for and certain of what we do not see" (11:1). Although we have no visible evidence of our future state, we take God at his word and the resurrected Christ as our example.

And this hope is how *we draw near to God.* We can enter God's presence because Jesus makes us righteous (2 Corinthians 5:17-21). With our sin completely obliterated, we can stand in God's presence. When we draw near to God, we have a better foundation for approaching God than those who tried to approach him through the law. Our hope is in Jesus (7:22). This is a hope that Old Testament followers of God never possessed. Our "hope" is not some vague wish; rather, we can be certain of what we hope for because of the character of the one who promised it to us.

DRAWING NEAR TO GOD

What does it mean that we can "draw near" to God? How can we do it?

While church buildings are often thought to be the "house of God," the Bible makes it clear that your own body is his temple. Mountaintops offer wonderful views, but you are not closer to God there than in the basement of your home. Your spirit needs and wants closeness with God. You want to know the living God personally, not as an idea or concept, not as a distant monarch.

We draw near to God through prayer, worship, and Bible meditation. You need not live like a monk, but you probably need more prayer in your life, and less work, less television. The habit of worship has become a convenience to be wedged between sports and other recreations. Instead, make worship your top priority. Bible meditation may include verse memory, songs, and quiet personal reading. The Bible is the word of God for you. Use it every day.

7:20-22 And it was not without an oath! Others became priests without any oath, but he became a priest with an oath when God said to him: "The Lord has sworn and will not change his mind: 'You are a priest forever.'" Because of this oath, Jesus has become the guarantee of a better covenant.[NIV] "And it was not without an oath" refers to the promise of a better hope and the ability to draw near to God (7:18-19). God did not have to take an oath because he cannot lie. Yet by taking an oath he added emphasis that what he said would definitely be so (see also 3:11; 4:3; 6:17). In the normal matter of the Levitical priesthood, men *became priests without any oath;* that is, their appointment was based on the law without any divine intervention by God. But this was not so with Jesus: *he became a priest with an oath.* Jesus' appointment came about by divine validation. God ordained Jesus' priesthood with an oath when he said, *"The Lord has sworn and will not change his mind: 'You are a priest forever'"* (quoted from Psalm 110:4). No similar, explicit oath is mentioned in the establishment of Aaron's priesthood (Exodus 28). The matter of God making an oath, in addition to the power of his word, underscores the argument that Jesus is truly superior in every way—the only Savior.

This "oath" emphasizes that *Jesus has become the guarantee of a better covenant* because his priesthood has a greater endorsement than the Aaronic priesthood. The name "Jesus" emphasizes this point. The writer was not talking about Melchizedek or any earthly high priest, but about the Son of God, who is now seated at the right hand of God. Therefore, he is the "guarantee" from God to us. Jesus guarantees God's forgiveness of us, and he guarantees our acceptability with God. The word "guarantee" means a pledge, bond, or collateral, but it goes beyond that. It stands for the person who stakes his life on the promise. Jesus is answerable for the fulfillment of the obligation that he guarantees. Because of what Jesus did for us, we are guaranteed this better covenant and better hope (7:18-19).

Jesus is "a priest forever" (7:15-17). Because Jesus lives forever, the better covenant is permanent. It will never need to be replaced, and it can never be improved upon. Originally, covenants were agreements between two parties. Each party had certain obligations and responsibilities. If either side failed, the covenant was broken. Jesus provided a way to guarantee the acts of both parties. He guaranteed the people's part by providing a perfect sacrifice. This ensured that the people would always be righteous before God. Jesus also guaranteed God's part by securing God's permanent forgiveness and presence.

THE BETTER COVENANT

This "better covenant" is also called the new covenant or testament. It is new and better because it allows us to go directly to God through Christ. We no longer need to rely on sacrificed animals and mediating priests to obtain God's forgiveness. This new covenant is better because, while all human priests die, Christ lives forever. Priests and sacrifices could not save people, but Christ truly saves. You have access to Christ. He is available to you, but do you go to him with your needs? He guarantees God's forgiveness to you. Trust him for forgiveness; he guarantees your acceptability to God. Thank him that your sin has been removed.

7:23-24 **Now there have been many of those priests, since death prevented them from continuing in office; but because Jesus lives forever, he has a permanent priesthood.**[NIV] The historian Josephus estimated that eighty-three high priests served Israel from the first high priest, Aaron, to the fall of the second temple in A.D. 70. Each served in his job, and each eventually died. But *Jesus lives forever.* Again the writer contrasted the many people with the perfect One (see also 1:1-3). Every high priest would hand off his job to his successor. Not Christ; *he has a permanent priesthood.* Only Jesus is qualified to become a permanent priest for the entire human race.

WHO ARE OUR PRIESTS TODAY?
Jesus has a permanent priesthood. He should be everyone's ultimate authority for spiritual life. In our culture today, however, many people have advisers and counselors whom they elevate almost to the role of priest. People look to financial advisers, lawyers, physicians, insurance agents, and political leaders to provide hope, long life, and security against all disasters. Many Christians regard the advice of priests and ministers, Christian friends, and even pop musicians before they consider the words of Jesus written in the Bible. Make sure your first allegiance and priority is to know and follow the advice given by Jesus.

7:25 **Therefore he is able to save completely those who come to God through him, because he always lives to intercede for them.**[NIV] Two themes portray Jesus' ministry for the community of believers:

1. Complete deliverance—Jesus *is able to save completely those who come to God through him.*

No one can add to what Jesus did to save us; our past, present, and future sins are all forgiven. In addition, Jesus is with the Father as a guarantee that our sins are forgiven and that we have access to God. If you are a Christian, remember that Jesus has paid the price for your sins once and for all (see also 9:24-28). He has saved you "completely." This unusual Greek construction (*eis to panteles*; the only other place it is used in the New Testament is Luke 13:11) conveys the meaning of extent—"completely and absolutely" and also the meaning of "for all time." It shows that Christ fulfills every need that sinners have. No sin is too great for this salvation. To point out that Christ's salvation is complete indicates that the old covenant could not save people in this way. The Greek for "those who come" denotes "those who constantly come" to God. Thus, salvation is open to all who come. "Come to God" means to approach or draw near in worship (see 10:22 and 12:22-24).

2. Eternally active intercession—Jesus *always lives to intercede for* those who come to God though him.

As our High Priest, Christ is our advocate, the mediator between us and God. His purpose is to "intercede" for those who follow God. He looks after our interests, presenting our requests to the Father. The Old Testament high priest went before God once a year to plead for the forgiveness of the nation's sins. Christ makes perpetual intercession before God for us. Christ's continuous presence in heaven as the Priest-King assures us that our sins have been paid for and forgiven (see Romans 8:33-34; Hebrews 2:17-18; 4:15-16; 9:24). This wonderful assurance frees us from guilt and spiritual failure. It allows us to have unlimited, immediate access to God. Christ's intercession means that he talks to God about you at this very moment. It means that God is never too far away, never too holy to meet with you.

CONSTANT INTERCESSION

Imagine having
- an expert mechanic with you on every car trip.
- an expert chef preparing every meal.
- an expert team of doctors at every athletic competition.
- an expert golf pro watching every swing.

Imagine having history's one and only Savior—an expert at solving your biggest, most worrisome problems as well as your little, trifling concerns—working on your case all the time. By faith, you don't have to imagine. He exists! He lives in you. And, according to Hebrews 7:25, he is constantly interceding for you with the Father. Don't wallow in your sin; don't carry around burdens too heavy to bear. In all your decisions, trust Jesus. Gather all your mistakes and weaknesses, and give them to him.

7:26-27 **Such a high priest meets our need—one who is holy, blameless, pure, set apart from sinners, exalted above the heavens. Unlike the other high priests, he does not need to offer sacrifices day after day, first for his own sins, and then for the sins of the people. He sacrificed for their sins once for all when he offered himself.**[NIV] Concluding the thought begun in 7:23-25, the writer explained again that the Old Testament system has been superseded by a full and final sacrifice. Not only is Jesus a suitable High Priest because he has an indestructible life, but he has certain other characteristics that show him as the High Priest who *meets our need;* that is, a High Priest who could truly save us. Jesus is

- *holy,* meaning that Jesus knew no sin. Jesus perfectly fulfilled all that God is and all that God required in a high priest who would bring salvation to sinful people (see 4:15).
- *blameless,* meaning he is without evil and is completely innocent. During his earthly life, even as he faced temptation, he remained completely obedient to God and completely without sin (see James 1:27).
- *pure*—that is, he remains undefiled even as he deals with sinful people in a defiled world (see 1 Peter 1:4).
- *set apart from sinners* because Jesus' sinless life separates him from sinful creation. Yet it was only through his separation by his sinlessness that he could act on our behalf.

- *exalted above the heavens.* He is greater than any other high priest because he represents people in the very throne room of God.

The final argument for Jesus' superiority shows the contrast between the essential nature of the priests and Jesus. A high priest under the old covenant was merely a sinful human being; thus, to fulfill his role, he had to make a sacrifice *first for his own sins* before he could offer the sacrifices *for the sins of the people.* And this had to be done *day after day* because no sacrifice could permanently remove the stain of sin. In Old Testament times when animals were sacrificed, they were cut into pieces, the parts were washed, the fat was burned, the blood was sprinkled, and the meat was boiled. Blood was demanded as atonement for sins, and God accepted animal blood to cover the people's sins (Leviticus 17:11). Because of the sacrificial system, the Israelites were generally aware that sin costs someone something and that they themselves were sinful.

Jesus, however, was completely sinless, never needing to offer a sacrifice for himself, nor did he need to repeat his sacrifice. *When he offered himself* as a sacrifice for sins, his perfect sacrifice obliterated the penalty of sins *once for all.* Because Jesus died "once for all," he brought the sacrificial system to an end. He forgave sins—past, present, and future. The Jews did not need to go back to the old system because Christ, the perfect sacrifice, had completed the work of redemption. You don't have to look for another way to have your sins forgiven—Christ was the final sacrifice for you.

WHAT'S LEFT FOR US TO DO?

So much is attributed to Jesus in this chapter that it might appear that there is nothing we need to do, or can do, to make salvation a reality for us.

True! Jesus has done it all. Nothing we do can improve his work. Nothing we do adds to God's acceptance of Jesus' sacrifice.

How do the benefits of Jesus' sacrifice become ours? We accept the gift of salvation by faith, trusting entirely in Jesus for salvation. You can do that now through a simple prayer: "Almighty God, I trust in Jesus alone. Please forgive my sins through him, and give me the eternal life secured by him. Amen."

7:28 For the law appoints as high priests men who are weak; but the oath, which came after the law, appointed the Son, who has been made perfect forever.[NIV] The writer here reviews the argument from the preceding chapter. *The law appoints as high priests men who are weak.* The high priests were not perfect; they were by nature sinful, and they eventually died. They could not bring sinners into the perfect presence of God. But God designed another way that he secured with *the oath.* The "oath" refers to God's words to Jesus, "You are a priest forever" recorded in 7:21. This "oath" was fulfilled and the new priesthood came *after the law* because the law had been surpassed by the appointment of *the Son, who has been made perfect forever.*

As we better understand the Jewish sacrificial system, we see that Jesus' death served as the perfect atonement for our sins. His death brings us eternal life. How callous, how cold, how stubborn it would be to refuse God's greatest gift. The original readers would be foolish to abandon Christianity and revert to a system that was now obsolete. In the same way, modern-day people are foolish if they attempt to reach contentment and spiritual satisfaction another way. Christ has provided the most superior way, which is guaranteed to stand forever. This High Priest knows the power of temptation. He can sympathize with our weaknesses and limitations as people (2:17-18; 4:14-16), though he does more than sympathize. For those who accept his sacrifice, he provides complete, uninterrupted access to God. When was the last time you took advantage of that free admission? Be careful not to treat this privilege lightly by neglecting to use it, trying to use it for selfish reasons, or by refusing to praise and thank God for it. Rather than trying to please God through our own efforts or win his approval by living a good life, we should approach God by placing our allegiance with the perfect High Priest, Jesus Christ.

HEBREWS 8

CHRIST IS THE HIGH PRIEST OF THE NEW COVENANT / 8:1-13

At one time, American car companies deliberately built obsolescence into auto-body styles so people would buy the new designs the next year. Distinctive body styles, such as the 1957 Chevy or the 1965 Mustang convertible, remain collector items. Recently, critics claim that computer manufacturers have raised built-in obsolescence to new heights.

We may not appreciate our products becoming obsolete, but we can be thankful for the obsolescence that God built into the old covenant, which has been superseded by the new covenant. Christ, the High Priest of the new covenant, will remain new and effective for all time; neither he nor his ministry to believers will ever grow obsolete. We can count on him.

8:1 **Now this is the main point of the things we are saying: We have such a High Priest, who is seated at the right hand of the throne of the Majesty in the heavens.**NKJV The writer now summarizes his message; what he has been saying is that Christ is superior to everything in the Jewish priesthood. Whatever the Jewish believers had previously trusted for salvation was merely a shadow of reality, not the reality itself. That shadow is now utterly replaced by the reality that *we have such a High Priest*—"one who is holy, blameless, pure, set apart from sinners, exalted above the heavens. Unlike the other high priests, he does not need to offer sacrifices day after day, first for his own sins, and then for the sins of the people. He sacrificed for their sins once for all when he offered himself" (7:26-27 NIV).

> It is shallow nonsense to say God forgives us because he is love. The only ground upon which God can forgive us is the Cross.
> *Oswald Chambers*

Chapter 7 explained that Jesus is a greater priest than any priest who had descended from Israel's first high priest, Aaron. Jesus is *a High Priest, who is seated at the right hand of the throne of the Majesty in the heavens.* In addition to being the greatest high priest, Christ also has received the greatest honor by being seated at the right hand of God (see 1:3). This is from Psalm 110:1, "The LORD says to my Lord: sit at my right hand" (NIV). This portrayal of Christ is a key argument for the deity of Christ in Hebrews. It was a primary Old Testament text on the exaltation of the Messiah for the early church. In Matthew 26:64, Jesus referred to the "Son of Man sitting at the right hand of the Mighty One" when he answered Caiaphas's challenge, "Tell us if you are the Christ, the Son of God" (NIV). This place at God's right hand belonged to Christ because he is more than just a high priest; he is God's Son. "The heavens" refers to the heavenly sanctuary (see 8:2), the dwelling place of God; it is the ultimate and eternal destination for all who believe (4:1; 6:19-20; 11:10; 12:22), and therefore an even greater reality than what we see. This present world is merely a representation or shadow of what will come (see 8:5). Because of this, Christ's ministry will be greater than that of the priests who served in the earthly tabernacle or temple, as we see in the following verse.

JESUS' HOME

In many churches, young Christians are introduced to the faith with the idea that Jesus lives in their hearts. In the book of Hebrews, Jesus clearly resides at the throne of God the Father. OK, where is he? The answer is . . .

- Jesus is very close to us. He is a personal Savior, a living presence, and an active guide. Jesus promised his disciples that when he ascended into heaven, he would send a Comforter, the Holy Spirit, through whom his presence would continue to minister to those who believe. So the Spirit of Jesus lives in us.
- Jesus is very close to God. He is a risen Savior, a heavenly Advocate, a High Priest whose sacrifice is a continuing reality in the presence of God. Jesus dwells with God in his physical resurrection body.

When we become Christians, we accept "into our heart" the living presence of Jesus through the Holy Spirit who indwells us. We trust Jesus for the salvation he secures as High Priest in heaven's court. Jesus' home is in God's presence, and our eventual home is where Jesus is.

8:2 There he ministers in the heavenly Tabernacle, the true place of worship that was built by the Lord and not by human hands.[NLT] Verse 1 describes Christ's exaltation at God's right hand; verse 2 describes his service. Christ, the exalted one, is a servant. What a vivid picture of the Savior, who *ministers in the heavenly Tabernacle*. In Judaism, the concept was commonly held by this time that there was in heaven a spiritual tabernacle that corresponded to the earthly one (see Exodus 25:40). The language, however, suggests that this heavenly tent is a spiritual sphere (in the presence of God himself) in which Christ, the heavenly High Priest, now ministers (see 9:11). We might ask, what is Jesus doing there? He is not offering additional sacrifices, because Jesus' death on the cross was the final sacrifice for sins (7:27). Nor is he trying to convince a reluctant God to accept the sacrifice as atonement for sin. Jesus' sacrifice fully met God's demand for holiness. Jesus serves by taking his rightful place as our Savior and Mediator. His ministry represents transcendent reality, not an earthly copy. His place in heaven secures our place there.

Christ returned to the presence of God in heaven, *the true place of worship that was built by the Lord and not by human hands.* God allows us to enter that same throne room and bring our worship and requests to him. This "true" place of worship does not imply that the tabernacle and temple on earth were false, but that they were imperfect shadows of the true and perfect place of worship (8:5). Before Christ, the high priest could only enter a special place, the Most Holy Place, to come into the presence of God. Today, through prayer, we can enter the throne room of heaven, and we will one day eternally live in that presence. By extension, then, the "old" way through the Jewish priesthood no longer exists, replaced by Jesus Christ, the way, the truth, and the life (John 14:6).

8:3 Every high priest is appointed to offer both gifts and sacrifices, and so it was necessary for this one also to have something to offer.NIV *Every high priest is appointed* by God for his work because each generation of high priests died and was replaced. The priests' work was *to offer both gifts and sacrifices.* "Gifts" probably refers to meal offerings, and "sacrifices" probably means blood offerings. God has stopped appointing priests, however, because his last appointment, Jesus, does not need to be replaced. The newest and last high priest, Jesus, can never lose his position.

Priests had been appointed to offer sacrifices to atone for sin, *so it was necessary for this one also to have something to offer.* Christ, as a high priest, was also appointed to offer a sacrifice. He offered his own life to God in our place—the perfect gift that could never be surpassed. "He sacrificed for their sins once for all when he offered himself" (7:27 NIV; see also 9:14). Christ's sacrifice is all-sufficient; that is, all sins are covered in his once-for-all offering to God. Therefore, his role as priest, his sacrifice, and his service to God all surpass the plan under the old covenant.

8:4 For if He were on earth, He would not be a priest, since there are priests who offer the gifts according to the law.NKJV Under the old Jewish system, priests were chosen only from the tribe of

Levi, and sacrifices were offered daily on the altar for forgiveness of sins. This system would not have allowed Jesus to be a priest, for according to the law, a priest had to come from the tribe of Levi, not Judah (see 7:12-14). *For if He were on earth, He would not be a priest, since there are priests who offer the gifts according to the law.* The use of the present tense in "there are priests who offer the gifts" indicates that this book was written before A.D. 70, when the temple in Jerusalem was destroyed, ending the sacrifices. But Jesus' perfect sacrifice had already ended the need for priests and sacrifices. Christ was appointed High Priest of a new and better system that allows God's people to enter directly into God's presence.

8:5 They serve at a sanctuary that is a copy and shadow of what is in heaven. This is why Moses was warned when he was about to build the tabernacle: "See to it that you make everything according to the pattern shown you on the mountain."[NIV] The priests who offered sacrifices *serve at a sanctuary that is a copy and shadow of what is in heaven.* This continues to show the insignificance of the Jewish priests' earthly service. Certainly it was important work, but their service was only an illustration of what was coming. Even the place where the priests served was only a pattern of the spiritual reality of Christ's sacrifice, looking forward to the future reality. Christ serves in the real, heavenly dwelling of God. (For "copy," see also 9:23; for "shadow," see 10:1.) The Jews considered their priestly service as a copy, a tracing of what is in heaven; they would never think of it as a shadow.

HOW CHRIST IS BETTER

The way to God that Christ opened was far suprior than the way provided in the Old Testament. Not only is the way better, but Hebrews says the old way is no longer an option. There remains one way to God, and that way is following Christ.

Christ provides better . . .

focus to life	6:9
hope	7:19
covenant	7:22
promises	8:6
sacrifice	9:23
spiritual possessions	10:34
future country	11:16, 35, 40

The concept of something earthly being a shadow of what is in heaven comes from Plato or Philo, whose ideas were prevalent in Alexandrian schools of interpretation. The apostle Paul also shows this influence when he said that earthly Jewish ceremonies are a shadow of Christ, who is the reality (Colossians 2:17).

FOLLOWING A PATTERN

The advice to Moses is good for us, too—not for building tent tabernacles but for building lives. As Moses followed a pattern given to him by God, so your life should be patterned after the virtues and aspirations Jesus displayed. The key to Jesus' character is others-directed care. This care rises above generosity ("I am here to help supply you") to a level that becomes "I am here for you." Jesus was fully given to the will of God and fully motivated by love for all that God created. The outcome of Jesus' character was a life that served every person he met. Not everyone followed him, but the gospel Jesus preached (and lived) was like a seed that spread the Good News through people he discipled. Even believers should be in that "service industry," helping by many means to spread God's truth. We would do well to follow his pattern.

God gave Moses the pattern for the tabernacle, and Moses was warned to follow it carefully. When Moses was about to build the tabernacle, he was warned: *"See to it that you make everything according to the pattern shown you on the mountain"* (Exodus 25:40). This earthly sanctuary was meant to reflect, however imperfectly, the heavenly tabernacle. The book of Hebrews does not try to describe heaven; instead, it shows how Christ serves in a better, more personal way than any other priest could. Because the temple at Jerusalem had not yet been destroyed, using the worship system there as an example would have had a great impact on this original audience. Their temple, and all they knew about the original tabernacle constructed by Moses, had been an imperfect picture, giving the people an appreciation of the heavenly reality that would one day be theirs.

> The covenant of grace is the saint's original title to heaven.
> *Thomas Brooks*

8:6 **But the ministry Jesus has received is as superior to theirs as the covenant of which he is mediator is superior to the old one, and it is founded on better promises.**[NIV] The writer has already proven that Jesus' priesthood is greater than the priesthood of Aaron (see chapter 7). Although the priests descended from Aaron possessed a job of high honor and dignity, *the ministry Jesus has received is as superior to theirs as the covenant of* *which he is mediator is superior to the old one.* Jesus' ministry and the new covenant are superior for several reasons:

- they completely fulfill and replace the priests' ministry and the old covenant;
- they last for eternity, because Jesus is High Priest forever;
- they require no further sacrifices;
- they accomplish what all the other sacrifices could not do—truly atone for sin;
- they provide sinful humanity the opportunity to have a personal relationship with God (see 8:10-11).

A "covenant" *(diatheke)* refers to a guaranteed agreement between two parties that was mutually beneficial to both parties. Each party agreed to responsibilities and sealed the covenant (many Old Testament covenants were sealed with blood; see Genesis 15; Exodus 24). If one party failed to fulfill the responsibilities, the covenant was broken. Often these agreements were initiated by the stronger party (or victorious king). In the Old Testament and in this case, the covenant was initiated by God, who invited people to enter the agreement. The old covenant fell apart because the people did not live up to their responsibilities (keeping the law). This new "covenant" of which Jesus is "mediator" was prophesied by Jeremiah (see Jeremiah 31:31-34) and is recorded in 8:8-12.

Jesus is described as the "mediator" of this new covenant. In Hebrews, the word "mediator" is always used in conjunction with the new covenant (see 8:6; 9:15; 12:24). The new covenant needed a new mediator—a "go-between" who could ensure that both sides fulfilled their part of the agreement. As High Priest and Advocate, Jesus ensures God's acceptance of us; as the one who sacrificed himself for our sins, Jesus ensures our acceptability before God. "For there is one God; there is also one mediator between God and humankind, Christ Jesus, himself human" (1 Timothy 2:5 NRSV). More of how Jesus mediates the new covenant is found in Matthew 26:27-28; 1 Corinthians 11:24-25; 2 Corinthians 3:6; Hebrews 9:15; 12:24.

This new covenant *is founded on better promises* that the writer will discuss in greater detail in 8:10-12. As the covenant is "better," so are the promises. As noted in Jeremiah 31:31-34 above, this promised new covenant focuses on forgiveness of sin and a relationship with God. "Promise" is a major term in the book of Hebrews. The promise refers to the Sabbath rest (4:1, 3, 9) and also to the unshakable kingdom (12:28) and the heavenly Jerusalem (12:22). It began with the promise to Abraham (6:13-15) and appears throughout chapter 11 as the reward of faith (11:8-11, 13, 33, 39).

A BETTER LIFE

In every way, the author of Hebrews gives superior grades to the new covenant over the old. For your life, that means

- God's presence is much more real to you than it was to believers under the old covenant. The promised Helper, the Holy Spirit, has come to guide and educate you in God's truth.
- The emotional quality of your life with God is better. You obey God because you love him, not because it is your duty.
- The mission to which your life is directed is greater. Your profession, for example—whether you're a plumber, a plastic surgeon, or a preacher—is a "calling" that God uses to advance his work. The barrier between sacred calling and secular employment washes away. In Christ, nothing is secular anymore. Everything shows the need for redemption, and everywhere God displays the possibility for it. You are a part of this great movement.

8:7 **If the first covenant had been faultless, there would have been no need for a second covenant to replace it.**[NLT] The *need for a second covenant* implies that the first covenant was faulty. Does this mean that God ordered Moses and Aaron to begin a way of worship that was mistaken or poorly contracted? No, but the old covenant was in every way preparatory for and pointing to the dynamic of the new covenant (see 7:11-19; also Romans 3–4; 9–11). In that way, the old covenant was not *faultless,* for without the new to complete the task, the old would not have been adequate. The old covenant was replaced because it was not eternal, not sufficient to completely deal with sin, and could not provide sinful humanity with a relationship with God. In its time, however, the old covenant was necessary. But it needed to be replaced by a better covenant, as was prophesied by Jeremiah and quoted in the following verses.

8:8 **Because finding fault with them, He says: "Behold, the days are coming, says the LORD, when I will make a new covenant with the house of Israel and with the house of Judah."**[NKJV] Since the people continually broke God's covenant, God kept *finding fault with them.* A part of the covenant involved keeping God's laws; however, the Israelites chose to disobey (see Jeremiah 7:23-24). When they failed to keep the requirements imposed on them, they broke the covenant. God, however, promised a new covenant that would be written on their hearts (see 8:10). This new covenant would not be filled with laws about sacrifices and other external responsibilities. Rather, it would bring about spiritual reconciliation by producing change in people's inner beings.

THE NEW COVENANT
In the old covenant God agreed to forgive people's sins if they brought animals for the priests to sacrifice. When this sacrificial system was inaugurated, the agreement between God and man was sealed with the blood of animals (Exodus 24:8). But animal blood did not in itself remove sin (only God can forgive sin), and animal sacrifices had to be repeated day by day and year after year. Jesus instituted a "new covenant" or agreement between humans and God. Under this new covenant, Jesus would die in the place of sinners. Unlike the blood of animals, his blood (because he is God) would truly remove the sins of all who put their faith in him. And Jesus' sacrifice would never have to be repeated; it would be good for all eternity (Hebrews 9:23-28). The prophets looked forward to this new covenant that would fulfill the old sacrificial agreement (Jeremiah 31:31-34), and John the Baptist called Jesus "the Lamb of God who takes away the sin of the world" (John 1:29). We need never struggle with the guilt of past sins. We have complete forgiveness in Christ.

Verses 8-12 quote Jeremiah 31:31-34, which is the longest Old Testament quotation in the New Testament. Jeremiah prophesied about a future time when a better covenant would be established, because the first covenant, given to Moses at Mount Sinai, was imperfect and provisional. The Israelites could not maintain faithfulness to it because their hearts had not been truly changed. This change of heart required Jesus' full sacrifice to remove sin and the Holy Spirit's permanent indwelling. When we turn our lives over to Christ, the Holy Spirit instills in us a desire to obey God.

This passage compares the new covenant with the old. The old covenant was the covenant of law between God and Israel. But God said, *"I will make a new covenant with the house of Israel and with the house of Judah."* The new and better way is the covenant of grace—Christ's offer to forgive our sins and bring us to God through his sacrificial death. God did not offer to renew the old covenant; instead, he replaced it with a new covenant. This covenant is new in extent—it goes beyond Israel and Judah to include all the Gentile nations. It is new in application because it is written on our hearts and in our minds. It offers a new way to forgiveness, not through animal sacrifice but through faith.

8:9 "Not according to the covenant that I made with their fathers in the day when I took them by the hand to lead them out of the land of Egypt; because they did not continue in My covenant, and I disregarded them, says the LORD."[NKJV] The old covenant was broken, not once, but many times. The Jewish readers' ancestors (their *fathers*) had been miraculously freed from slavery in Egypt. In the wilderness, they had received God's laws and had made a covenant of obedience. However, they *did not continue in My [God's] covenant,* and by that disobedience, they voided their part of the agreement. "Did not continue" brings back the apostasy theme of chapter 6. Grieved and offended by the willful disobedience of his chosen people, God *disregarded them.* This means that they faced the consequences of sin instead of receiving the blessings of obedience. "Disregarded" brings back the judgment theme from Psalm 95 of chapters 3 and 4. While God may have allowed such consequences, he never abandoned his people. Instead, he promised something better for all who would remain faithful.

STILL OLD-FASHIONED?

With the coming of Christ, the old covenant became dated. If you are trying hard to deal with your sin and appease God with charitable deeds of generosity and human care, you are old-fashioned. If you go about the chore of getting yourself and the family to church every Sunday because it's expected, you're out of step. If you're trying to obey with mere force of willpower and human effort, you're behind the times.

It's time you woke up to the new covenant and enjoyed a new relationship with God won by Jesus, the Mediator of a new covenant.

8:10 **"For this is the covenant that I will make with the house of Israel after those days, says the LORD: I will put My laws in their mind and write them on their hearts; and I will be their God, and they shall be My people."**[NKJV] Under God's new covenant, God's law is inside us. It is no longer an external set of rules and principles. The Holy Spirit reminds us of Christ's words, activates our consciences, influences our motives and desires, and makes us want to obey. Now we desire to do God's will with all our heart and mind.

> Faith believes implicitly in the new heart, with the law written in it, because it believes in the promise, and in the God who gave and fulfills the promise.
>
> *Andrew Murray*

This new covenant has four provisions (covered in verses 10-12):

1. The new covenant provides inward change: *"I will put My laws in their mind and write them on their hearts."* More than just memorizing Scripture, this means having a new "heart," and with it a new sense of intimacy with God where he is known as Father *(Abba)* and where Christians are known as children of God and heirs. This new heart will bring the people's relationship with

God to a personal level (not just through intermediaries). Having these laws written on our hearts means that we will want to obey God. If our hearts are not changed, we will find it difficult to follow God's will and we will rebel against being told how to live. The Holy Spirit, however, gives us new desires for God (see Philippians 2:12-13). With new hearts, we will find serving God to be our greatest joy. Is your life devoted to obeying God?

2. The new covenant provides intimacy with God: *"I will be their God, and they shall be My people."* This reveals a positive, close relationship between God and his people. In the first covenant, people continually failed to live up to this relationship. It began with God's covenant to Abraham and was affirmed to the people of Israel (Exodus 6:7). It is a key Old Testament promise. In the new covenant, this relationship is secured through Jesus Christ. Although the promise was always there, it now has a newer and richer meaning because of the provision of Christ. It reaches its highest fulfillment in the return of Christ to rule the new heaven and new earth (Revelation 21:1-3). Have you experienced this close relationship with God?

8:11 "And they will not need to teach their neighbors, nor will they need to teach their relatives, saying, 'You should know the LORD.' For everyone, from the least to the greatest, will know me already."NLT

3. The new covenant provides knowledge of God: *"everyone, from the least to the greatest, will know me already."* The new covenant brings a new relationship between people and God. Intermediaries (priests), who were vital under the old covenant, have changed roles under the new covenant. No longer is God's truth apprehended and applied through priestly mediation. Rather, the new covenant made each believer a priest (1 Peter 2:5, 9). Every believer has access to God through prayer. Every believer can understand God's saving promises as revealed in the Bible because he or she has God as a living presence in his or her heart. Of course, there will still be the need for teachers, but every believer will be able to know God—not just priests or a select few. Twenty years after this was written, John would echo this truth: "But you have been anointed by the Holy One, and all of you have knowledge. . . . As for you, the anointing that you received from him abides in you, and so you do not need anyone to teach you. But as his anointing teaches you about all things, and is true and is not a lie, and just as it has taught you, abide in him" (1 John 2:20, 27 NRSV). Do you know God's truth in your heart?

8:12 "For I will forgive their wickedness and will remember their sins no more."NIV

4. The new covenant provides complete forgiveness from sins: *"For I will forgive . . . and will remember their sins no more."* People of the old covenent had forgiveness of sins (see Exodus 34:6-8; Micah 7:18-20), but they had experienced an incomplete, unlasting forgiveness as determined by the incessant need to make sacrifices for sins. In the new covenant, sin and its effect of separating people from God are eliminated. God wipes out memory of sin and renders sin as if it had never occurred. Sin's impact is completely overcome, making it possible for believers to receive the promised blessing. There is no longer any barrier to our relationship with God. We have received once-for-all cleansing. Have you received forgiveness for your sins?

All four of these characteristics (noted in the commentary on verses 10-12) bring about a true righteousness that could not be known under the old covenant.

8:13 By calling this covenant "new," he has made the first one obsolete; and what is obsolete and aging will soon disappear.NIV Introducing and *calling this covenant "new"* means that God *has made the first one obsolete.* The old one was fulfilled by Christ and completed by him; therefore, it was no longer needed. When God initiated a new covenant, the old one was no longer valid. The observation that the old covenant is *obsolete and aging [and] will soon disappear* was visually demonstrated just a few years after this book was written when Jerusalem and its temple were destroyed by the Romans in A.D. 70.

The "new" covenant implies that the "old" covenant and its way have now passed. Old systems, old sacrifices, and the old priesthood now have no value in securing God's approval. "Hang on to the old covenant if you will," warns Hebrews, "but you're hanging on to a shadow, a bubble ready to burst, a moment passing into history. The old covenant has served its purpose and will soon be just a memory. You can't live in the past, so your real choice is clear: accept the new covenant or none at all." Believers have become "ministers of a new covenant—not of the letter but of the Spirit; for the letter kills, but the Spirit gives life" (2 Corinthians 3:6 NIV).

But how can these words be reconciled with Jesus' words in Matthew 5:17-19, where he says he had not come to abolish the law, but to fulfill it? When Jesus said he came to "fulfill" the Old Testament law, he meant that: (1) He would exemplify the full meaning of the law and prophecy, because it all pointed to him, and (2) he would also bring the law and prophecy to their

THE OLD AND NEW COVENANTS

Like pointing out the similarities and differences between the photograph of a person and the actual person, the writer of Hebrews shows the connection between the old Mosaic covenant and the new Messianic covenant. He proves that the old covenant was a shadow of the real Christ.

The Old Covenant under Moses	*The New Covenant in Christ*	*Application*
Gifts and sacrifices by those guilty of sin	Self-sacrifice by the guiltless Christ	Christ died for you.
Focused on a physical building where one goes to worship	Focuses on the reign of Christ in the hearts of believers	God is directly involved in your life.
A shadow	A reality	Not temporal, but eternal
Limited promises	Limitless promises	We can trust God's promises to us.
Failed agreement by people	Faithful agreement by Christ	Christ has kept the agreement where people couldn't.
External standards and rules	Internal standards—a new heart	God sees both actions and motives—we are accountable to God, not rules.
Limited access to God	Unlimited access to God	God is personally available.
Based on fear	Based on love and forgiveness	Forgiveness keeps our failures from destroying the agreement.
Legal cleansing	Personal cleansing	God's cleansing is complete.
Continual sacrifice	Conclusive sacrifice	Christ's sacrifice was perfect and final.
Obey the rules	Serve the living God	We have a relationship, not regulations.
Forgiveness earned	Forgiveness freely given	We hve true and complete forgiveness.
Repeated yearly	Completed by Christ's death	Christ's death can be applied to your sin.
Human effort	God's grace	Initiated by God's love for you
Available to some	Available to all	Available to you

intended completion. Jesus' fulfillment of the law was the means of setting it aside. When all the terms of a contract have been fulfilled, it is no longer needed.

God does not change his mind. He did not send his Son to repeal, abolish, or annul what he had told his people previously. Instead, the Father sent his Son as the fulfillment. Jesus' coming had been part of God's plan from Creation (see Genesis 3:15). The disciples did not thoroughly understand how Jesus fulfilled the Scriptures until after his death and resurrection (Luke 24:25-27).

SPIRITUALLY OBSOLETE

Some of the Jewish believers were clinging to the obsolete old ways instead of embracing Christ's new covenant. What could be worse? All the joy of newfound faith and all the relief of fresh forgiveness had given way to a kind of boredom that was never supposed to be. Growth had stopped. What should be done if this happens to you?

First of all, realize that life in Christ is never complete. Heaven promises completeness; until then, growth is the normal pattern. Growth often endures seasons of drought and drabness. That's also normal.

What are you doing that might be spiritually ineffective or obsolete? The key to growth includes daily devotion to Christ through Bible study and prayer. Perhaps you need to intensify your study and find helps that provide more substance. Perhaps you need to grow by engaging in new areas of service that express your faith. Seek God for how he would have you keep growing in your faith.

HEBREWS 9

RULES FOR WORSHIP UNDER THE OLD COVENANT / 9:1-10

As the Israelites learned God's laws and how to worship him, God gave them instructions for building a place of worship (8:5; see Exodus 25:40). Called the tabernacle, this portable building traveled with the Hebrews as they traveled to the Promised Land. It became the place where God lived among them. To Jewish minds, the tabernacle had wider appeal than the temple. In order to worship, Jews had to travel to the temple, located in Jerusalem. But before the temple was built, the tabernacle had traveled with the people, representing God's presence and availability.

9:1 **Now the first covenant had regulations for worship and also an earthly sanctuary.**[NIV] The end of chapter 8 explains that the old (or first) covenant has been made obsolete by the new covenant. The original readers of Hebrews would have known all about the *regulations for worship* that were required by *the first covenant.* The first covenant also had made provision and instructions for *an earthly sanctuary* (first the tabernacle, later the temple). Calling this sanctuary "earthly" (Greek, *kosmikon*) again contrasts it with the heavenly sanctuary, thereby showing that worship in the new covenant is better than the old.

The "regulations" and the elements found in the "earthly sanctuary" are discussed in greater detail in 9:2-10 (the furnishings in 9:2-5 and the rituals in 9:6-10).

9:2 **There were two rooms in that Tabernacle. In the first room were a lampstand, a table, and sacred loaves of bread on the table. This room was called the Holy Place.**[NLT] "Earthly sanctuary" (9:1) refers to the *Tabernacle* (or tent) that God's people used for worship before the temple was built. Constructed while the Israelites were en route to the Promised Land, it was a portable structure that could be taken apart and carried when the people moved from place to place. God's instructions for building the tabernacle are in Exodus 25–31.

The tent had *two rooms:* an inner room (called the Most Holy

KEY TABERNACLE PIECES

What can we learn today from the details involved in the building of God's tabernacle? First, the high quality of the precious materials making up the tabernacle shows God's greatness and transcendence. Second, the curtain surrounding the Most Holy Place shows God's moral perfection as symbolized by his separation from the common and unclean. Third, the portable nature of the tabernacle shows God's desire to be with his people as they traveled. For a description of these items, see Exodus 25–31.

Name	*Function and significance*
Ark of the Covenant	• A golden rectangular box that contained the Ten Commandments • Symbolized God's covenant with Israel's people • Located in the Most Holy Place
Atonement Cover	• The lid to the ark of the covenant • Symbolized the presence of God among his people
Curtain	• The curtain that divided the two sacred rooms of the tabernacle—the Holy Place and the Most Holy Place • Symbolized how the people were separated from God because of sin
Table	• A wooden table located in the Holy Place of the tabernacle • The holy bread and various utensils were kept on this table
Holy Bread (Bread of the Presence)	• Twelve loaves of baked bread, one for each trible of Israel • Symbolized the spiritual nourishment God offers his people
Lampstands and Lamps	• A golden lampstand located in the Holy Place, which held seven burnng oil lamps • The lampstand lighted the Holy Place for the priests
Altar of Incense	• An altar in the Holy place in front of the curtain • Used for burning God's special incense and symbolic of acceptable prayer
Anointing Oil	• A speical oil used to anooint the priests and all the pieces in the tabernacle • A sign of being set apart for God
Altar of Burnt Offering	• The bronze altar outside the tabernacle used for the sacrifices • Symbolized how sacrifice restored one's relationship with God
Basin	• A large washbasin outside the tabernacle used by the priests to cleanse themselves before performing their duties • Symbolized the need for spiritual cleansing

Place or Holy of Holies) and an outer room. A priest on duty would enter the outer room *(the first room),* called *the Holy Place,* each day to commune with God and to tend to the other elements located in this room:

- *Lampstand*—the lampstand was the Menorah, a seven-branched candlestick standing in the south side of the room (Exodus 25:31-40; 37:17-24). Its candles burned day and night and provided light for the priests as they carried out their duties. The light also symbolized God's presence. The Menorah still remains as a major symbol of the Jewish faith.
- *Table*—the table was made of wood and overlaid with pure gold (Exodus 25:23-30; 37:10-16). On this table sat the *sacred loaves of bread* (called "shewbread" in the KJV or "bread of the Presence" in modern versions). Once a week on the Sabbath, a priest would enter the Holy Place and set twelve freshly baked loaves of bread on a small table. This bread symbolized God's presence among his people as well as his loving care in meeting their physical needs. The bread that was replaced was to be eaten only by the priests on duty.

9:3-4 Then there was a curtain, and behind the curtain was the second room called the Most Holy Place. In that room were a gold incense altar and a wooden chest called the Ark of the Covenant, which was covered with gold on all sides. Inside the Ark were a gold jar containing manna, Aaron's staff that sprouted leaves, and the stone tablets of the covenant.[NLT] Beyond the first room, the Holy Place, *there was a curtain* (described in Exodus 26:31-33). This curtain closed off the Most Holy Place, preventing anyone from entering, gazing into, or even getting a fleeting glimpse of the interior of the Most Holy Place, symbolizing that sinful people could not approach the holy God. The curtain formed the separation between the holy God and sinful people (see 6:19). The original readers would have known of the magnificent curtain in Herod's temple. It was made of blue, purple, and scarlet woven linen. Figures of the cherubim were embroidered on it. *Behind the curtain was the second room called the Most Holy Place.* The Most Holy Place was where God himself dwelt. Only the high priest could enter the Most Holy Place, and then, only once a year (on the Day of Atonement) to make atonement for the sins of the whole nation. The elements in the Most Holy Place included

- *a gold incense altar*—in Exodus, this incense altar was placed just outside the curtain, for it was used daily (see Exodus 30:6-8; 37:25-28; 40:5). It stood in front of the ark of the covenant

The Tabernacle

From the Wilderness of Sinai until the building of Solomon's Temple in 950 B.C.

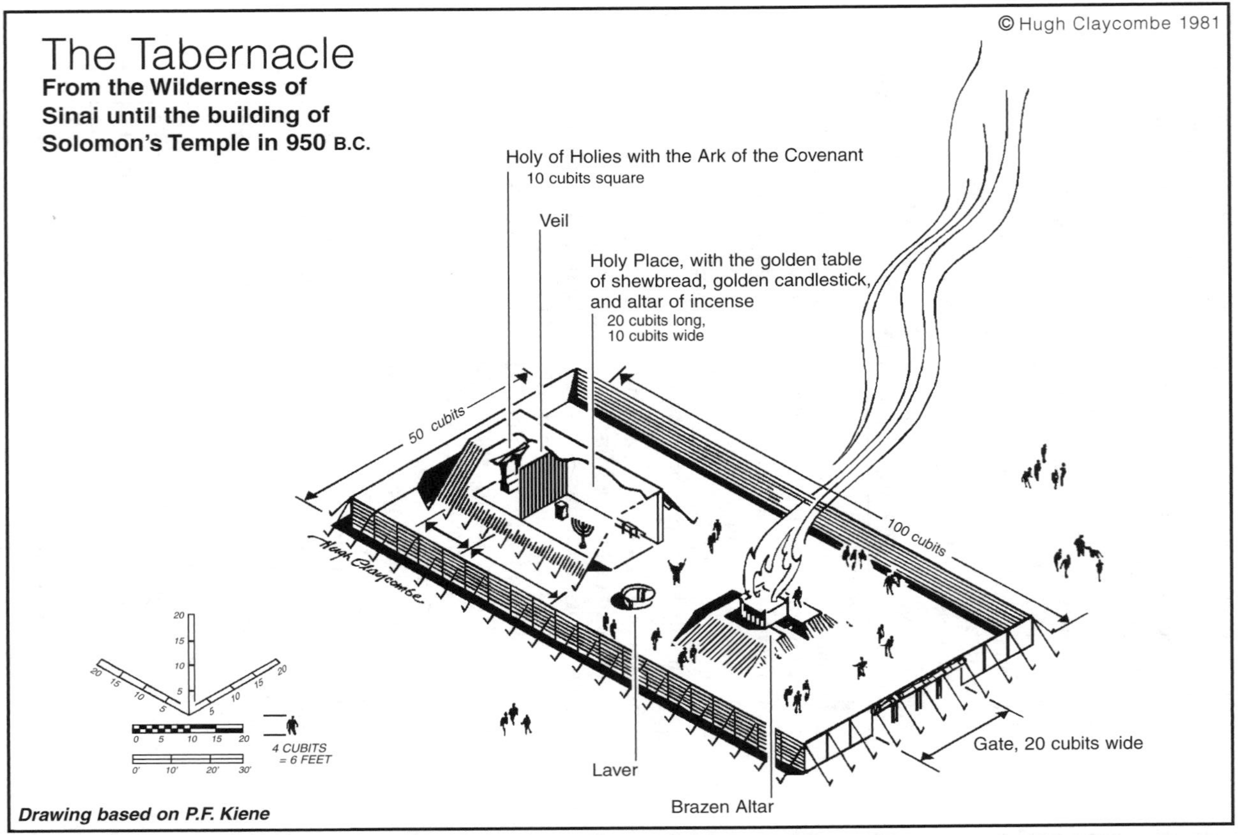

Drawing based on P.F. Kiene

© Hugh Claycombe 1981

(which was directly behind the curtain). The high priest burned incense on the altar twice daily. The incense altar eventually became a symbol for the prayers of the believers (see Luke 1:8-10; Revelation 5:8; 8:3-4). The altar also had a special part in the ceremony of the Day of Atonement when the high priest would enter the Most Holy Place. Thus the altar is mentioned as part of the "second room."

- *the Ark of the Covenant*—this sacred object was *a wooden chest,* the most holy piece of furniture in the tabernacle. The wood was acacia wood. Acacia trees flourished in barren regions and were fairly common in Old Testament times. The wood was brownish-orange and very hard, making it an excellent material for furniture. The ark was then *covered with gold on all sides* (Exodus 25:10-22; 37:1-9). Many of the items in the tabernacle were covered with gold. The high quality of the precious materials symbolized God's greatness and transcendence. Also called the ark of the testimony, the ark symbolized God's covenant with his people. Two gold angels called cherubim were placed on its top. On the annual Day of Atonement, the high priest would enter the Most Holy Place to sprinkle blood on the top of the ark (called the atonement cover) to atone for the sins of the entire nation.

The ark of the covenant itself contained certain holy objects:

- *a gold jar containing manna*—first described in Exodus 16:32-35, this symbolized God's care in providing food for his people in the wilderness. It may have been lost when the Philistines captured the ark and held it for a time (see 1 Samuel 4–6).
- *Aaron's staff that sprouted leaves*—first described in Numbers 17:1-11, this staff showed that Aaron's descendants had indeed been chosen by God to care for the priesthood. It certified their authority as priests. This staff was also probably lost during the Philistine control of the ark (see 1 Samuel 4–6).
- *the stone tablets of the covenant*—these two stone tablets were put in the ark at Mount Sinai (called tablets of the covenant, see Exodus 34:27-29). When the ark was placed in Solomon's temple, only the tablets of the Ten Commandments were still inside (1 Kings 8:9).

9:5 Above the ark were the cherubim of the Glory, overshadowing the atonement cover. But we cannot discuss these things in detail now.[NIV] Next the author described what decorated the top of the ark of the covenant: *cherubim of the Glory* (Exodus 25:18-22). Cherubim are mighty angels. One of the functions of the cherubim was to serve as guardians. These angels guarded the entrances to both the tree of life (Genesis 3:24) and the Most Holy Place (Exodus 26:31-33). The living creatures carrying God's throne in Ezekiel 1 may have been cherubim. With their wings *overshadowing the atonement cover,* these two gold statues were believed to support God's invisible presence. They stood at the ends of the atonement cover, facing each other. They may have been represented with bodies of animals and faces of humans. Often they symbolized the glory of God (see Psalm 80:1; 99:1). Here they are called "cherubim of the Glory," referring to the glory of God. The glory of God's presence hovered over the ark of the covenant (see Exodus 40:34-36; Leviticus 16:2).

The atonement cover was also called "the mercy seat." The word for "mercy" *(hilastarion)* is the same word used for "propitiation" elsewhere in the New Testament (Romans 3:25). The mercy seat was significant because it was where sin was taken away. The blood from the sacrifice given on the Day of Atonement was sprinkled by the high priest on the mercy seat (Leviticus 16:15-17). Here the people experienced God's forgiveness.

The original readers would have been very well acquainted with the apparatus of the tabernacle. The intention was not to give a commentary on these things; so the writer explained, *we cannot discuss these things in detail now.*

9:6 When everything had been arranged like this, the priests entered regularly into the outer room to carry on their ministry.[NIV] Having reminded the people of the basic arrangement of the holy rooms in the tabernacle, the writer gets to the reason for this discussion. The priests would serve regularly in the outer rooms—daily offering incense (see Exodus 30:7), setting out the holy loaves on the Sabbath (Leviticus 24:8-9), and trimming the wicks on the candles in order to keep them burning (Exodus 27:20-21). Because the worship that the priests led had to be done continually, *their ministry* was inferior to the ministry and sacrifices of Christ.

Why were priests needed in Israel? Exodus 19:6 instructs the Israelites to be a kingdom of priests; ideally all the people would be holy and relate to God. But from the time of Adam's fall, sin has separated people from God, and people have needed mediators to help them find forgiveness. At first, the patriarchs—heads of households like Abraham and Job—were priests of the house or clan and would make sacrifices for the family. When the Israelites left Egypt, the descendants of Aaron were chosen to serve as priests for the nation. After the nation was established in the land of Canaan, they ministered to God by working at the temple, managing its upkeep, teaching the people the Scriptures, and directing the worship services. At this time, there were about twenty thousand priests throughout the country—far too many to minister in the temple at one time. Therefore the priests were divided into twenty-four separate groups of about a thousand each, according to David's directions (1 Chronicles 24:3-19). Each of these twenty-four groups of priests served two-week shifts each year at the temple (the rest of the time they served in their hometowns). Each morning a priest was to enter the Holy Place in the temple and burn incense. Lots were cast to decide who, from the division on duty, would enter the sacred room (see Luke 1:8-10).

The priests stood in the gap between God and human beings. They were the full-time spiritual leaders and overseers of offerings. In Christ, this imperfect system was transformed. Jesus Christ himself is our High Priest. Now all believers can approach God through him.

9:7 **But only the high priest ever entered the Most Holy Place, and only once a year. And he always offered blood for his own sins and for the sins the people had committed in ignorance.**[NLT] In addition to these regular services, *the high priest* goes into *the Most Holy Place* but *only once a year* on the Day of Atonement. This day was strictly observed (see Leviticus 23:26-32), and no one was permitted to enter the Most Holy Place on any other day. On this day, the blood sprinkled on the mercy seat on the ark of the covenant symbolized atonement for the sins of the nation (Leviticus 16:15-30). Even if the people had diligently sacrificed throughout the year, they may not have realized that they had committed certain sins. This sacrifice would cover unintentional and unknown sins.

Hebrews reminds us that the priest was only allowed to enter with *blood.* The Most Holy Place was the most sacred spot on earth for Jews. Only the high priest could enter—the other priests and the common people were forbidden to come into the room. Their only access to God was through the high priest, who would offer a sacrifice and use the animal's blood to atone for his own sins and then for the people's sins (see also 10:19). As part of the yearly ritual, the priest would enter the Most Holy Place with the blood of a bull. This blood would serve to cover *his own sins.* Then the priest would leave the room and return with the blood of a goat. This blood would cover *the sins the people had committed in ignorance.* The blood that the priest brought into the Most Holy Place would be sprinkled on the altar of incense and on the front of the mercy seat. (In the day of the original readers, the ark of the covenant was missing, so the priest would simply sprinkle the blood into the Most Holy Place.)

The argument continues, showing that this earlier priestly practice was insufficient in bringing the people into a good relationship with God. It failed in three primary ways: (1) The Most Holy Place could only be entered by the high priest, and only once a year. (2) When the high priest did enter the Most Holy Place, he needed to bring blood for his own sins and then blood for the people. (3) The high priest's effort had to be repeated every year.

Why was blood so important? From the beginning God had said, "For the life of a creature is in the blood, and I have given it to you to make atonement for yourselves on the altar; it is the blood that makes atonement for one's life" (Leviticus 17:11 NIV). In Old Testament times, animal sacrifices were continually offered at the tabernacle and temple. These animals brought to the altar had two important characteristics: they were alive, and they were without flaw. The sacrifices showed the Israelites the seriousness of sin: innocent blood had to be shed before sins could be pardoned. But animal blood could not really remove sin (10:4); and the forgiveness provided by those sacrifices, in legal terms, was more a stay of execution than a pardon. Those animal sacrifices could only point to Jesus' sacrifice that paid the penalty for all sin. Jesus' life was identical with ours, yet unstained by sin; therefore, he could serve as the flawless sacrifice for our sins. In him, our pardon is complete.

In God's new covenant, the Most Holy Place, that is, God's presence, is open to all who come in the name of Jesus. No blood or sacrifice is required other than the blood provided by Jesus Christ. No sacrifice needs to be repeated because Christ's sacrifice is completely effective.

UNINTENTIONAL SINS

In Old Testament times, the priests made sacrifices for unintentional sins. Will God hold us responsible for sins we did not intend to commit or did not know we committed?

Think about it. Is ignorance of the speed limit an excuse in court? Will a teacher overlook poor homework if a student had good intentions? Will the IRS write off tax due on bartered goods merely because someone thought the law did not require payment?

God is patient and kind above all earthly courts and classrooms, but sin is sin, and God judges sin. God cannot overlook unintentional sin. That is why we must come to him for forgiveness.

9:8 **The Holy Spirit was showing by this that the way into the Most Holy Place had not yet been disclosed as long as the first tabernacle was still standing.**[NIV] In giving instructions for the tabernacle, *the Holy Spirit was showing by this that the way into the Most Holy Place had not yet been disclosed.* The ceremony carried out on the Day of Atonement revealed that people had no direct approach to God. Ordinary people could never enter God's presence and had to depend on the high priest. A heavy curtain blocked the Most Holy Place; thus, this place "had not yet been disclosed." The way had not yet been revealed—Christ would do that. "As long as the first tabernacle was still standing" means more than the physical tent itself; it also refers to the system that revolved around the first tent. This would include the practices of temple worship.

The Holy Spirit showed that the sacrifice system was ineffective for bringing unhindered fellowship with God, but one day, people would experience a new kind of relationship with God that would effectively remove sin. This old covenant pointed to what Christ would do in the new covenant. Hebrews says that the Holy Spirit was teaching the people to look forward because there was more to come—God would provide a better way.

9:9 **This is an illustration pointing to the present time. For the gifts and sacrifices that the priests offer are not able to cleanse the consciences of the people who bring them.**[NLT] This older way was simply *an illustration pointing to the present time.* Under the old covenant, the people did not have direct access to God. But under the new covenant made available through Christ, God's people can have access to God and be free from guilt. This guilt was never fully relieved in the old covenant, *for the gifts and sacrifices that the priests offer are not able to cleanse the consciences of the people who bring them.* These sacrifices symbolized atonement for sin and provided a way for the people to continue to worship God, but the sacrifices could not change the people's hearts and lives. Only through Christ can people's consciences be cleansed—purified and made perfect (see also 9:14; 10:22; 13:18). Christ dealt decisively with the root cause of sin and made it possible for people to be cleansed from sin.

> The really effective barrier to a man's free access to God is an inward and not a material one; it exists in his conscience. *F. F. Bruce*

9:10 **They are only a matter of food and drink and various ceremonial washings—external regulations applying until the time of the new order.**[NIV] The writer continues to show why the old system of sacrifice through the priests was inadequate. The people had to keep the Old Testament dietary laws and ceremonial cleansing laws until Christ came with God's new and better way. Even the food and drink laws (Leviticus 10:8-9; 11) and various ceremonial washings (Leviticus 15:4-27; Numbers 19:7-13) dealt only with *external regulations* that were required under the old covenant.

CLEAR CONSCIENCE

Forgiveness has two sides. On God's side, his demand for holiness is satisfied by the sacrifice of Jesus on the cross. On our side, guilty consciences are scrubbed clean.

There's no reason for you to feel defeated by a guilty conscience. When God forgives sin, he satisfies his requirement of holiness and wipes your record clean.

If you're bothered by guilt today, two reasons may explain it:

1. You have not understood that God can make your conscience clean. Perhaps no one has ever explained that to you.
2. You have not received God's forgiveness because you have not asked.

Bring your guilt-ridden life to Christ, confess your inability to clean up your own conscience, ask him to forgive you. Thank him for his deliverance. God can forgive you and clear your record.

God replaced this old system at *the time of the new order*. This order began with the new covenant in Christ when God's laws were written on people's hearts (see commentary on 8:10-12). Perhaps some of the original readers had been considering reverting back to certain ceremonial rules. The book of Hebrews points out that these rules are no longer necessary or spiritually beneficial. The "external regulations" have been replaced by the "new order," initiated through Christ's death. The old order passed away, as illustrated by the torn curtain in the temple, opening the way for believers to directly access God (Mark 15:38).

Paul wrote in Colossians 2:16-17: "Therefore do not let anyone judge you by what you eat or drink, or with regard to a religious festival, a New Moon celebration or a Sabbath day. These are a shadow of the things that were to come; the reality, however, is found in Christ" (NIV).

CHRIST IS THE PERFECT OFFERING FOR SIN / 9:11-28

Before bar codes and electronic checkout devices, every item in most stores had a price tag that clearly told the cost. Sin, in God's eyes, carries a clear price tag: punishment.

Under the first covenant, sins were covered temporarily by the blood of bulls and goats. Under the second covenant, the blood of the supreme sacrifice, Jesus Christ, covered all believers' sins. Under the first convent, the blood had to be shed and offered to

God again and again. Under the new covenant, Jesus' blood was shed once for all. Under the old covenant, the priest physically sprinkled blood on the ceremonially unclean. Under the new covenant, we who believe in Christ are covered by his blood, which was shed two thousand years ago.

9:11 **When Christ came as high priest of the good things that are already here, he went through the greater and more perfect tabernacle that is not man-made, that is to say, not a part of this creation.**NIV Although the people worshiped under the old covenant for nearly fifteen hundred years, God provided a new way that arrived *when Christ came.* Christ fulfilled perfectly and completely all that had been illustrated in the old covenant (described in 9:1-10). Christ did not come under the old covenant; he came as a priest of the new covenant (described in 8:10-12). This new covenant is described as *the good things that are already here.* With Christ, the new covenant has arrived, changing the way people are forgiven. While alive on earth, Christians experience some of the blessings of the new covenant. In heaven, Christians will experience all of the blessings fully. Ephesians 1:3 says, "Blessed be the God and Father of our Lord Jesus Christ, who has blessed us in Christ with every spiritual blessing in the heavenly places" (NRSV).

As a high priest, Christ also served in the tabernacle, but his ministry was not limited to the earthly tabernacle. Instead, *he went though the greater and more perfect tabernacle that is not man-made . . . not a part of this creation.* Christ served in the real, heavenly tabernacle because the earthly tabernacle had simply been an illustration of what was to come (see commentary on 8:1-5). Although some early Christians saw the phrase "more perfect tabernacle" as a reference to Christ's incarnation, that could not be what the author of Hebrews had in mind. The writer clearly says that this tabernacle is "not a part of this creation," so it couldn't refer to Christ's human body. Christ's ministry on our behalf was in God's presence, a place where the blood of goats and bulls would have no effect. This point again reveals Christ's superiority. Verse 24 further explains this: "For Christ did not enter a man-made sanctuary that was only a copy of the true one; he entered heaven itself" (NIV).

> One drop of Christ's blood is worth more than heaven and earth.
> *Martin Luther*

9:12 **Not with the blood of goats and calves, but with His own blood He entered the Most Holy Place once for all, having obtained eternal redemption.**NKJV This imagery comes from the Day of Atonement rituals described earlier. Just as a priest would enter the earthly Most Holy Place, Christ *entered the Most Holy Place* in heaven. Just as a priest would enter with the blood of animals, Christ entered, *not with the blood of goats and calves, but with His own blood.* By his own blood, Christ *entered the Most Holy Place once for all.* Having entered by his own blood, he was able to obtain *eternal redemption* for all who would believe. He did not literally carry his blood with him, but rather, his death secured the result needed. The real work was done on the cross. It was "eternal" in the sense of being complete and unrepeatable.

To speak of Jesus' "blood" was an important first-century way of speaking of his death. Christ's death redeems us. "Redemption" was the price paid to gain freedom for a slave (see Leviticus 25:47-54). Through his death, Jesus paid the price to release us from slavery to sin. Now we are forgiven on the basis of the shedding of Jesus' blood—he died as the perfect and final sacrifice. (See also Romans 5:9; Ephesians 1:7; 2:13; Colossians 1:20; 1 Peter 1:18-19.) Christ's sacrifice was so perfect and effective that it never needs to be repeated. Unlike the earthly priests, who offered sacrifices every year on the Day of Atonement, Christ was able to offer his sacrifice "once for all." Having provided the sacrifice at the Cross by offering his blood, the high-priestly sacrificial work is done. Now Christ sits at the right hand of God the Father (see 1:3; 8:1).

FREEDOM

Christ provided our redemption. Although you know Christ, you may still believe that you have to work hard to make yourself good enough for God. But rules and rituals have never cleansed people's hearts. By Jesus' blood alone we are forgiven, are freed from death's sting and sin's power, and can live to serve God. If you are carrying a load of guilt because you are finding that you can't be good enough for God, take another look at Jesus' death and what it means for you. Christ can heal your conscience and deliver you from the frustration of trying to earn God's favor.

9:13 Under the old system, the blood of goats and bulls and the ashes of a young cow could cleanse people's bodies from ceremonial impurity.[NLT] Christ's sacrifice was superior to any of the sacrifices offered under the old covenant. *Under the old system,* the priests offered *goats and bulls* as sacrifices (see commentary on 9:7). The phrase "ashes of a young cow" refers to a ceremony described in Numbers 19:1-10. This ceremony was performed when someone was made unclean and needed to be purified. For example, someone might become defiled by touching a dead body. In such a case, the carcass of a red heifer was burned with cedar wood, hyssop, and scarlet wool; then the ashes were used with water for cleansing the person. This ceremony served to purify an unclean person; thus, it *could cleanse people's bodies from ceremonial impurity* (literally, "to the purifying of the flesh"). A ceremonially defiled person, as described above, could not participate in Jewish ceremonies until he or she was cleansed (see also Mark 7:15-23; Acts 10:15; 21:28). The ceremony kept people from being cut off from God. But the Levitical offering only provided ceremonial purity on a temporary basis. Such a temporary act was effective. Christ's sacrifice was even more effective, as is noted in the following verse.

9:14 How much more shall the blood of Christ, who through the eternal Spirit offered Himself without spot to God, cleanse your conscience from dead works to serve the living God?[NKJV]
If the old way of ceremonial cleansings allowed people to be made clean (as described in 9:13), *how much more shall the blood of Christ, who through the eternal Spirit offered Himself without spot to God?* "How much more" points to the surpassing greatness of Christ and what his sacrifice did for us compared to the ceremonial system of the old covenant. As evidence of the greatness of Christ's sacrifice, note that all three members of the Trinity were involved—Jesus offered himself, through the eternal Spirit (referring to the Holy Spirit), to God (the Father). Is the "eternal Spirit" the Holy Spirit or Christ's personal spirit? Because there is no article in the Greek text, some have taken this to be Christ's spirit whereby he made spiritual sacrifice for us. But it seems likely that the author would have said "*his* spirit" if that was what he had meant. In Isaiah 42:1, the prophet gave God's message, "I have put my Spirit upon him" (NKJV), indicating the empowering of the servant of the Lord by the Holy Spirit. Based on that connection, it seems likely that the eternal Spirit is the Holy Spirit. Empowered and ordained by the Holy Spirit, Christ made his sacrifice. Christ willingly offered himself as the sacrifice for the new covenant. Only he could do so because only he was *without spot,* that is, without sin. Christ's all-surpassing sacrifice obtains our cleansing.

Christ's sacrifice did more than *cleanse* the person ceremonially, which is all the ashes could do, but it cleansed the person's *conscience.* When the people sacrificed animals, God considered the people's faith and obedience, cleansed the people from sin, and made them "ceremonially" clean and acceptable according to Old Testament law. But Christ's sacrifice transforms our lives and hearts and makes us clean on the inside. His sacrifice is infinitely more effective than animal sacrifices. No barrier of sin or weakness on our part can stop his forgiveness.

Christ's blood cleansed his followers from *dead works.* Before people follow Christ, they are filled with sinful thoughts, actions, and behavior. These "dead works" defile people, placing them in need of atonement (see 6:1). Some believe that "dead works" refers to the now outdated sacrifices of the old covenant. This seems unlikely because all people, whether or not they have ever participated in the Levitical sacrifices, must be saved from their dead works. It is the dead works that required the original sacrifices and the new covenant. However, any attempt to please God either by works of the Old Testament law or by doing good deeds is worthless. These are ineffective and invalid. We are saved only by God's gracious kindness, not by our works.

It could be that the original readers were tempted to revert to sacrifices because of guilty feelings. It could be that they had difficulty trusting in Christ's forgiveness and felt the urge to do something themselves. In a similar way, Christians today often try to appease their consciences by doing good deeds, giving money, living up to leaders' expectations, or taking on extra responsibilities. For the original readers and for us, the message is clear. Our consciences can be clean on account of what Christ has done. No human activity can restore a conscience. If you feel guilty, don't look for something you can do. Look to Christ, whose sacrifice you can trust.

SUCCESSFUL LIVING

The Bible says that dead works are not only sinful deeds, but ways in which we attempt to reach God without accepting his gracious kindness. Our culture, however, glorifies self-effort and personal achievement. More and more, our culture suggests that a successful person seeks certain goals: financial security, health and fitness, and the respect of others (especially in your career field).

But here and in many other places, the Bible gives us another picture of successful living: accept Jesus' sacrifice for your sin, escape the futility of dead works, and let God cleanse your conscience.

Are you trying to reach God through the dead works of personal achievement, self-improvement, or even active service to help others? Instead, accept his forgiveness, allow him to cleanse and change you, and let your service to others be motivated by your love and gratitude to God.

The purpose of all the cleansing was to allow the people to *serve the living God.* The Greek word for "serve" used here *(latreuo)* means to carry out religious duties. Now that sins are forgiven, we can worship truly and freely. We are not limited to external actions, but we can worship in spirit. Our worship does not need to be mediated through a priest, but we can worship God on our own with unlimited access to him. If we were not cleansed from our consciences, we might be inhibited from worshiping. But being freed from our dead works and having a clean conscience allows us to put off our guilt so we can serve and worship effectively. (For more on the role of works in service, see 13:16.)

9:15 For this reason Christ is the mediator of a new covenant, that those who are called may receive the promised eternal inheritance—now that he has died as a ransom to set them free from the sins committed under the first covenant.[NIV] Here the two themes, mediator and new covenant, previously discussed in 8:6-13, are reintroduced. Under this new covenant, believers are not just ritually cleansed on the outside, which is all that the animal sacrifices could do under the old covenant. Instead, they are cleansed from within, consciences cleansed by the blood of Christ, who died on our behalf (9:14). Christ can mediate the new covenant because of his sacrificial death. (For more on the "new covenant," see 8:6-13 and commentary.) *For this reason,* that is, because Christ offered himself to God (9:14), Christ is able to be *the mediator of a new covenant.* He mediates on the basis of his self-sacrifice and shed blood. As our High Priest, Christ acts as the mediator, or advocate, between us and God. He intercedes for all who believe, looking after their interests and presenting their requests to God. Christ *died as a ransom,* the price paid to release a slave. The Greek word for "ransom to set them free" here contains the root word used for eternal redemption in 9:12. Here the word is *apolutrosis.* This is the only occurrence in Hebrews of this word to refer to redemption from sin (see also Romans 3:24; Ephesians 1:7; Colossians 1:14). In 9:12, the related word *lutrosis* is used. Jesus paid a ransom for us because we could not pay it ourselves. His death released all of us from our slavery to sin. God redeemed us from the tyranny of sin, not with money, but with the precious blood of his own Son (Matthew 20:28; Romans 6:6-7; 1 Corinthians 6:20; Colossians 2:13-14; 1 Timothy 2:6; 1 Peter 1:18-19). We cannot escape from sin on our own; only God's Son can free us.

> The only thing that a man can contribute to his own redemption is the sin from which he needs to be redeemed.
> *William Temple*

Because Christ serves as our Mediator, *those who are called may receive the promised eternal inheritance.* The phrase, "those who are called," refers to all who believe in Jesus Christ and accept his sacrifice on their behalf. That they are "called" points to God's initiative in giving salvation. The "promised eternal inheritance" is the final end of the new covenant—believers one day living in heaven with God. This inheritance will last forever.

Christ's sacrificial death saves not only those who died after Christ, but it also saves those who died *under the first covenant.* People in Old Testament times were saved through Christ's sacrifice, although that sacrifice had not yet happened. Those who offered unblemished animal sacrifices were anticipating Christ's coming and his death for sin. There was no point in returning to the sacrificial system after Christ had come and had become the final, perfect sacrifice.

9:16-17 **Now when someone leaves a will, it is necessary to prove that the person who made it is dead. The will goes into effect only after the person's death. While the person who made it is still alive, the will cannot be put into effect.**[NLT] These two verses introduce a parenthetical thought that shows when the new covenant was actually initiated. Through a play on words, the author speaks of someone who *leaves a will.* The word for "will" is the same word elsewhere used as "covenant." The new covenant was inherited by God's people at the death of Christ. In essence, he left the new covenant in his will. When he died, it was received by God's people. When Jesus died, the will was enacted and the promised inheritance (salvation and eternal life) was received. His death also provided the blood needed to put the covenant into effect.

LAST WILL AND TESTAMENT

From the simplest facts about wills, the writer of Hebrews makes an argument about the grandest facts of salvation. What about wills, and specifically, your will? Is it just a list of items given to relatives and friends? A document to reduce family squabbles over your estate?

A will can be much more:

- A tool to help people in the name of Christ. Reach out with your assets to people in need. Designate a portion to important Christian work.
- A last loving message to your dearest ones on earth. Tell them how much they meant to you.
- A final testimony to Christ's saving grace in your life. In your own words, tell about God's power in your life.

Make your will a record of encouragement and support for those you leave behind.

9:18 **That is why even the first covenant was put into effect with the blood of an animal.**NLT After a brief pause, the discussion returns to the covenant. The author reminds the readers that *the first covenant was put into effect with the blood of an animal.* To understand the reason for blood under the first covenant, we need to understand the Bible's view of sin and forgiveness. God is the sovereign judge of the universe. He is also absolutely holy. As the holy judge of all, he condemns sin and judges it worthy of death. In Old Testament times, God accepted the death of an animal as a substitute for the sinner. The animal's shed blood was proof that one life had been given for another. So on the one hand, blood symbolized the death of the animal, but it also symbolized the life that was spared as a result. (See also 9:22.)

SUBMITTING TO GOD

Moses held nothing back. Every commandment was in his message to the people, and everybody received the sprinkled blood, a sign of their submission to God's law.

Someone might have objected. "It's icky! I don't want that smelly blood on my clean clothes!"

Someone might have deferred. "Moses' sermon is basically correct, but the second paragraph under point six raises pertinent issues of . . ."

But the proper response is submission. When God's law is the topic, we do right to listen, accept, and obey. Of course, we also do right to understand what God's law requires of us (to rightly interpret its meaning). We should be as eager to obey as were the original hearers of God's law.

9:19 **When Moses had proclaimed every commandment of the law to all the people, he took the blood of calves, together with water, scarlet wool and branches of hyssop, and sprinkled the scroll and all the people.**NIV This passage looks back to Exodus 24:3-8, which describes the covenant sacrifice of Sinai. In this ceremony, an animal would be killed. Then its blood would be sprinkled on the altar and on the people. *When Moses had proclaimed every commandment of the law to all the people,* he sealed the covenant with blood. The meaning of this sprinkling went beyond this ceremony. It demonstrated the ratification of the whole ceremonial system. The entire old covenant was ratified and sealed with blood. The blood that sealed the covenant, *the blood of calves,* was mixed *together with water* to symbolize cleansing. *Scarlet wool* was tied onto the *branches of hyssop* and was used to sprinkle the blood on *the scroll and all the people.* In the ceremony described here, Moses would sprinkle half the blood from the sacrificed animals on the altar to show that the sinner could once again approach God because something had died in his or her place. Moses then would sprinkle the other half of the blood on the people to show that the penalty for their sin had been paid and they could be reunited with God. Through this symbolic act, God's promises to Israel were reaffirmed and lessons were taught about Christ's future sacrificial death.

9:20-21 **He said, "This is the blood of the covenant, which God has commanded you to keep." In the same way, he sprinkled with the blood both the tabernacle and everything used in its ceremonies.**[NIV] In the same way that Moses sprinkled the *blood of the covenant,* Christ shed his blood in order to inaugurate the new covenant. As the old covenant was sealed with the blood, so the new covenant was sealed with Christ's blood. This quote has been adapted from the Septuagint (the Greek version of the Old Testament). Rather than reading, "This is the blood of the covenant that the Lord has made with you" (Exodus 24:8), the quote here reads, "This is the blood of the covenant, which God has commanded you to keep." This may have been used to bring to mind the words of Christ from Mark 14:24, "This is My blood of the new covenant, which is shed for many" (NKJV). The sprinkling of blood on *the tabernacle and everything used in its ceremonies,* while not noted in the Pentateuch, symbolized the purification of the earthly sanctuary and sacrificial system.

THE SYMBOL OF THE CROSS

Shed blood means something living has died. In the Old Testament, it was an animal, carefully selected and ritually sacrificed. In the New Testament, it was Jesus Christ on the cross, supremely and for all time satisfying God's holiness in our place.

- Where there is no loss of life, there is no forgiveness.
- Where there is no forgiveness, there is no freedom.
- Where there is no freedom, there is no hope.

The next time you see a cross or crucifix on a building or as jewelry, send a quick prayer to God—"Thank you, almighty God, for the hope, assurance, and freedom won by Jesus on the real cross, and thank you that the cross symbolizes the proof that I am forgiven."

9:22 **In fact, the law requires that nearly everything be cleansed with blood, and without the shedding of blood there is no forgiveness.**[NIV] Blood from a sacrifice symbolized cleansing and forgiveness, thus *nearly everything* was cleansed with blood. In fact, *without the shedding of blood there is no forgiveness.* Why does forgiveness require the shedding of blood? This is no arbitrary decree on the part of a bloodthirsty God, as some have suggested. There is no greater symbol of life than blood because blood keeps us alive. Jesus shed his blood—gave his life—for our sins so that we wouldn't have to experience spiritual death, eternal separation from God. Jesus is the source of life, not death. He gave his own life to pay the penalty for us so that we might live. After shedding his blood, Christ rose from the grave and proclaimed victory over sin and death. (For more on the reason for blood, see commentary on 9:7 and 9:18.)

9:23 **That is why the Tabernacle and everything in it, which were copies of things in heaven, had to be purified by the blood of animals. But the real things in heaven had to be purified with far better sacrifices than the blood of animals.**[NLT] The *Tabernacle and everything in it* were, in a way that we don't fully understand, *copies of things in heaven,* illustrating God's heavenly originals, which are far better than the earthly copies. Just as the copies had to be purified, so *the real things in heaven had to be purified with far better sacrifices than the blood of animals.* This purification of the heavenly things can best be understood as referring to Christ's spiritual work for us. Of course, the "better sacrifices" were, in fact, only one sacrifice. The real spiritual work of forgiveness continues in the presence of God as he forgives us because of Christ's death in our place. Why did the heavenly tabernacle need to be purified? Heaven and God's presence are already holy, so this probably refers to the cleansed people of God, who can now stand in God's presence.

9:24 **For Christ did not enter a man-made sanctuary that was only a copy of the true one; he entered heaven itself, now to appear for us in God's presence.**[NIV] Again the author contrasts the earthly and heavenly sanctuaries. Christ's work was superior to that of the priests because he was not limited to a *man-made sanctuary that was only a copy of the true one.* The priests appeared in a symbolic, man-made place. Christ *entered heaven itself,* appearing before the actual face of God, *now to appear for us in God's presence.* Among references to priests, tabernacles, sacrifices, and other ideas unfamiliar to us, we come to this description of Christ as our Mediator, appearing in God's presence on our behalf. No intermediary priests or saints are necessary. Christ is our perfect representative and Advocate. We can relate to this role and be encouraged by it. Christ is on our side at God's side. He is there *now,* always available. He is our Lord and Savior. He is not there to convince or remind God that our sins are forgiven, but to present both our needs and our service for him as an offering (see 6:20; 7:25; also Romans 8:34).

9:25 And he did not enter heaven to offer himself again and again, like the high priest here on earth who enters the Most Holy Place year after year with the blood of an animal.[NLT] Again, unlike the priests, Christ did not *offer himself again and again, like the high priest here on earth* whose job never ended, but continued *year after year.* Here is another contrast between the earthly priest and Christ's role as priest. Christ's sacrifice was once for all (9:12). The high priest's job (by requirement) meant that he would go into *the Most Holy Place* and offer *the blood of an animal* to bring cleansing to the nation year after year. Christ's sacrifice invalidated any other sacrifice.

9:26 Then Christ would have had to suffer many times since the creation of the world. But now he has appeared once for all at the end of the ages to do away with sin by the sacrifice of himself.[NIV] If Christ's sacrifice had followed the pattern of the old covenant, *then Christ would have had to suffer many times since the creation of the world.* Christ's sacrifice, however, initiated a new covenant and was the perfect sacrifice. As a result *he has appeared once for all* and, by doing so, has done *away with sin by the sacrifice of himself.* "Once for all" indicates the final removal of sin and contrasts with "many times" (see also 9:25 and 10:11, which refer to the Levitical sacrifice that must be repeated). Sin is more than just covered; it is obliterated. Forgiven and forgotten. Jesus sacrificed himself by freely giving his life for us. He told his disciples, "For this reason the Father loves me, because I lay down my life in order to take it up again. No one takes it from me, but I lay it down of my own accord. I have power to lay it down, and I have power to take it up again. I have received this command from my Father" (John 10:17-18 NRSV).

"End of the ages" refers to the time of Christ's coming to earth in fulfillment of the Old Testament prophecies. This is similar to "in these last days" of Hebrews 1:2. Christ ushered in the new era of grace and forgiveness. We are still living in the time period called "the end of the ages." The Day of the Lord has begun and will be completed at Christ's return.

9:27 And just as each person is destined to die once and after that comes judgment.[NLT] This parenthetical remark shows the certainty of death and judgment. Each person will live on earth and then die. All people will stand before God. Those who follow Christ have hope. Christians can know that just as death and judgment are certain, so is their hope (9:28). All people die physically, but Christ died so that we would not have to die spiritually. We can have wonderful confidence in his saving work for us, doing away with sin—past, present, and future. He has forgiven our past sin—when he sacrificed himself once for all (9:26); he has given us the Holy Spirit to help us deal with present sin; he appears for us now in heaven as our High Priest (9:24); and he promises to return (9:28) and raise us to eternal life in a world where sin will be banished.

JUDGMENT

It's not a popular theme today, but it is nevertheless true that judgment is coming. Do you look forward to Christ's return, or do you see it as a threat? As sure as death itself, judgment awaits. At God's judgment there will be no higher court of appeal should the verdict not be to your liking.

- If you hope for a favorable verdict in this court, put your hope entirely on Jesus.
- Pray today—now if you haven't before—for the freedom and pardon Jesus has won for you.
- Rejoice that God's judgment of you will be in favor of his Son, Jesus, your heavenly Advocate.
- Tell others, for many face an unfavorable judgment.

9:28 **So Christ was sacrificed once to take away the sins of many people; and he will appear a second time, not to bear sin, but to bring salvation to those who are waiting for him.**NIV The phrase "so Christ was sacrificed once" means that Christ died once for all and not repeatedly. His sacrifice was the turning point in history. The word "once" *(hapax)* indicates the completeness and finality of Jesus' sacrifice. "To take away the sins of many people" literally means "to bear the sins of many" (see also Isaiah 53:12; 1 Peter 2:24). "Many people" refers to everyone—all humanity (see 2:9).

> He who came in humility and shame will return in spectacular magnificence.
> *John R. W. Stott*

Jesus went into heaven and likewise will *appear a second time.* Because his death took care of sin completely and finally, he will not need *to bear sin* when he returns. That work was finished. Instead, at his second coming, he will *bring salvation to those who are waiting for him.* The imagery behind the picture of Christ appearing a second time to bring salvation gets its force from the Day of Atonement, when the priest stood (appeared) before the people, then disappeared inside the Most Holy Place to present the blood on the mercy seat. Then the priest came out (a second time) and proclaimed forgiveness on the people. So Jesus appeared on our behalf the first time. When he returns, he

BIBLE "WAITERS"

In the Bible we find many people who had to "wait on the Lord," just as believers today must patiently wait for Christ's return. We can learn a lesson in patience from these Bible waiters.

Noah waited for God's timing before leaving the ark.	Genesis 8:10, 12
Moses waited on God on the mountain.	Exodus 24:12
Job waited for God's answers.	Job 14:14
Isaiah waited for God to work in Israel.	Isaiah 8:17; 25:9; 26:8; 30:18; 33:2; 40:31; 49:23; 59:9, 11; 64:4
Jeremiah understood the need to wait quietly for God's salvation.	Lamentations 3:25
Hosea warned the people to return to God and wait for him to work.	Hosea 12:6
Micah waited for the God of his salvation.	Micah 7:7
Habakkuk warned the people to hold on to their hope and to wait because it would surely come.	Habakkuk 2:3
Zephaniah explained that the Lord wanted his people to wait for him.	Zephaniah 3:8
Joseph of Arimathea was waiting for God's kingdom.	Luke 23:51
The disciples were ordered by Jesus to wait in Jerusalem for the coming of the Holy Spirit.	Acts 1:4
Believers are called to wait for heaven, for the promise is sure.	Romans 8:23, 25; Galatians 5:5; 1 Thessalonians 1:10; Titus 2:13 2 Peter 3:12-14

will proclaim the full benefits of salvation. "Those who are waiting for him" conveys a warning, reminding the readers to remain faithful to Christ during their time of testing and persecution on earth.

HEBREWS 10

A SACRIFICE ONCE FOR ALL / 10:1-18

At high school and college reunions, renewed friends repeat the phrase "Do you remember?" Momentarily, a person or event long forgotten springs to mind. Memory can be a warm friend or a cruel adversary, depending on past deeds and activities.

In the new covenant between God and his people covered by Christ's once-for-all sacrifice, God promises through Jeremiah and the author of Hebrews that he will remember our sins no more. How wonderful to realize that someday we can ask God, "Do you remember my sins?" and know he will answer, "No!"

10:1 **The law is only a shadow of the good things that are coming—not the realities themselves. For this reason it can never, by the same sacrifices repeated endlessly year after year, make perfect those who draw near to worship.**NIV The old covenant contained the old requirements (or *the law*). But just as the old covenant prefigured and illustrated the new covenant, so the law *is only a shadow of the good things that are coming—not the realities themselves.* The law simply offered a preliminary sketch (a foreshadow) of what was coming. The realities ("the good things") are the new covenant described in 8:10-12, including direct access to God. The law was not (nor could it be) the means of forgiveness and true access to God. "The law never made anything perfect" (7:19 NLT). The law only illustrated what would be available later. The law was "a shadow" in the same sense as this word was used in 8:5. Some scholars believe that the word "shadow" refers to a painting metaphor. As an artist draws a shadow or preliminary sketch before the final portrait, so the law was the preliminary sketch of the later masterpiece.

Because the law was not the final plan, it could never *by the same sacrifices repeated endlessly year after year, make perfect those who draw near to worship.* In 9:6-10, the problem with the inferior sacrifices of the old covenant was discussed. These sacrifices showed that without blood there can be no forgiveness (9:22). Yet these very sacrifices could not effectively provide the forgiveness that was needed because they were not completely effective and had to be "repeated endlessly." Christ's sacrifice, the final sacrifice, removed the need for any other sacrifice. Until Christ, these sacrifices took place "year after year" on the Day of Atonement, reminding the people of their guilt. Their guilt kept them far from God. They could not "draw near to worship" him.

FOLLOWING SHADOWS

If the law was only a shadow, how do we find the reality?

Some men "fall in love" with a woman they cannot win. Some women imagine a blissful married life that no man can fulfill. Although music urges people to climb mountains and follow dreams, people who chase shadows have lost touch with reality.

To satisfy spiritual hunger, people chase the shadows of rigorous do-goodism, pious meditationism, or strict adherence to rules of all kinds—all futile evasions of what is real.

To satisfy your soul, turn to the living Christ. You do that by granting him supreme allegiance, depending on him for daily needs, and trusting him completely for every part of life. It's the only real way.

10:2 **If they could have provided perfect cleansing, the sacrifices would have stopped, for the worshipers would have been purified once for all time, and their feelings of guilt would have disappeared.**NLT If sacrifices could have made people perfect, *the sacrifices would have stopped.* If the sacrifices could have made people perfect, then people *would have been purified once for all time.* Then no one would ever need to feel guilty over sin because *feelings of guilt would have disappeared.* But the endless nature of the sacrifices proved their inability to purify worshipers, remove their guilt, and provide closeness with God. None of these happened under the old covenant, but they did happen as a result of Christ's sacrifice (see commentary on 9:14).

Only Christ's sacrifice can purify people once for all time (see 9:12). Only Christ's sacrifice can remove the guilt from sin and offer clean consciences (see 9:14). Gathered for the offering of sacrifices on the Day of Atonement, the people were reminded of their sins, and they undoubtedly felt guilty all over again. "Feelings of guilt" literally means "consciousness of sins." The Day of Atonement, with its solemn ceremony of fasting and confession, was a constant reminder of the people's sin. Hence, it heightened their awareness of sin. That this ceremony had to be repeated every year showed that the conscience was only temporarily cleansed. In Christ, sins are blotted out (9:26) and completely removed from the conscience. What the people needed most was total forgiveness—the permanent, powerful, sin-destroying forgiveness available through Christ. When we confess a sin to him,

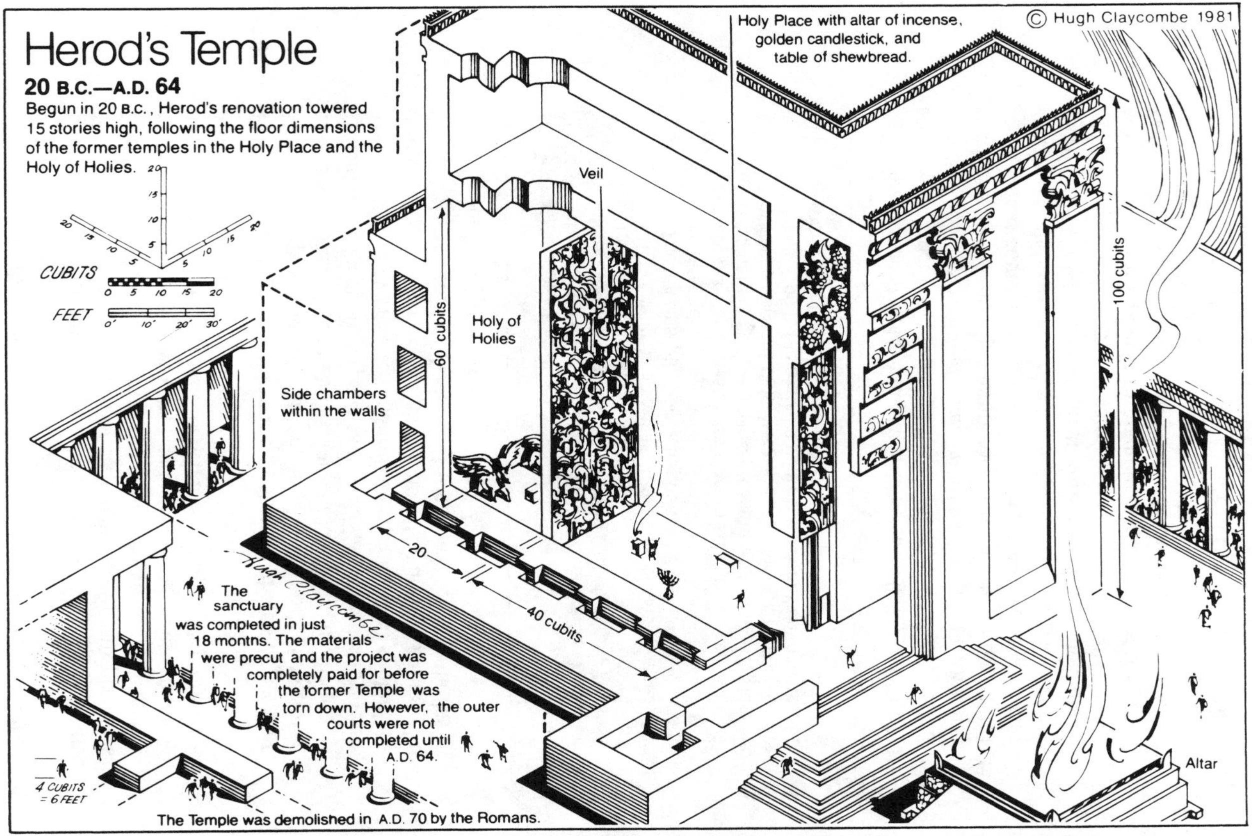

Herod's Temple
20 B.C.—A.D. 64
Begun in 20 B.C., Herod's renovation towered 15 stories high, following the floor dimensions of the former temples in the Holy Place and the Holy of Holies.
CUBITS
FEET
Side chambers within the walls
60 cubits
Holy of Holies
Veil
Holy Place with altar of incense, golden candlestick, and table of shewbread.
© Hugh Claycombe 1981
100 cubits
20
40 cubits
The sanctuary was completed in just 18 months. The materials were precut and the project was completely paid for before the former Temple was torn down. However, the outer courts were not completed until A.D. 64.
4 CUBITS = 6 FEET
Altar
The Temple was demolished in A.D. 70 by the Romans.

we need never think of it again. Christ has forgiven us, and the sin no longer exists (see 1 John 1:9).

These words would have been another encouragement for the Jewish audience not to return to their Jewish religious practices. Following the law could never put someone back into a right relationship with God. Modern readers must be careful not to substitute something weaker for what is stronger. Don't settle for a weak substitute. Trust Jesus.

10:3-4 But in those sacrifices there is a reminder of sins every year. For it is not possible that the blood of bulls and goats could take away sins.NKJV The Old Testament law and the worship system served a good purpose as *a reminder of sins every year.* These sacrifices were a reminder that God punished sin but also offered forgiveness through repentance. The apostle Paul said that this was the purpose of the law, "If it had not been for the law, I would not have known sin" (Romans 7:7 NRSV).

REMINDERS
What do you most want to remember? Look around your kitchen. Whose pictures are stuck to the refrigerator? Whose notes are posted at eye level?

Do you hang on your walls reminders of sins—the really gross and costly sins—that once trapped you? Not unless you're mentally deranged.

For the same reason, don't try to satisfy your soul with reminders of spiritual failure—like the old sacrifice system was, or newer versions of it. Feed your memory with the joy of freedom in Christ. Memorize a verse a week for two months. Start with two or three from Hebrews 10.

While the sacrifices could teach them these lessons, the daily and yearly repetition reminded the people that *it is not possible that the blood of bulls and goats could take away sins.* Animal sacrifices provided only a temporary way to deal with sin until Jesus would come to deal with sin permanently. Animals, ignorant beasts and part of a fallen world, could not provide the same sacrifice as Christ—the God-man, fully rational, completely sinless, who willingly went to the cross.

How, then, were people forgiven in Old Testament times? When Old Testament believers followed God's command to offer sacrifices, he graciously forgave them. When they made their sacrifices by faith (9:15), God guaranteed forgiveness. But that practice looked forward to Christ's perfect sacrifice.

As Christians, God has completely forgiven our sins because of Christ's death for us. God even forgets about our sins (10:17).

Many Christians, however, still wallow in guilt over past sins. They might even offer the modern counterpart to sacrifices to God (repeated prayers of confession, giving time and money) in order to compensate for their wrong behavior. While these actions may have been appropriate for someone living under the old law, they are no longer needed for someone who lives under the new covenant.

10:5-7 **Therefore, when Christ came into the world, he said: "Sacrifice and offering you did not desire, but a body you prepared for me; with burnt offerings and sin offerings you were not pleased. Then I said, 'Here I am—it is written about me in the scroll—I have come to do your will, O God.'"**NIV Christ did not leave people under the old covenant; the phrase "when Christ came into the world" speaks of a new order. This new order (the new covenant discussed in chapter 8) demonstrated that the old covenant was not intended to be permanent. This is demonstrated with a quote from Psalm 40:6-8.

Although sacrifices were necessary to pay the price of sin, this quotation reveals that God never took pleasure in sacrifices—

OBEDIENCE VERSUS SACRIFICES

Often in Scripture, God states that he doesn't want our gifts and sacrifices when we give them out of ritual or hypocrisy. God wants us first to love and obey him.

1 Samuel 15:22-23	Obedience is far better than sacrifice.
Psalm 40:6-8	Instead of burnt offerings, God wants our lifelong service.
Psalm 51:16-19	Instead of penance, God wants a broken and contrite heart.
Jeremiah 7:21-23	Instead of sacrifices, God wants our obedience, and he promises that he will be our God and we will be his people.
Hosea 6:6	Instead of sacrifices, God wants our loving loyalty. Instead of offerings, he wants us to acknowledge him.
Amos 5:21-24	God hates pretense and hypocrisy; he wants to see justice roll on like a river.
Micah 6:6-8	God is not satisfied with offerings; he wants us to ge fair and just and merciful, and to walk humbly with him.
Matthew 9:13	Instead of sacrifices, God wants us to be merciful.

sacrifice and offering you did not desire. In many places in the Bible, God revealed that he didn't want the sacrifices of a person whose heart was not right (see the chart "Obedience versus Sacrifices" on page 151). God "did not desire" these sacrifices; instead, he wanted his people to obey him. The sacrifices were necessary, however, because the people did not live up to the regulations that God had given them.

Central to the Old Testament is the teaching that God desires obedience and a right heart, not empty compliance to a set of rules and regulations. The book of Hebrews applies to Christ the words of the psalmist in Psalm 40:6-8. Christ came to offer his body *(a body you prepared for me)* on the cross for us as a sacrifice that is completely acceptable to God. God's new and living way for us to please him comes not by keeping laws or even by abstaining from sin, but by turning to him in faith for forgiveness and then following him in loving obedience.

Christ willingly obeyed God, saying, *Here I am,* and that's what God wants his people to do. This was what set Christ's sacrifice apart. He followed God's will, obeyed him, and offered the perfect sacrifice of perfect obedience: *I have come to do your will, O God.*

The entire Old Testament pointed to Christ: he *is written about . . . in the scroll.* All the law and all the sacrificial system was a shadow of what was to come. Christ fulfilled the law as well as the prophecies that announced the coming of the new covenant.

OUR FIRST PRIVILEGE

Jesus' first priority was doing God's will. We should try the same life plan. Ask a group of mature Christian friends how God's will is done today with respect to:

- spending, tithing, and savings;
- service time, work (for pay) time, family time, and personal recreation;
- Bible study, exposure to arts and entertainment, and political participation.

Wise friends help sharpen our sense of following Jesus' lead. Pray together after your talks.

10:8-9 **First, Christ said, "You did not want animal sacrifices or sin offerings or burnt offerings or other offerings for sin, nor were you pleased with them" (though they are required by the law of Moses). Then he said, "Look, I have come to do your will." He cancels the first covenant in order to put the second into effect.**[NLT] These two verses repeat the ideas from 10:5-7, reinforcing the contrast between the old way and the new. God

THE OFFERINGS

Listed here are the five key offerings the Israelites made to God. The Jews made these offerings in order to have their sins forgiven and to restore their fellowship with God. The death of Jesus Christ made these sacrifices unnecessary. Because of his death our sins were completely forgiven and fellowship with God has been restored.

Offering	*Purpose*	*Significance*	*Christ, the Perfect Offering*
Burnt Offering (Levicitus 1: voluntary)	To make payment for sins in general	Showed a person's devotion to God	Christ's death was the perfect offering (10:12).
Grain Offering (Leviticus 2: voluntary)	To show honor and respect to God in worship	Acknowledged that all we have belongs to God	Christ was the perfect man, who gave all of himself to God and others (9:14).
Fellowship Offering (Leviticus 3: voluntary)	To express gratitude to God	Symbolized peace and fellowship with God	Christ is the only way to fellowship with God (10:9-10).
Sin Offering (Leviticus 4: required)	To make payment for unintentional sins of uncleanness, neglect, or thoughtlessness	Restored the sinner to fellowship with God; showed seriousness of sin	Christ's death restores our fellowship with God (4:14-16).
Guilt Offering Leviticus 5: required)	To make payment for sins against God and others, and to compensate the injured parties	Provided compensation for those who had been injured	Christ's death takes away the deadly consequences of sin (9:26).

never took pleasure in the sacrifices of the Old Testament: *You did not want animal sacrifices or sin offerings or burnt offerings or other offerings for sin, nor were you pleased with them* (from Psalm 40:6). Five offerings were required by the Old Testament law (see the chart, "The Offerings" above). These offerings had important purposes and were *required by the law of Moses.*

God had never planned for the old system to be the final system. Instead, he provided a new way, a new covenant through Christ, who obeyed God and willingly gave up his life as a perfect sacrifice. *He said, "Look, I have come to do your will,"* quoting from Psalm 40:7-8. Christ *cancels the first covenant in order to put the second into effect.* Setting aside the first system in order to establish a far better one meant doing away with the system of sacrifices contained in the ceremonial law. (It didn't mean eliminating God's "moral" law, contained in the Ten Commandments.) The ceremonial law prepared people for Christ. With his coming, that system was no longer needed.

10:10 **And by that will, we have been made holy through the sacrifice of the body of Jesus Christ once for all.**[NIV] The phrase "by that will" is probably taken from the last sentence of the psalm quoted above (Psalm 40:6-8), for verse 8 says, "I delight to do Your will, O my God" (NKJV). God's will was accomplished *through the sacrifice of the body of Jesus Christ once for all.* For the seventh time in less than two chapters, the phrase "once for all" is used to underscore the finality of Christ's sacrifice.

WHO'S MAKING IT HAPPEN?

Christ's sacrifice of obedience saved us (10:10). When you wonder if you've got the energy for another day . . . where the time will come from to get it all done . . . where the money will come from to get it all paid for . . . where your relationships are heading and where your future is pointing . . . think about how Christ obeyed. He said, "Here I am. I have come to do what you want" (10:9).

When you wonder why you're such a weak Christian, so easily tempted, so confused by a friend's betrayal, so hurt by a child's remark . . . think about how Christ obeyed. He said, "Not what I want but what you want" (Matthew 26:39 NRSV).

When you wonder who's in charge of your spiritual journey . . . think about how Christ obeyed.

How have we *been made holy*? The God of Israel and of the Christian church is holy—he sets the standard for morality. Unlike the Roman gods, he is not warlike, adulterous, or spiteful. Unlike the gods of the pagan cults popular in the first century, he is not bloodthirsty or promiscuous. He is a God of mercy and justice who cares personally for each of his followers. Our holy God expects us to imitate him by following his high moral standards. Like him, we should be both merciful and just; like him, we should sacrifice ourselves for others. Holiness means being totally devoted or dedicated to God, set aside for his special use, and set apart from sin and its influence. Holiness comes from a sincere desire to obey God and from wholehearted devotion to him. God's qualities make us different. A follower of Christ becomes "holy" (sanctified) through believing and obeying the word of God. Daily application of the word of God purifies our minds and hearts. It points out sin, motivates us to confess, renews our relationship with Christ, and guides us back to the right path. We cannot become holy on our own, but God gives us his Holy Spirit to help us obey him and to give us power to overcome sin.

10:11-12 Day after day every priest stands and performs his religious duties; again and again he offers the same sacrifices, which can never take away sins. But when this priest had offered for all time one sacrifice for sins, he sat down at the right hand of God.[NIV] Here again is the point of 10:1 that the priests had to offer sacrifices *day after day . . . again and again.* Even then, these sacrifices could *never take away sins.* The priests were decreed by the law to stand and perform their *religious duties* (see Numbers 18:5); their posture of "standing" indicated that their work was never finished. By contrast, however, *this priest* (referring to Christ) *offered for all time one sacrifice for sins* (dying in our place), and then he *sat down.* The sacrificial system couldn't completely remove sin; Christ's sacrifice did so.

Christ now sits *at the right hand of God* (see commentary on 1:3, 13; 8:1). He is able to sit because his sacrifice was completely sufficient to take care of sin. The other priests' work was never done, so, in a sense, they could never sit down. But Christ's once-for-all sacrifice allows him to sit—his work finished. The place where Christ sits shows his exalted position. Christ sits enthroned at the right hand of God. This is the place of highest honor. Even the angels must stand in God's presence (Luke 1:19). This place at the right hand of God rightfully belongs to Christ because he is God's Son.

A GOOD WORK

If the Jewish readers of this book were to return to the old Jewish system, they would be implying that Christ's sacrifice wasn't enough to forgive their sins. Adding anything to his sacrifice or taking anything from it denies its validity. Following any system to gain salvation through good deeds essentially rejects the significance of Christ's death and spurns the Holy Spirit's work.

Beware of anyone who tells you that Christ's sacrifice still leaves you incomplete or that something else is needed to make you acceptable to God. When you believe in Christ, he makes you completely right with God. Then your loving relationship will lead you to follow him in willing obedience and service.

10:13-14 **Since that time he waits for his enemies to be made his footstool, because by one sacrifice he has made perfect forever those who are being made holy.**[NIV] *Since that time* when Christ offered the final sacrifice for sins, he has been sitting at the right hand of God (10:12), and he *waits for his enemies to be made his footstool.* The phrase "enemies to be made his footstool" refers to the prophecy in Psalm 110:1. It is also quoted in Hebrews 1:13 (see commentary there). In the context of Hebrews, it might refer to any reader who apostatizes.

Christ paid the penalty for our sins, and by his *one sacrifice he has made perfect forever those who are being made holy.* We are "perfect forever" because we are new creations whom God sees as holy. The second half of these verses contrast believers "who are being made holy" with people who refuse to believe—the "enemies" mentioned in the first half of the verse.

Although we are made holy when we accept Christ as Savior, we are also continually "being made holy." This means persevering in holy living. How can we be holy, and yet continue to do wrong? Through Christ's death and resurrection, he, once for all, made his believers holy in God's sight. At the same time, he makes them holy (progressively cleansed and set apart for his special use) in their daily pilgrimage here on earth. In Christ, we are free from the penalty of sin (judgment) and the power of sin (compulsion to sin, death). But while still alive on earth, we are not free from the presence of sin (temptations) and the possibility of sin (failures). We are saved by God's grace, but we still need to grow. We can encourage this growth process by deliberately applying Scripture to all areas of our lives, by accepting the discipline and guidance Christ provides, and by giving God control of our desires and goals.

10:15-17 **But the Holy Spirit also witnesses to us; for after He had said before, "This is the covenant that I will make with them after those days, says the LORD: I will put My laws into their hearts, and in their minds I will write them,"** ***then He adds,*** **"Their sins and their lawless deeds I will remember no more."**[NKJV] Again Hebrews states that *the Holy Spirit* is the author of the Old Testament (see also 3:7; 9:8). The Holy Spirit inspired the writers; thus, it is the Holy Spirit who *witnesses to us* through the words of Scripture. The Holy Spirit witnesses to us through inspiring Scripture, and also by helping us understand and internalize it.

Quoting again from Jeremiah 31:33-34 (as in 8:10-12), Hebrews makes the connection between Christ's sacrifice and the new covenant (see commentary on 8:10-12). Here again we see a close connection between the forgiveness of sins (that comes with the new covenant) and the ability to know God. The new covenant and new sacrifice brought forgiveness in a better way than the Levitical system could provide. With sins forgiven, Christians can now enter the real presence of God. The guilt that remained under the old covenant has been permanently removed.

GOD'S MEMORY LOSS

God says that he will not remember our sins and lawless deeds (10:17). Typically a sign of degenerative disease, acute memory loss is one of God's great promises to us—his own memory loss concerning our sins.

Think of that friend you've offended. Reparations may have patched wounds, but the memory remains.

Think of that former spouse and your hurtful divorce. Counseling may settle your anger but never erase your memory.

When God forgives, he forgets. OK, how can an all-knowing God forget anything? In this way: there's no more separation between offender and offendee over the offense. It's gone, completely disappeared. Such forgetting is a gift that few people can give, and none so completely as God. When you pray in faith today for forgiveness, you can forget your sins too. Don't hurt yourself by holding on to guilt over sin that God has wiped from his memory.

10:18 And when sins have been forgiven, there is no need to offer any more sacrifices.[NLT] In 10:17, we read the powerful statement that God will remember our sins no more. Christ forgives completely, so there is no need to confess past sins repeatedly. As believers, we can be confident that the sins we confess and renounce are forgiven and forgotten. Because this has happened, because *sins have been forgiven, there is no need to offer any more sacrifices.* God requires no more sacrifices to make people acceptable to him because Christ's once-for-all sacrifice makes people acceptable.

Have you thanked God for his full forgiveness? Your sin caused you to owe more to God than you could ever repay. Rather than punish you, however, he has shown grace and kindness. Thank him for his kindness.

LIVING BY FAITH / 10:19-39

The second section of Hebrews begins here. The first section, 1:1–10:18, developed the superiority of Christ. The second section, 10:19–13:25, develops the church's responsibility to live in faith. Verses 19-25 of this chapter introduce the second section.

Megachurches command headlines, but experts indicate that

more than half of American churches have congregations less than one hundred. Smaller churches often reflect their communities, which may have a total population smaller than some megachurches' membership. Hebrews exhorts believers to meet together regularly and to encourage one another (10:25), an appropriate message for any congregation. A first-century tradition of encouraging one another, sometimes still emulated at Easter, involved one Christian greeting another believer with "The Lord is risen!" The appropriate response: "The Lord is risen, indeed." Christians could encourage each other by adopting a similar practice of greeting other Christians regularly with, "The righteous will live by faith" (10:38), and the response, "Live by faith, indeed."

10:19-20 Therefore, my friends, since we have confidence to enter the sanctuary by the blood of Jesus, by the new and living way that he opened for us through the curtain (that is, through his flesh).[NRSV] Hebrews now applies the doctrines that have been discussed up to this point. These verses summarize the argument in the first ten chapters, focusing on 8:1-2 and its further explanation in 9:1–10:18. The phrase "Therefore, my friends" in essence says, "In light of all Christ has provided, let us . . ." What has Christ provided? Through his death on our behalf, *we have confidence to enter the sanctuary by the blood of Jesus.* The word for "enter" used here in Greek *(parresia)* means admission, authorization for access. Believers have access to the heavenly sanctuary; that is, they have free access to God. Christ now sits at God's right hand as our High Priest in this heavenly sanctuary (see 6:19-20; 8:1-2; 9:11-12, 24).

Christians can now enter this Most Holy Place with boldness *by the blood of Jesus.* The "blood" refers to Jesus giving his life for us (see 9:12, 14; 10:19, 29; 12:24; 13:12, 20). This encouragement for boldness is remarkable because, under the old covenant, the Most Holy Place was sealed from view by a curtain. Only the high priest could enter this holy room. This he would do only once a year on the Day of Atonement when he offered the sacrifice for the nation's sins. The curtain represented the mystery of God's holiness because only the consecrated priest could go behind it. In a similar way, we cannot have access to God without the appropriate sacrifices and cleansing from sin. But Jesus' death in his human body (flesh) removed *the curtain.* When Jesus died on the cross, the curtain in the temple (which had replaced the tabernacle) tore from top to bottom (Mark 15:38), thereby unveiling the glorious reality that believers now have free access to God. More than just the curtain was torn; Christ's body was also torn. As Christ's body was torn in his excruciating death on the cross, people received access to God. *Through his flesh* Jesus opened *the new and living way.* He truly was "the way" itself (John 14:6). This way was "new" because it had not existed before; it was new because this was the "new covenant," opening the way to fellowship with God. Because of Christ, all believers may walk into God's presence at any time (4:16).

Do not miss the amazing reality in these words. We believers have access to God—the sovereign king of the universe! When was the last time you utilized the full value of this privilege? The presence and closeness of God is available to you.

10:21-22 And since we have a great priest over the house of God, let us draw near to God with a sincere heart in full assurance of faith, having our hearts sprinkled to cleanse us from a guilty conscience and having our bodies washed with pure water.NIV

"Since we have confidence to enter the sanctuary" (10:19) and *since we have a great priest,* we have been offered a tremendous privilege: *let us draw near to God* (see also 4:16 where a similar statement is made). To "draw near" means to approach God so as to come into his presence.

What Christ has done for Christians is the focus of the next three exhortations—the first dealing with their faith in God (10:21-22), the second dealing with their hope in their salvation (10:23), and the third dealing with their love for each other (10:24-25).

The writer calls Christians *the house of God.* In the Old Testament, God's "house" referred exclusively to his people, the Jews. But under the new covenant, God's "house" refers to all who believe in Jesus Christ as Savior, accepting his sacrifice for their sins—whether they are Jews or Gentiles. Over this house rules "a great priest" (Jesus Christ) who opened the way into God's presence. As the perfect Mediator, Christ accompanies Christians into the very throne room of God.

The book of Hebrews exhorts us, as members of that house, to approach God: *let us draw near to God.* This is the first of five "let us" phrases that encouraged the people to persevere (all are from NIV):

1. "Let us draw near to God" (10:21).
2. "Let us hold unswervingly to the hope we profess" (10:23).
3. "Let us consider how we may spur one another on" (10:24).
4. "Let us not give up meeting together" (10:25).
5. "Let us encourage one another" (10:25).

The book of Hebrews encourages readers to draw near to God with four characteristics:

1. *With a sincere heart.* We come not halfheartedly or with improper motives or pretense, but with pure, undivided, and sincere worship. We can know we have a sincere heart if we evaluate our thoughts and motives according to his Word (see 4:12).
2. *In full assurance of faith.* The Greek word for "assurance" used here *(plerophoria)* means literally openness or outspokenness. Christians can approach God boldly, free from guilt because of the work of Jesus Christ. James 1:6-8 carries this same thought. We can go to God without doubting, knowing that he will hear and answer us.
3. *Having our hearts sprinkled to cleanse us from a guilty conscience.* This is sacrificial language. Under the new covenant, hearts and consciences are cleansed (see 9:14). This differed from the old covenant in that it completely cleansed the conscience, not partially or temporarily. This clean conscience allows people to enter God's presence with boldness.
4. *Having our bodies washed with pure water.* The imagery of an external action actually pictures an inward cleansing. Just as baptism is an outward sign that represents the purification that Christ does inside us, so this washing speaks of an internal cleansing from sin. Once cleansed, Christians can approach God.

The "full assurance of faith" is a key term and leads into chapter 11. Our trust in God enables us to have this access (see commentary on 4:2, 14; 6:1, 12).

A NEW LEADER

Every four years in American politics, voters look for a new vision, a new agenda, a new leader. Every day on the sandlot or basketball court, teams look for leaders to emerge, with victory hanging in the balance.

The "house of God" refers to you and all believers across the globe. The great High Priest, in ancient times the spiritual leader of God's people, is Jesus—crucified once for sin, risen to life, ascended to heaven—a leader for all times.

With this new leadership, you should.

- Feel your own life has vitality and purpose, serving Jesus with energy and devotion.
- Feel anew the hope of promises yet to come, following the leader to a heavenly home.
- Feel the courage swell to carry your load, however heavy, with our leader close at hand.
- Drop whatever holds you back and follow close—in prayer, study, and service—every day.

10:23 Let us hold fast the confession of our hope without wavering, for He who promised is faithful.[NKJV] This second *let us* would help the people persevere. The readers were encouraged to *hold fast the confession of our hope.* The New Testament uses the phrase "hold fast" to speak of remaining true to tradition or doctrine. The readers are encouraged to remain true to their "confession"—referring both to what they believe about God and what they say to others. When they were converted and baptized, early Christians confessed what they believed about Christ. Here they were told to hold on to what they had previously claimed.

They were to hold fast *without wavering*. It may have been easy to waver during the early days of the church because there was no New Testament for the believers to study for themselves. At this time, many New Testament books had not yet been written. Yet the Christians had good reason to hold on to their confession: *He who promised is faithful.* God made the promise; because God is faithful, we know that what he promised will come to pass. Security is linked to the promise of God. The idea here is, "God is faithful—will you be?" There might be times when Christians feel like quitting or giving up their faith. During those times, Hebrews encourages us to remember God's faithfulness.

> Those that would enjoy the dignities and privileges of Christ's family must submit to the discipline of it.
> *Matthew Henry*

HOLDING FAST

How do we develop skill at "holding fast"—staying faithful to Jesus during life's stormy days? Here are three suggestions:

1. Practice the habit of transparency with God and others. When you feel happy, express it. When you feel down, say so. When storms hit, the worst response is a veneer of gaiety covering misery inside. Be an honest person.
2. Practice the habit of meditation on the word of God. Memorize verses of Scripture. Wonder over those promises during the day. Sing a little praise for God's promises.
3. Practice the habit of giving God priority. Pray early in the day. Worship regularly. Share your resources generously. Study the Bible systematically.

Many diversions will crowd your schedule, but as God comes first in your day, so the dike of faith will hold against the flood of trouble.

10:24-25 And let us consider how we may spur one another on toward love and good deeds. Let us not give up meeting together, as some are in the habit of doing, but let us encourage one another—and all the more as you see the Day approaching.[NIV]

ENCOURAGE ONE ANOTHER

Christians are to encourage one another. A word of encouragement offered at the right moment can be the difference between staying strong in the faith or collapsing along the way. Believers ought to be sensitive to one another's needs for encouragement, ready to offer supportive words or actions. The Bible gives several examples of encouragement and commands for believers to encourage each other (verses quoted from NRSV, italics ours):

Deuteronomy 3:28	"But change Joshua, and *encourage* and strengthen him, because it is he who shall cross over at the head of this people and who shall secure their possession of the land that you will see."
Acts 4:36	"There was a Levite, a native of Cyprus, Joseph, to whom the apostles gave the name Barnabas (which means 'son of *encouragement*')."
Acts 15:32	"Judas and Silas, who were themseslves prophets, said much to *encourage* and strengthen the believers.
Romans 12:6, 8	"We have different gifts, according to the grace given us. If a man's gift is . . . *encouraging*, let him *encourage* (NIV).
Romans 15:4-5	"For whatever was written in former days was written for our instruction, so that by steadfastness and by the *encouragement* of the scriptures we might have hope. May the God of steadfastness and *encouragement* grant you to live in harmoney with one another, in accordance with Christ Jesus."
Ephesians 6:22	"I am suffering [Tychicus] to you for this very purpose, to let you know how we are, and to *encourage* your hearts."
1 Thessalonians 3:2	"We sent Timothy, our brother and coworker for God in proclaiming the gospel of Christ, to strengthen and *encourage* you for the sake of your faith."
1 Thessalonians 4:18; 5:11, 14	"Therefore *encourage* one another with these words . . . *encourage* one another and build up each other, as indeed you are doing . . . *encourage* the faint hearted, help the weak, be patient with all of them."
2 Timothy 4:2	"Proclaim the message; be persistent whether the time is favorable or unfavorable; convince, rebuke, and *encourage*, with the utmost patience in teaching."
Philemon 1:7	"I have indeed received much joy and *encouragement* from your love, because the hearts of the saints have been refreshed through you, my brother.
Hebrews 3:13	"But *encourage* one another daily, as long as it is called Today, so that none of you may be hardened by sin's deceitfulness" (NIV).
1 Peter 5:12	"Though Silvanus, whom I consider a faithful brother, I have written this short letter to *encourage* you and to testify that this is the true grace of God. Stand fast in it."

The third, fourth, and fifth *let us* statements appear in these two verses. Believers ought to *consider how we may spur one another on toward love and good deeds.* This word "spur" *(paroxysm)* means to "stimulate strongly," "arouse," or "incite to riot." Christians need to spur or stimulate each other in two areas: (1) *Love:* not an emotion but a choice to act regardless of our feelings. We are to act lovingly toward other believers. (2) *Good deeds:* works done for the good of others, and which attract others to Christ. (For more on good deeds, see notes on 6:10; 13:16, 20-21.)

Believers also must *not give up meeting together.* Some Christians (then as well as today) were *in the habit of* not going to the church meetings. For whatever reason, these believers were trying to survive on their own. This individualistic attitude is prevalent today, as well. God did not design Christians to be completely independent of each other, however; he designed believers to need and encourage each other. To withdraw from corporate strength is to invite disaster, like a soldier in battle who lags behind the rest of his platoon and becomes an easy target.

> There is nothing more unchristian than a solitary Christian.
> *John Wesley*

Finally, believers must *encourage one another.* These words reveal that Christians are responsible for each other (a similar theme is found elsewhere, see 3:13). Christians cannot be concerned just for their own spiritual well-being; they must also encourage others to keep fervent in their love and active in their service to God. This encouragement should happen *all the more as you see the Day approaching.* This "day" (Christ's return) is guaranteed; Christ will return. Through the centuries, many Christians have been discouraged because they believed that Christ should have already returned. But Christ has not forgotten, and he has not changed his plans. Christians must live as if the Lord will come back at any moment. Christ must not find us lax in our devotion and preparation.

CHURCHGOING

To neglect Christian meetings is to give up the encouragement and help of other Christians. We gather together to share our faith and to strengthen one another in the Lord. As we get closer to the day when Christ will return, we will face many spiritual struggles, and even times of persecution. Anti-Christian forces will grow in strength. Difficulties should never be excuses for missing church services. Rather, as difficulties arise, we should make an even greater effort to be faithful in attendance.

TOGETHER

In a former era, no one tried to compete with church for the Sunday morning time slot, a slot now regarded as open time to be filled by almost any recreational attraction. Yet gathering for worship is both an essential witness to Christ and a valuable time for spiritual nourishment. Want to grow as a Christian?

- Don't go it alone. You have been called to participate in a wonderful "body," the church, a large group of brothers and sisters.
- Don't try to squeeze it in. Worship should be a top priority.
- Don't rationalize when you skip church. Worshiping God with the body of believers cannot be substituted with personal study or watching a church service on television. Of course, physical limitations could keep you from attending a worship service. If so, ask some believers to come to your home for personal fellowship.

10:26 **Dear friends, if we deliberately continue sinning after we have received knowledge of the truth, there is no longer any sacrifice that will cover these sins.**NLT This is the second great warning against apostasy; 6:4-6 gave the first great warning: "For it is impossible for those who were once enlightened . . . if they fall away, to renew them again to repentance, since they crucify again for themselves the Son of God" (NKJV). For those who *have received knowledge of the truth* of the gospel and yet reject Christ, the consequences are severe. For those who learn the truth and then *deliberately continue sinning,* no sacrifice is left. When people deliberately reject Christ's offer of salvation, they reject God's most precious gift. They ignore the leading of the Holy Spirit, the one who communicates God's saving love.

This warning was given to Jewish Christians who were tempted to reject Christ for Judaism. It applies, however, to anyone who turns away from Christ to another religion or, having understood Christ's atoning work, deliberately turns away from it (Mark 3:28-30). Under the old covenant, the Jews had this threat of punishment if they rejected God's way (see also Numbers 15:30-31). There is no other acceptable sacrifice for sin than the death of Christ on the cross. If, after understanding the gospel message, someone deliberately rejects the sacrifice of Christ, that person cannot be saved because God has not provided any other name under heaven for salvation (see Acts 4:12).

This threat of God's punishment is aimed at those who reject Christ and determine to live by their own standard. For these people *there is no longer any sacrifice that will cover these sins.* Someone who treats Christ in this way acts as his enemy, subjecting him to public disgrace (see 6:6).

Chapter 6 points out that just because someone seems like

a Christian doesn't mean that he or she necessarily is one. Only perseverance in the faith demonstrates true Christians from impostors. When these impostors leave, they will never find a superior sacrifice to Christ's. Indeed, there is no other effective sacrifice for sins.

10:27 There is only the terrible expectation of God's judgment and the raging fire that will consume his enemies.[NLT] For those who have rejected Christ, the only future they can look forward to is *God's judgment,* namely *the raging fire that will consume [God's] enemies.* The book of Hebrews is filled with the message of the hope that Christians have. They can look forward to their guaranteed salvation. Those who do not follow Christ, however, also have a guarantee. They will face God's wrath as experienced in the "raging fire" of hell. Like the followers of Korah (Numbers 16:1-35) who faced severe punishment for rebelling against God when "they with all that belonged to them went down alive into Sheol" (NRSV), so God promises eternal punishment for those who reject him (see Isaiah 26:11; Revelation 20:11-15).

GIMME ONE GOOD REASON

If promises don't grab you and "hope" seems too distant, if forgiveness isn't your thing and worship is equivalent to "boring," there's still one very good reason to confess sins and trust fully in Christ.

If God's good promises seem pale to you, consider the alternative: terrifying destruction. Without God there will be no second chance and no other appeal.

10:28 Anyone who has rejected Moses' law dies without mercy on the testimony of two or three witnesses.[NKJV] Under the old covenant, anyone who *rejected Moses' law* was punished by death *on the testimony of two or three witnesses.* This meant the person had rejected the authority of the Mosaic law; this was as serious as the sin of idolatry. There were sacrifices available for sins that were unintentional, but if someone willfully rejected God's covenant and followed after another god, there was no *mercy* and no sacrifice (Deuteronomy 17:2-7). If God required physical death for breaking the old covenant, the new covenant's punishment would be much greater (10:29).

10:29 Just think how much worse the punishment will be for those who have trampled on the Son of God, and have treated the blood of the covenant, which made us holy, as if it were common and unholy, and have insulted and disdained the Holy

Spirit who brings God's mercy to us.[NLT] Those who reject Christ and deliberately continue to sin (10:26) will receive a terrible punishment, worse than those who refused to follow the old covenant. Those who treated the old covenant in this way received physical death (10:28). Those who treat the new covenant (and Christ) with contempt, however, will receive something far worse than physical death. Because the blessings under the new covenant are greater, there awaits even greater *punishment* for those who scorn it. The book of Hebrews issues a strong warning and gives three specific indictments against these people.

They have

1. *trampled on the Son of God.* To refuse to accept the sacrifice of his life on our behalf is to show contempt and disdain for Christ. The word for "trample underfoot" is vivid and conveys strong antagonism. See Matthew 5:13 where salt that loses its flavor is "trampled underfoot." The person who treats Christ's death for sin as worthless deserves great punishment. This indictment is particularly strong because the book of Hebrews has built the case for the superiority of the Son of God.
2. *treated the blood of the covenant, which made us holy, as if it were common and unholy* (or "defiled"). The "blood of the covenant" refers to Christ's blood and thus to his death. The importance of the blood has been established in previous verses (7:22; 9:15-18; 10:12-18). Christ's blood inaugurated the new covenant (Matthew 26:28; Mark 14:24; 1 Corinthians 11:25), just as blood established the old covenant (Exodus 24:8). To treat something holy as if it were defiled would have been seen as a terrible sin by these Jewish readers. Since blood ratified the covenant, to reject the consecrated blood of Christ was the ultimate rejection. The person who treats the holy blood of Christ as if it were common and unholy deserves great punishment!
3. *insulted and disdained the Holy Spirit* (in other translations, "Spirit of grace") *who brings God's mercy to us.* We read in 9:14, "How much more will the blood of Christ, who through the eternal Spirit offered himself without blemish to God, purify our conscience from dead works to worship the living God!" (NRSV). The sacrifice of Christ is tied with the Holy Spirit; therefore, to scorn Christ's sacrifice is to insult and enrage the Holy Spirit. "Insult" and "enrage" are two words used to convey the meaning of one strong Greek word. To enrage the Holy Spirit means to reject him arrogantly. He is the Spirit of grace; the Holy Spirit is a person, not just a force or influence. To reject him is to cut off the means of God's acceptance. This is equivalent to blasphemy against

> the Holy Spirit (see Matthew 12:31-32). Deserving of great punishment is the person who insults the Holy Spirit who brings mercy!

This verse pictures a person who is hard-hearted and stubborn (see 3:7-15). This person shows complete contempt for the Christian faith. Perhaps you've run across such people. Terrible punishment awaits them.

WASHED-OUT BRIDGES

In very few places does the Bible cease to offer words of hope and recovery. But this is one—Hebrews 10:29. Like a stranded traveler who can't return because a flood has washed out the bridges leading home, so is the person who rejects the gospel and abandons God's way.

Careful now! Many people go through spiritual storms. Many teenagers turn against strict church upbringings. But the bridges remain intact. If you're grieved over rebelling children, keep communication strong and pray every day. Your prayers and love keep tidal waves from washing out bridges.

10:30-31 **For we know him who said, "It is mine to avenge; I will repay," and again, "The Lord will judge his people." It is a dreadful thing to fall into the hands of the living God.**[NIV] The terrible punishment (10:29) will come from the hands of God. Two lines quoted from Moses' farewell song in Deuteronomy 32 emphasize this truth. In this song, Moses warned the people against apostasy and unbelief. These words reveal two truths:

1. *It is mine to avenge, I will repay.* God's judgment will come and will be severe. God, the Sovereign of the universe, has the right to punish those who disobey him. God's holiness and perfect justice demand that he punish those who sin. Only God is allowed to avenge, for he alone is perfect, and he has been wronged by those who reject him.
2. *The Lord will judge his people.* Those who heard the gospel and then treated it with contempt will be judged because they have rejected God's mercy. Those who have accepted Christ's love and his salvation need not worry about the coming judgment. Being saved through his grace, they have nothing to fear (see 1 John 4:18).

These quotations show that *it is a dreadful thing to fall into the hands of the living God.* God's power is awesome, and his punishment terrible. These words give us a glimpse into the awesome holiness of God. He is sovereign; his power is unlimited;

he will do as he promises. Those who reject the covenant will be punished. For them, falling into God's hands will be a dreadful experience. They will have no more excuses. They will discover that they were wrong, but it will be too late.

10:32 Think back on those early days when you first learned about Christ. Remember how you remained faithful even though it meant terrible suffering.NLT Chapter 6:4-8 includes a similar harsh warning about falling away from the faith. While terrible punishment awaits those who scorn the gospel, this passage acknowledges that these readers are not like that. After a harsh warning, the readers are encouraged that their past actions demonstrate their genuine faith. Remembering their past faithfulness should encourage them to persevere in their faith: *Think back on those early days when you first learned about Christ.* Like many Christians, these people had a deep desire for Christ at their conversion. The memory of that closeness and their deep desire to serve him would encourage them during difficult days.

During those "early days," these believers had remained faithful *even though it meant terrible suffering.* This literally means, "you endured a great struggle with suffering." The word for "struggle" is *athlesis,* from which we get our word "athletics." Christians are in a contest requiring faithful endurance. We must stand our ground as if we are in a great contest. Despite feeling pressure from Romans and fellow Jews, these Christians had remained firm in their faith.

GOOD SUFFERING

Hebrews encourages believers to persevere in their Christian faith when facing persecution and pressure. We don't usually think of suffering as good for us, but it can build our character and our patience. During times of great stress, we may feel God's presence more clearly and find help from Christians whom we never thought would care. Knowing that Jesus is with us in our suffering and that he will return one day to put an end to all pain helps us grow in our faith and our relationship with him. Stand your ground in times of suffering.

10:33-34 Sometimes you were publicly exposed to insult and persecution; at other times you stood side by side with those who were so treated. You sympathized with those in prison and joyfully accepted the confiscation of your property, because you knew that you yourselves had better and lasting possessions.NIV These believers had indeed remained faithful through terrible suffering (10:32)—being *publicly exposed to insult and persecution.* During

CALLED TO SUFFER

The New Testament abounds with warnings about suffering and words of comfort for those who are suffering.

Speaker	*Reference*	*Words about Suffering*
Jesus	Matthew 5:10-12	Those who are persecuted are called "blessed."
Jesus	Matthew 20:23	The Son of Man will return and end all suffering.
Jesus	John 15:20	Jesus was persecuted; we will be persecuted.
The Apostles	Acts 5:41	We can rejoice for being considered worthy to suffer for Christ.
Jesus	Acts 9:16	Paul was called to suffer for Jesus' name.
Paul	Romans 8:17	As children and heirs, we will share in Jesus' suffering.
Paul	2 Corinthians 1:37	God gives comfort in suffering.
Paul	2 Corinthians 4:7-12	Paul suffered so that others might be saved.
Paul	2 Corinthians 6:4-5, 9-10	Paul suffered yet rejoiced.
Paul	Ephesians 3:13	Our sufferings can glorify God.
Paul	Philippians 1:29	Suffering for Christ's name is a privilege.
Paul	2 Timothy 1:12	We must not be ashamed of suffering; trust Christ.
Paul	2 Timothy 2:10	Paul suffered for the sake of other believers.
Paul	2 Timothy 3:11	God will rescue us from suffering—now or in eternity.
Paul	2 Timothy 4:5	We are called to endure hardship.
Author of Hebrews	Hebrews 10:32-34	We can face suffering because we know we have God's inheritance.
James	James 1:2	We can consider it pure joy to face trials.
Peter	1 Peter 1:6	Our suffering is refining our faith.
Peter	1 Peter 2:21	We suffer because Christ suffered.
Peter	1 Peter 3:13-14	We are blessed for suffering for what is right.
Peter	1 Pter 4:1, 13, 16	We suffer yet rejoice because we suffer for Christ.
Jesus	Revelation 2:10	We must be faithful, even to death; the crown of life awaits us.

those difficult times of persecution, they had encouraged each other, helping each other remain firm by standing *side by side with those who were so treated.* These Christians had seen fellow believers publicly insulted in their trials or punishments. They had seen others become prisoners. Apparently the recipients of this letter had risked their own reputation and public standing as they *sympathized with those in prison* by visiting and providing for them. The risk of being associated with those in jail did not discourage them from this good work.

In addition, they even *joyfully accepted the confiscation of [their] property.* The text does not say whether this action was from the local government or from angry neighbors. Either way, the writer points to the good attitude that the people maintained. At that time, they were able to endure because they remembered that they had *better and lasting possessions awaiting them.* The word "better" means superior in quality and reality. The believers trusted in God's promises of future tremendous rewards. These believers had the right attitude toward their earthly possessions, understanding that everything comes from God's hand and could be taken away without changing their status with him. They did not allow their possessions to come between them and God, or between them and their service for God on behalf of other believers (see also Matthew 6:19-20; 19:21; Luke 12:13-21; 1 Timothy 6:17-19). What happened to these early Christians and so many other early believers serves as an indictment to us. Perhaps we desire too much approval from nonbelievers. Are we too willing to compromise our convictions just to be accepted by others?

LONG-TERM OUTLOOK

Because God's people have better and lasting "possessions," they are long-term investors. They will give up everything except God's promises. If your life is marred by losses you did not foresee, by premature deaths, unfair treatment at work, broken relationships—God's promise is still your best hope. Your life today should reflect the buoyancy of that promise:

- Share what little you have with someone else.
- Whatever hardship you may face, pray for a friend.
- When people offer help, witness to the hope God has put deep in your heart.

10:35 **Therefore do not cast away your confidence, which has great reward.**[NKJV] Back in the "early days" of their faith, the believers had had great confidence (10:32). This great confidence often caused them to experience great hardships (10:33-34). These hardships would not cease, so they would need to continue to endure. This verse implores, *Do not cast away your confidence;* that is, do not abandon your faith in times of persecution, but show by your endurance that your faith is genuine and sincere. Such faith means resting in what Christ has done in the past, but it also means trusting him for what he will do in the present and in the future (see Romans 8:12-25; Galatians 3:10-13). Doing so will bring *great reward*—joy today and heavenly possessions in the future—the greatest of which is eternal life.

10:36 **You need to persevere so that when you have done the will of God, you will receive what he has promised.**NIV For the time being, these believers needed to *persevere,* that is, to remain steadfast, to bear down to reach the goal, to "hold firm" (3:6; 10:32). Because Christ lives in us, we can persevere to the end. Endurance grows out of commitment to Jesus Christ. Jesus predicted that his followers would be severely persecuted by those who hated what he stood for: "And you will be hated by all because of my name. But the one who endures to the end will be saved" (Matthew 10:22 NRSV). In the midst of terrible persecution, however, they could have hope, knowing that salvation was theirs. Times of trial serve to sift true Christians from false or fair-weather Christians. When you are pressured to give up and turn your back on Christ, don't do it. Remember the benefits of standing firm, and continue to live for Christ. Standing firm to the end is not a way to be saved but the evidence that a person is really committed to Jesus.

Persistence is not a means to earn salvation; it is the by-product of a truly devoted life. This perseverance will help us do *the will of God.* In the end, we *will receive what he has promised.* This refers to the rewards mentioned in 10:34-35, and these promises will be further elaborated with specific metaphors in chapters 11–12, specifically God's promise of eternal life (see 9:15).

10:37-38 **"For yet a little while, and He who is coming will come and will not tarry. Now the just shall live by faith; but if anyone draws back, My soul has no pleasure in him."**NKJV One of the promises that believers will receive (10:36) is the return of the Christ. Through this quote of Habakkuk 2:3-4, readers are reminded that the day is drawing near (see also 10:25). This second coming of Christ and all the blessings that come with him outweigh any discomfort faced by believers in this life. Those who remain faithful to God are *the just* who will *live by faith.* These people will persevere to the end. However, those who have drawn back forfeit the heavenly blessing because they prove that they do not belong to God's household. "Draw back" is an allusion to apostasy. People who defect from the Christian faith when persecution comes will be forfeiting the ultimate goal of salvation—living forever with Christ.

When the prophet Habakkuk penned these prophetic words, evil and injustice seemed to have the upper hand in Israel. Like Habakkuk, Christians often feel angry and discouraged as they see what goes on in the world. Habakkuk complained vigorously to God about the situation. God's answer to Habakkuk is the same answer he would give us, "Be patient! I will work out my plans in my perfect timing." It isn't easy to be patient and to persevere during persecution and trials, but it helps to remember that God hates sin even more than we do. Punishment of sin will certainly come. As God told Habakkuk, "Wait for it." To trust God fully means to trust him even when we don't understand why certain events occur. This verse has inspired countless Christians. Paul quoted it in Romans 1:17 and Galatians 3:11. It is quoted here, just before the famous chapter on faith. And it is helpful to all Christians who must live through difficult times without seeing signs of hope. Christians must trust that God is directing all things according to his purposes.

JUST AHEAD

Around the bend, just a little further on, there's a staging area where angels are standing ready and Jesus himself is poised for . . . history's marvelous day.

It could be soon, and you could be part of it.

It will be powerful, and you need not fear it.

It must be coming, for God has promised it.

And everything you venture today can be done in the hope of it—Jesus' return, just ahead. Keep steadfast in your faith and active in your worship and service for him. God's very best still lies ahead.

10:39 But we are not of those who shrink back and are destroyed, but of those who believe and are saved.NIV The writer knew that these readers were *not of those who shrink back* and thus would be *destroyed.* Such people are hard-hearted and stubborn, rejecting Christ as Savior (10:29). Instead, the readers were *of those who believe and are saved.* This vote of confidence readies the believers to learn from the examples of faith and perseverance that will be cited in the next chapter. Living by faith is far better than merely fulfilling rituals and rules. The examples of faith in chapter 11 can challenge us to grow in faith and to live in obedience to God each day.

TWO DIRECTIONS

The Bible gives us a clear choice between two life directions. Because life often forks off in two directions, you must take the higher road.

It gets steep in places. The climb takes a toll on your energy. It gets lonely in places. Not many on it, but more than you imagined, and some because of your example. It gets slippery in places. The devil blows ice on the narrow passages.

Despite its dangers, the higher road is bound for the peak, and you'll make it—God has a lifeline around you. When you are tempted to falter in your faith or to turn back from following Christ, keep focused on what he has done for you and what he offers in the future.

HEBREWS 11

GREAT HEROES OF FAITH / 11:1-40

Most people love to read about heroes. Writers relish building the exploits of athletes, politicians, soldiers, medical researchers, and social reformers into heroic stories. Christian preachers enjoy expounding this passage that describes the faithful heroes of the early books of the Old Testament, properly called a "great cloud of witnesses" (12:1).

However, 11:36-40 presents the moving stories of other heroes of faith, seldom glorified. They were people who trusted God, even when they were ridiculed and persecuted, hunted and killed. They maintained their faith even though they never received in their lifetime all the blessings that God had promised them. This chapter provides examples for two key terms, faith and hope, from 10:19-25.

> Faith is to believe what we do not see, and the reward of this faith is to see what we believe.
> *Augustine*

These few verses present more than a verbal capsule of past history; they also comment on today and our vision for tomorrow. While followers of Christ experience a period of unprecedented creditability and respectability in certain areas of the world, Christians in other parts of the globe are being martyred. Real heroes maintain their faith in God despite brutal persecution.

11:1 Now faith is the assurance of things hoped for, the conviction of things not seen.[NRSV] Chapter 11 serves as a parenthesis; 12:1 resumes the theme of the last part of chapter 10. The words of 10:39 regarding "those who believe" lead to the description of the faith that causes Christians to hold on and not lose hope in the face of persecution and trials. In this wonderful and well-known chapter (probably the most well-known in the entire book), "faith" is explained as *the assurance of things hoped for, the conviction of things not seen.* Two words describe faith: "assurance" and "conviction." Faith starts with believing in God's character, that he is who he says he is. Faith culminates with believing in God's promises, that he will do what he says he will do. When we believe that God will fulfill his promises even though we don't yet see any evidence, we demonstrate true faith (see John 20:24-29).

"The assurance of things hoped for" means the person has complete confidence that God will fulfill his promises. We often think of the word "hope" in terms of uncertain desire—"I hope it doesn't rain on Saturday," "I hope I do well on this test." For believers, however, "hope" is a desire based on assurance, and the assurance is based on God's character.

"The conviction of things not seen" means that the person believes in the reality of something that he or she cannot see, taste, hear, or touch. The "things not seen" include eternal life, future rewards, heaven, and so forth. Faith regards these to be as real as what can be perceived with the senses. Faith means that if God promised something, he will fulfill that promise. Faith allows Christians to make God-honoring decisions based on unseen realities. This conviction about God's unseen promises allows Christians to persevere in their faith regardless of persecution, opposition, and temptation.

BETTER VISION

Faith gives believers confidence to see more clearly. Faith is like putting on

- fisherman's sunglasses that remove much of the glare so that you can see the fish better. Faith enables you to perceive realities most people cannot because they can't see beneath the surface; they are blinded by the glare of sinful attractions.
- night-vision lenses that penetrate the darkness surrounding you, enabling you to identify enemies or see danger ahead. Faith enables you to follow God's clear leading, even though Satan attempts to deceive you and places pitfalls in your path.
- corrective lenses that compensate for weaknesses in your eyes. Faith corrects your perception so that God's teaching makes sense to you, and you can see his leading in your daily activities.

Want to see better? God is the great optometrist. Utilize his lenses of faith. The lenses he crafts are just right for you.

11:2 **Through their faith, the people in days of old earned a good reputation.**[NLT] "Faith" is a word with many meanings. It can mean faithfulness (Matthew 24:45). It can mean absolute trust, as shown by some of the people who came to Jesus for healing (Luke 7:2-10). As James points out, it can even mean a barren belief that does not result in good deeds (James 2:14-26). Or, as noted in the book of Hebrews, it is assurance and conviction that help believers to persevere through tough times (11:1).

Through their faith, the people in days of old earned a good reputation. People with faith please God very much. But faith is not something we must do in order to earn salvation. If that were true, then faith would be just one more deed, and human deeds can never save us (Galatians 2:16). Instead, faith is a gift God gives us because he is saving us (Ephesians 2:8). It is God's grace, not our faith, that saves us. In his mercy, however, when he saves us he gives us faith—a relationship with his Son that helps us become like him. Through the faith he gives us, he carries us from death into life (John 5:24).

Even in "days of old" (Old Testament times), grace, not deeds, was the basis of salvation. This is why the book of Hebrews says, "It is not possible that the blood of bulls and goats could take away sins" (10:4 NKJV). God intended for his people to look beyond the animal sacrifices to him, but too often they instead put their confidence in fulfilling the requirements of the law—that is, performing the required sacrifices. When Jesus triumphed over death, he canceled the charges against believers and opened the way to the Father (Colossians 2:12-15). Because God is merciful, he gives us faith. It would be tragic to turn faith into a deed and try to develop it on our own! We can never come to God through our own faith, any more than his Old Testament people could come through their own sacrifices. Instead, we must accept his gracious offer with thanksgiving and receive the seed of faith he plants within us.

When believers have faith, that is, when they have confidence in God, they receive God's approval. The rest of the chapter presents examples of men and women who received God's approval because of their faith. Without this faith, it is impossible to please God (11:6).

11:3 By faith we understand that the entire universe was formed at God's command, that what we now see did not come from anything that can be seen.NLT Here is an illustration of faith. Faith allows us to understand that God created the world from nothing by his creative word alone. Believing this fact requires spiritual perception—that we receive only by faith. This passage reminds us that all of creation was new, not made from preexistent materials. The visible world did not come from anything that can be seen. God called the universe into existence out of nothing; he declared that it was to be, and it was. The entire universe was formed at God's command—God simply said the words, "Let there be . . ." and what he wanted came into being (see Genesis 1). We understand this by faith, not because we saw it happen but because we understand from what we read in Scripture and from our relationship with the loving Father that the world was created with a purpose and that we are part of that purpose.

This passage is very important for the debate about creation because it supports the Christian view that God created out of nothing. If any material or force existed prior to creation, then that material or force would also be eternal and therefore on the same level with God. Just how God created the earth is still a subject of great debate. Almost every scientist has an opinion on the origin of the universe, and many do not agree. But the Bible shows one supreme God creating the world by his word alone.

The Jewish believers reading this letter were in danger of returning to Judaism. Many may have desired to turn back because the "visual" nature of the rituals and sacrifices made their faith seem more real. Christianity, however, was based on so many invisible realities that many Jewish Christians may have begun to doubt its reality. Hebrews shows that Christianity's "unseen truths" are more real and more certain than what can be seen.

To make this point, the author goes back into the Jewish Scriptures, focusing on the heroes of faith. What these men and women had in common was a perspective that looked beyond this present world to God and his promises for the future. As the chapter unfolds, we'll review the lives of these many believers for whom the consolation of their faith (i.e., the fulfillment of the promises) was invisible. Yet they believed that God could bring to pass what they could not yet see. For them, the invisible would eventually appear.

11:4 By faith Abel offered God a better sacrifice than Cain did. By faith he was commended as a righteous man, when God spoke well of his offerings. And by faith he still speaks, even though he is dead.[NIV] Abel's faith is the first demonstrated in the Old Testament. Cain and Abel were Adam and Eve's first two sons (see Genesis 4:2-5). Cain, a farmer, brought an offering to God from the ground. Abel, a shepherd, brought firstborn sheep. Abel's sacrifice (an animal substitute) was *a better sacrifice* because it was acceptable to God, while Cain's sacrifice was unacceptable. Cain became so angry that he killed his brother, Abel.

The Bible does not say why God rejected Cain's sacrifice. Perhaps Cain's attitude was improper, or perhaps his offering was not up to God's standards. Proverbs 21:27 says, "The sacrifice of the wicked is detestable—how much more so when brought with evil intent!" (NIV). God evaluates both our motives and the quality of what we offer him (see Genesis 4:7). From the very beginning of creation, God was concerned more about the heart than the actual sacrifice. God, who later accepted grain offerings, would have accepted Cain's sacrifice if Cain's spiritual state had been proper (see 1 John 3:12). The real difference in the sacrifices seems to be that Abel offered his by faith.

Therefore, Abel *was commended as a righteous man* (see Matthew 23:35). Because of Abel's faith, he *still speaks* by his example, *even though he is dead.* These words play on Genesis 4:10, "Your brother's blood cries out to me from the ground" (NIV). Abel continues to be an example, therefore "he still speaks" to us.

PLEASING TO GOD

Hebrews reminds us that God spoke well of Abel's offering. Yet Abel was murdered. The first victim of crime in recorded history was a person at whose burial it could have been said, "He followed God." Why did God allow this to happen?

For similar victims, Abel's appearance as first in the "faith hall of fame" is encouraging. God hates evil, but in his providence he allows evil to happen, even to people very close to him. Through it all, God's will is accomplished, mysteriously and sometimes painfully. Nonetheless,

- Abel's life was good. He did his work and worship well.
- Abel's life was complete—shorter than most, but God was pleased.
- Abel's life was faithful, for which he is remembered even today.

Other victims of crime or disease, take heart. God leads you through the dark valleys to a sunlit home.

11:5 **By faith Enoch was taken from this life, so that he did not experience death; he could not be found, because God had taken him away. For before he was taken, he was commended as one who pleased God.**[NIV] Enoch is the next example of faith (see Genesis 5:20-24). Enoch was a popular figure in Jewish speculations. Jewish tradition says that he received special revelations about the world to come and was able to mediate between God and human beings because of his pure life. The book of 1 Enoch is a pseudepigraphal book written during the time between the two Testaments (the intertestamental period). The 106 chapters of the book are thought to be the record of visions that Enoch received. His book became so popular that even Jude quoted from it (see Jude 14).

Enoch was a righteous man and, as a result, *he did not experience death.* This passage states that God took him away (literally: God "translated" him). Enoch was translated from earthly life to heavenly life. Enoch is one of two Old Testament characters who never died (the other being Elijah, 2 Kings 2:11-12). God chose to take Enoch without dying because Enoch lived *by faith.* He was a righteous man who was commended as one who pleased God. The Hebrew Old Testament says that Enoch "walked with God," but the Septuagint (the Greek translation of the Hebrew Old Testament) translated it "pleased God." Enoch pleased God because he had faith; that is, Enoch kept his attention on the unseen things of God.

11:6 **And without faith it is impossible to please God, because anyone who comes to him must believe that he exists and that he rewards those who earnestly seek him.**[NIV] God gave his approval to these Old Testament people because of their faith (11:2). In fact, *without faith it is impossible to please God.* This would have functioned as a warning to those Hebrew Christians whose faith was wavering. No one (not Abel, Enoch, or anyone else) can please God without faith. It is an absolute requirement. All the rituals mean nothing without faith. Those who believe can come to God and discover that he is approachable (see 4:16; 7:25; 10:1, 22).

> Faith begins where man's power ends.
> *George Muller*

"Pleasing God" has two presuppositions here: (1) *People must believe that he exists* and then (2) endeavor to have a personal relationship with him. Drawing from the example of Enoch, in 11:5, we see that Enoch pleased God because he had a personal relationship with him. Before this relationship could happen, Enoch obviously had to believe that God exists. However, believing that God exists is only the beginning; even the demons believe in God's existence (James 2:19-20). God will not settle for mere acknowledgment of his existence. He wants a personal, dynamic relationship with you that will transform your life.

This is the message that Enoch's example should give to the Jewish Christians. Undoubtedly, they wanted to please God, but they couldn't do so without faith, particularly faith in his existence and in his promises to reward those who seek him. This reward is the rest and inheritance spoken of in chapters 3–4 and the reward of unlimited access to God as discussed in 4:14–10:18. Those who might wonder whether their faith in God is worthwhile are reminded that those who seek God will find that they are rewarded with his intimate presence. We may wonder about the fate of those who haven't heard of Christ and have not even had a Bible to read. God assures us that all who *earnestly seek him* will be rewarded. To "earnestly seek" means to act in faith on the knowledge of God that one possesses, and then to determine to devote oneself to him. When you tell others the gospel, encourage them to be honest and diligent in their search for truth. Those who hear the gospel are responsible for what they have heard (see 2 Corinthians 6:1-2).

WHAT TO BELIEVE

Do you believe because faith makes sense, or because faith doesn't need to make sense? Some Christians think people cannot understand God and should not try. Others believe that nothing true is irrational, including true faith.

The great church leader Augustine was among the first to ponder the relationship of faith to reason. He concluded, "I believe in order to understand," meaning that true understanding follows commitment to God, and that we cannot hope to understand God by human reason alone.

Almost nine hundred years later, the great theologian Thomas Aquinas wrote that reason, while marred by sin, can know God through arguments and proofs.

God gave us minds, which should be developed and used. To ignore intellectual growth is to live a stunted and naive life.

God wants our trust and faith, even while we ponder and wonder about so many matters mysterious to us.

God has spoken to us—to the mind, heart, and will—in Jesus Christ. We do not believe in a void, nor leap into the dark. Faith is reasonable, though reason alone cannot explain the whole of it.

So use your mind to think things through. But leave room for the unexplainable works of God.

11:7 **By faith Noah, being divinely warned of things not yet seen, moved with godly fear, prepared an ark for the saving of his household, by which he condemned the world and became heir of the righteousness which is according to faith.**[NKJV] Old Testament examples of faith continue with Noah who, by faith, believed God's warnings of *things not yet seen.* This relates to the comments in 11:1. God *divinely warned* Noah about coming events that the world had never seen—God warned that it would rain, and it had never rained before. God also promised to bring the animals to Noah! (Noah's story is found in Genesis 6–9.)

Noah believed God, *moved with godly fear,* and *prepared an ark,* following God's construction plans. Noah's story involves not one, but two great and tragic floods. The world in Noah's day was flooded with evil. The number of those who remembered the God of creation, perfection, and love had dwindled to one family. God's response to the severe situation was a 120-year-long last chance, during which he had Noah build a graphic illustration of the judgment to come. "Godly fear" refers to Noah's love and obedience out of reverence and respect for God. Noah trusted that

God would do as he said (bring a flood) and so he obeyed God's seemingly outrageous plan (build a ship). There's nothing like a huge boat on dry land to make a point!

While the ark accomplished *the saving of his household,* Noah's faith *condemned the world* because it illustrated what the people lacked. Those without faith faced God's judgments; those with faith were saved. While Noah believed God and was willing to sacrifice his reputation and public standing, the people around him were only interested in pursuing their own selfish lusts. As a result, Noah became *heir of the righteousness which is according to faith.* Noah is the first person in the Bible to be called "righteous" (see Genesis 6:9). To say that Noah was righteous and blameless does not mean that he never sinned (the Bible records one of his sins in Genesis 9:20-21). Rather, it means that he wholeheartedly loved and obeyed God. For a lifetime, Noah walked step-by-step in faith as a living example to his generation and future generations (see also Matthew 24:37-39; Luke 17:26-27; 1 Peter 3:20; 2 Peter 2:5).

> The life of faith is not a life of mounting up with wings, but a life of walking and not fainting. . . . Faith never knows where it is being led, but it loves and knows the One who is leading.
>
> *Oswald Chambers*

The early believers could learn this lesson from Noah: requiring no physical evidence of what was coming, he simply trusted God and obeyed. For Noah, obedience meant a long-term commitment to God's will in the face of scorn and ridicule.

TOO DIFFERENT

Noah experienced rejection because he was different from his neighbors. God commanded him to build a huge boat in the middle of dry land. Although God's command seemed foolish, Noah obeyed. Noah's obedience made him appear strange to his neighbors, just as the new beliefs of Jewish Christians undoubtedly made them stand out. As you obey God, don't be surprised if others regard you as "different." Your obedience makes their disobedience stand out. Remember, if God asks you to do something, he will give you the necessary strength to carry out that task.

11:8 By faith Abraham obeyed when he was called to go out to the place which he would receive as an inheritance. And he went out, not knowing where he was going.[NKJV] Abraham is the next Old Testament example of faith. Genesis records his faith in Genesis 15:6, and Hebrews has already mentioned his faith in 6:13-15. Two other notable New Testament passages speak of Abraham: Paul used Abraham as an example of justification by faith (Romans 4); James used Abraham as an example of faith that results in works (James 2:20-24). Hebrews explains that *by faith Abraham obeyed,* and it describes three actions resulting from Abraham's faith: (1) he moved to a new home (11:8); (2) he became a father in his old age (11:11); (3) he was willing to obey God's command to sacrifice his only son (11:17). Abraham demonstrated his faith through his actions. His faith made him right with God.

Abraham's faith is first seen in his obedience to leave his home and *go out to the place which he would receive as an inheritance.* Abraham left his home on the basis of God's promise—*he went out, not knowing where he was going* (see Genesis 12:1-9). God promised to bless Abraham and make him great, but there was one condition. Abraham had to do what God wanted him to do. Abraham obeyed, leaving his home, his assured wealth, and his established reputation for a nomadic life in an unknown land. He trusted in God's promises of even greater blessings in the future. Abraham's life was filled with faith. He believed the covenant that God had made with him (Genesis 12:2-3; 13:14-16; 15:1-6). In obedience to God, Abraham was even willing to sacrifice his son Isaac (Genesis 22:1-19).

Believers can take heart from Abraham's example of faith. God may ask us to give up secure, familiar surroundings in order to carry out his will; he may ask us to do some difficult tasks. But we can be sure that the outcome always will be for our best, drawing us closer to him.

HEADING OUT

Abraham obeyed God and left home for a far place, not knowing where he was going. Faith has that quality to it—not knowing quite where you are heading. If you're the type of person who needs to plan every move, get ready . . .

. . . for stepping into the unknown. You haven't seen where faith may lead you. Faith often carries with it an element of adventure.

. . . for becoming more of a pilgrim than a tour guide. Each day faith will stretch your vision.

. . . for following close to Jesus. In faith we follow his teaching and example, and through faith we grow to know him personally.

That's faith—always heading out. Jesus knows the way, and that's enough for you to take the next step.

11:9 And even when he reached the land God promised him, he lived there by faith—for he was like a foreigner, living in tents. And so did Isaac and Jacob, who inherited the same promise.NLT Abraham lived by faith throughout the rest of his life, continuing to trust God as he lived in *the land God promised him.* This land was to be his "as an inheritance" (11:8), yet Abraham never possessed the land. Instead, he lived in "his" land *like a foreigner, living in tents.* He didn't build cities and take over the land, and neither did his son and grandson, *Isaac and Jacob.* That job would be left to their descendants, hundreds of years later. Abraham lived like a nomad, moving around the land and even down to Egypt for a time (Genesis 12:10; 20:1; 21:23; 35:27). Nomads lived in tents and carried everything with them when they moved. Generally nomads moved in order to find better water or grazing for their flocks. Though Abraham had been promised the whole land, he had no house to dwell in. The only land he ever owned was the place where he buried his wife Sarah (Genesis 23). God gave Abraham "no inheritance here, not even a foot of ground. But God promised him that he and his descendants after him would possess the land, even though at that time Abraham had no child" (Acts 7:5 NIV). Yet even all that time, they understood that the land was not their final destination. Their real home was in heaven. Isaac and Jacob, *who inherited the same promise,* also remembered that promise and lived by faith.

Abraham influenced a great gift of faith in the one true God. Isaac had his weaknesses and committed sins, but we must remember that God works through people in spite of their shortcomings and, often, through them. God's words to Isaac are recorded in Genesis 26:2-5.

Jacob also had his record of sins and deceptions as recorded in Scripture. Jacob was the third link in God's plan to start a nation from Abraham. God's words to Jacob are recorded in Genesis 28:12-22. The success of that plan was more often in spite of than because of Jacob's life. Before Jacob was born, God promised that his plan would be worked out through Jacob and not his twin brother, Esau. Although Jacob's methods were not always respectable, his skill, determination, and patience have to be admired.

While we don't read much about Isaac's and Jacob's faith directly, we can see from their lives that despite their weaknesses and sins, they were part of God's plan. They kept heading in the right direction, trusting in the promise of God.

11:10 Abraham was confidently looking forward to a city with eternal foundations, a city designed and built by God.NLT Abraham lived by faith (11:9) because he was *confidently looking forward to a city.* The verb "looking forward" connotes intensely looking forward to and waiting for that city. This was not an earthly city, but a city with eternal foundations. This contrasts with the tents in which Abraham lived. This city, though as yet unseen, stretches to eternity; thus, it is permanent and secure. The readers would have remembered the psalmist's words praising God for laying the foundations of Jerusalem (Psalm 87:1-5). It was understood that God laid the foundations of the heavenly city as well. This city, *designed and built by God,* will indeed be both beautiful and *eternal.* He builds on real foundations that are stable and lasting. Having God as builder means that everything will be perfect. Revelation 21:2 states, "I saw the Holy City, the new Jerusalem, coming down out of heaven from God, prepared as a bride beautifully dressed for her husband" (NIV).

TOWARD SOMETHING NEW

Abraham had seen enough of human architecture; he had seen the great cities of the Chaldean empire. But he looked forward to something more: a city kept from disrepair, where bridges worked and rivers held their banks. No slums or crumbling tenements. No don't-walk-at-night areas where dealers do business in drugs and guns. No sullen police. No sirens wailing someone's grief.

What's your city like?

With a group of friends, elaborate on your dreams about God's eternal city. Then pray for (1) the energy to do all you can for Jesus' sake here on earth to resist the present disrepair, and (2) the faith to trust all Jesus has done and to follow him daily.

11:11 **By faith Abraham, even though he was past age—and Sarah herself was barren—was enabled to become a father because he considered him faithful who had made the promise.**NIV

There are two basic translations of this verse, influenced by variation in some of the Greek manuscripts: the NIV and NRSV focus on Abraham's faith, while the NKJV focuses on Sarah's faith: "By faith Sarah herself also received strength to conceive seed, and she bore a child when she was past the age, because she judged Him faithful who had promised." Most likely, the focus of this verse continues to be Abraham and the examples of faith from his life (starting from 11:8). Obviously, however, it took faith on both Abraham's and Sarah's parts, trusting in God's divine intervention in their physical bodies that were both well past the age of childbearing. In addition, Sarah was *barren* (unable to have children) in her childbearing years. God promised

Abraham a son, but Sarah at first doubted that she could become pregnant in her old age. Abraham was one hundred and Sarah was ninety when Isaac was conceived (Genesis 17:1, 15-16; 21:1-7). Although Sarah laughed when God told her she would have a son in her old age (Genesis 18:12), it appears that Sarah's approach changed; thus she, like Abraham, had faith that God could and would do as he promised *because he considered him faithful who had made the promise* (see 1 Peter 3:6). The faithfulness of God picks up the theme from 10:23.

Promises from God (no matter how unlikely or even impossible they may seem as we look around at our circumstances) can be trusted because we can trust God's character. God cannot lie, and he will not make a promise that he does not intend to keep.

11:12 And so a whole nation came from this one man who was as good as dead—a nation with so many people that, like the stars in the sky and the sand on the seashore, there is no way to count them.[NLT] Abraham and Sarah became parents because of their faith. It didn't matter to them that they seemed to be too old to have any children. Because they believed God, he rewarded their faith with a child whose descendants became *a nation with so many people that, like the stars in the sky and the sand on the seashore, there is no way to count them.* This had been part of God's covenant with Abraham: "I will indeed bless you, and I will make your offspring as numerous as the stars of heaven and as the sand that is on the seashore" (Genesis 22:17 NRSV; see also Genesis 12:2; 15:5). The contrast is being made between Abraham *(one man)* and his countless descendants (the Jews, and eventually all Christians), all because of that one man's faith. God had indeed been faithful to his promise.

11:13 All these people died still believing what God had promised them. They did not receive what was promised, but they saw it all from a distance and welcomed it. They agreed that they were foreigners and nomads here on earth.[NLT] *All these people* so far described (except for Enoch) *died* and *did not receive what was promised*—the new, eternal city (see 11:10). But these heroes saw and welcomed the promise even though it was, as it were, *from a distance.* For them it existed on the distant horizon, and they merely greeted it. They had faith and believed in God's promises, which they could not see (as 11:1 introduced). Faith is indeed a "hope" in that which has not yet come to pass.

These people of faith died without receiving all that God had promised, but they never lost their vision of heaven ("a better country—a heavenly one," 11:16 NIV). Many Christians become frustrated and defeated because their needs, wants, expectations, and demands are not immediately met when they believe in Christ. They become impatient and want to quit. They expect instant, not distant, answers. Take courage from these heroes of faith who lived and died without seeing the fruit of their faith on earth and yet continued to believe (see 11:35-39).

These faithful people knew that heavenly bliss could never be achieved on earth through status, money, or other means. Their future hope was not for this earth. Thus *they agreed that they were foreigners and nomads here on earth.* Their "agreement" was not passive receptivity, but an active declaration and pronouncement because of their faith in God. The patriarchs of the Jewish nation called themselves "foreigners and nomads" even after they had arrived at the Promised Land (see Genesis 23:4; 28:4). They knew that this world does not contain the ultimate fulfillment of God's promises. Loss of a job or relocation may force us to realize that we are "foreigners and nomads." This world is not our home, and there is no heaven on earth. We cannot live here forever (1 Peter 1:1). It is best for us to stay unattached to this world's desires and possessions so that we can move out at God's command.

We are not at home in this world because we are made for a better one. *Vance Havner*

FOREIGNERS

Citizens have rights. Capitalists control wealth. Politicians exert power. Majorities elect. Minorities (some at least) are specially treated. Scholars publish. Athletes compete.

Who are you?

You may not have special rights, not much wealth, uncertain status, not owning bylines or trophies, not fawning for power. You are just a pilgrim and a foreigner.

Do your inventory. For this special role, what do you need? What can you do without? You'll need the Holy Spirit as your Guide; you'll need the word of God as your road map. You'll need fellow believers as traveling companions and for aid on your journey. Keep looking ahead.

11:14-16 **People who say such things show that they are looking for a country of their own. If they had been thinking of the country they had left, they would have had opportunity to return. Instead, they were longing for a better country—a heavenly one.**[NIV] The first part of Hebrews has proven that Christ is higher in authority and status than Moses and higher than any other high priest. Here the emphasis is that the world to come will be better than this present world. This "better world" was the country of

WHAT DOES GOD HAVE IN MIND FOR US?

We need only go to the end of the story, recorded in Revelation 20–22, to find out what God has in mind for his faithful people from across the ages.

Satan is defeated	20:10
Death is defeated	20:14
Sin is banished	21:27
We live with God forever	21:3; 22:5
There will be no more sin, tears, or sorrow	21:4
The heavenly city is revealed	21:2, 10-14
The earth is made new	21:5
Paradise is gained	22:1-3

their own that the people of faith "saw in the distance" (11:13). These people were foreigners and nomads, but they were not seeking to return to their old homeland, Mesopotamia. If that were the case, they could have easily returned there. *Instead, they were longing for a better country—a heavenly one.* Instead of an earthly Promised Land, they looked ahead for a "heavenly one." As they served God and walked with him in this land, they knew that this world was not their home, and they looked forward to that "better country."

Therefore God is not ashamed to be called their God, for he has prepared a city for them.NIV Because these people looked forward to their new home, *God is not ashamed to be called their God* (see also Exodus 3:6), and *he has prepared a city for them.* This city is heaven (see John 14:2ff.).

11:17-18 **It was by faith that Abraham offered Isaac as a sacrifice when God was testing him. Abraham, who had received God's promises, was ready to sacrifice his only son, Isaac, even though God had told him, "Isaac is the son through whom your descendants will be counted."**NLT Abraham trusted God's promises so much that when God commanded him to offer Isaac (his only son) *as a sacrifice,* Abraham obeyed. The book of Hebrews does not try to show why God tested Abraham in this way, nor does it try to explain the command. The purpose of the account is to show that God was testing him and that Abraham had passed the test.

TWELVE TESTS OF ABRAHAM

Abraham's faith was tested at least twelve specific times. Some of them were not what we might call big tests, but together they establish a picture of Abraham as a person whose faith was genuine. After the last of these, God said, "Now I know that you fear God, because you have not withheld from me your son, your only son" (Genesis 22:12). Each of Abraham's tests can have applictions for us:

Reference	*Test*	*Application*
Genesis 12:1-7	Abraham left Ur and Haran for an unknown destination at God's direction.	Do I trust God with my future? Is his will part of my decision making?
Genesis 13:8-13	Abraham directed a peaceful separation from Lot and settled at the oaks of Mamre.	Do I trust God with my interests even when I seem to be receiving an unfair settlement?
Genesis 14:13-16	Abraham rescued Lot from the five kings.	Does my faithfulness to others bear witness to my trust in God's faithfulness?
Genesis 14:17-24	Abraham gave a tithe of loot to the godly kin of Salem, Melchizedek, and refused the gift of the king of Sodom.	Am I watchful in my dealings with people that I give proper honor to God and refuse to receive honor that belongs to him?
Genesis 15:1-6	Abraham trusted God's promise that he would have a son.	How often do I consciously reaffirm my trust in God's promises.
Genesis 15:7-11	Abraham received the Promised Land by faith, through the fulfillment would not come for many generations.	How have I demonstrated my continued trust in God during those times when I have been required to wait?
Genesis 17:9-27	At God's command, Abraham circumcised every male in his family.	In what occasions in my life have I acted simply in obe4dience to God and not becuase I understood the significance of what I was doing?
Genesis 18:1-8	Abraham welcomed strangers, who turned out to be angels.	When was the last time I practiced hospitality?
Genesis 18:22-33	Abraham prayed for Sodom.	Am I eager to see people punished, or do I care for people in spite of their sinfulness?
Genesis 20:1-17	Abraham admitted to wrong-doing and took the actions needed to see things right.	When I sin, is it my tendency to cover up or confess? Do I practice the truth that an apology must sometimes be accompanied by restitution?
Genesis 21:22-24	Abraham negotiated a treaty with Abimelech concerning a well.	Can people depend on my words and promises.
Genesis 22:1-2	Abraham prepared to sacrifice his son Isaac.	In what ways has my life demonstrated that I will not allow anything to come before God?

SOMETHING BETTER
For Christians, our better days are always ahead. People of faith get real testy with the phrase "This is as good as it gets." Because no matter how good it is,
It doesn't last.
It grows old.
It, when often repeated, gets dull.
It can become a real pain.

Christians seek a place that has that feel of constancy and goodness that doesn't fade with time. We catch glimpses of it, feel impulses of it, sense the beginnings of it, and follow the one who knows where it is.

Don't be sidetracked by thats and thoses, which may burn hot but will surely burn out. Jesus has something better—we have a glimpse of it today; we'll experience it in abundance in heaven.

Abraham passed because he *had received God's promises* and believed them. When God promised that many descendants would be born through Isaac, Abraham believed. Abraham brought Isaac to the altar, tied him up, placed him on the altar, and was about to sacrifice him, but God intervened at the last minute, sparing Isaac (Genesis 22:1-19). Abraham's obedience demonstrated his faith. He had learned many tough lessons about the importance of obeying God. Although he didn't understand God's command, his obedience was prompt and complete.

TRUSTING GOD
Abraham was willing to give up his son when God commanded him to do so (Genesis 22:1-19). God did not let Abraham take Isaac's life because God had given the command in order to test Abraham's faith. Instead of taking Abraham's son, God gave Abraham a whole nation of descendants through Isaac. If you are afraid to trust God with your most prized possession, dream, or person, pay attention to Abraham's example. Because Abraham was willing to give up everything for God, he received back more than he could have imagined. What we receive, however, is not always immediate, or in the form of material possessions. Material things should be among the least satisfying of rewards. Our best and greatest rewards await us in eternity.

11:19 Abraham reasoned that if Isaac died, God was able to bring him back to life again. And in a sense, Abraham did receive his son back from the dead.[NLT] Abraham had believed God's promise to bring a great nation out of Isaac; so *Abraham reasoned that if Isaac died, God was able to bring him back to life again.* Abraham even had told his servant that the boy would come back alive (see Genesis 22:5).

As a result of Abraham's faith, he figuratively received *his son back from the dead.* When Isaac was on the altar, he was as good as dead, but God spared him and restored him to Abraham. This illustrated what would happen to Christ. In reality, however, Christ actually did die and then came back from the dead.

11:20 **By faith Isaac blessed Jacob and Esau concerning things to come.**[NKJV] Other patriarchs are discussed in 11:20-22. The book of Hebrews notes that it was by faith that *Isaac blessed Jacob and Esau.* Isaac was the son whom God had promised to Abraham and Sarah in their old age. Through Isaac, God began to fulfill his promise to give Abraham countless descendants. Isaac had twin sons, Jacob and Esau. God chose the younger son, Jacob, to continue the fulfillment of his promise to Abraham (see Genesis 25–36 for the story of Esau; Jacob's story continues to the end of Genesis). The ancient story of deception, greed, birthright, and blessing is of no concern here. Verses 20-21 focus on the "blessing" conferred by aged fathers on their sons. Before the father died, he performed a ceremony of blessing in which he officially handed over the birthright to the rightful heir. Although the firstborn son was entitled to the birthright, it was not actually his until the blessing was pronounced. Before the blessing was given, the father could take the birthright away from the oldest son and give it to a more deserving son. But after the blessing was given, the birthright could no longer be taken away. This is why fathers usually waited until late in life to pronounce the blessing. They were looking forward to the future as they conferred blessings on their children. They trusted in God's future promises and were able to trust their children to the future. Faith in the promises of God allowed Isaac to bless his sons *concerning things to come.*

More important in these verses, however, is the picture of these two fathers, Isaac and then Jacob, giving blessings "out of order." For example, Isaac blessed his younger son, Jacob, over the older son, Esau.

11:21 **By faith Jacob, when he was dying, blessed each of the sons of Joseph, and worshiped, leaning on the top of his staff.**[NKJV] Isaac had blessed Jacob and Esau; Jacob's sons had become the fathers of Israel's twelve tribes. Even when Jacob (also called "Israel") was dying in a strange land (in Egypt), he believed the promise that Abraham's descendants would live in the Promised Land, be numerous, and would become a great nation. In this case, Jacob blessed not his son Joseph, but his grandsons, Ephraim and Manasseh, *the sons of Joseph* (this blessing is recorded in Genesis 48:1-22). As noted in Isaac's case, Jacob blessed "out of order"; that is, he blessed the younger son over the older, *by faith,* realizing that it was God's plan. This blessing was directed from God.

Jacob offered this blessing and worship *when he was dying.* This illustrates what it means to persevere—true faith will endure until the end.

FAITH FOR YOUR FAMILY
Moses' parents trusted God to protect their son's life. More than proud parents, they were believers who had faith that God would care for him. If you are a parent, are you trusting God to care for your children? God has a plan for every person, and your important task is to pray for your children and prepare them to do the work God has planned for them to do. Faith allows us to entrust even our children to God.

11:22 **By faith Joseph, when he was dying, made mention of the departure of the children of Israel, and gave instructions concerning his bones.**[NKJV] Other than Abraham, Joseph may have lived the greatest life of faith. He lived *by faith* while he remembered God's promises to him and to his descendants. Joseph, one of Jacob's sons, was sold into slavery by his jealous brothers (Genesis 37). Eventually, Joseph was sold again—this time to an official of the pharaoh of Egypt. Because of Joseph's faithfulness to God, he was promoted to a top-ranking position in Egypt. Although Joseph could have used that position to build a personal empire, he remembered God's promise to Abraham. After he had been reconciled to his brothers, Joseph brought his family to be near him. Joseph believed God's promise that Israel would return to Canaan and *gave instructions concerning his bones* (Genesis 50:24-25; Exodus 13:19; Joshua 24:32). Like Isaac, Joseph gave these instructions *when he was dying.* At that same time, Joseph *made mention of the departure of the children of Israel* (a departure that occurred under Moses about four hundred years later). Even on his deathbed, Joseph persevered in his faith, looking forward to the promises God had made.

11:23 **By faith Moses' parents hid him for three months after he was born, because they saw he was no ordinary child, and they were not afraid of the king's edict.**[NIV] *Moses' parents* are listed among these great people of faith. Through their faith they recognized that God's hand was on Moses and that *he was no ordinary child* (see Exodus 2; 12; 14). The Greek wording here indicates that Moses was a beautiful child, and that beauty convinced his parents that he was not ordinary. Moses' parents disobeyed the king by faith, not being *afraid of the king's edict.* Pharaoh's "edict" stated that all male children born to the Hebrew slaves were to be killed. Instead, Moses' parents *hid him for three months after he was born,* trusting God to take care of them and their child. Moses' mother knew how wrong it would be to destroy her child. But there was little she could do to change Pharaoh's new law. Her only alternative was to hide the child and later place him in a tiny papyrus basket on the river. God used her courageous act to place her son, the Hebrew of his choice, in the house of Pharaoh.

DEFYING THE LAW

Civil disobedience means to deliberately break the law for a higher moral purpose, such as Rosa Parks's refusal to move to the back of the bus or Corrie ten Boom's hiding Jewish refugees. Few people today contest the moral rightness of their lawbreaking. Moses' parents disobeyed the law when they hid him as a baby.

It's risky, but . . .

- when a law is so unjust as to be utterly opposed to God's way and desperately hurtful to many victims,
- when a Christian consensus (the judgment of many wise leaders) opposes the unjust law,
- when your lawbreaking perpetrates no violence,

then you are in the position of Moses' parents. Act with courage, and have compassion even for those responsible for the legal corruption you protest.

11:24-25 **It was by faith that Moses, when he grew up, refused to be called the son of Pharaoh's daughter. He chose to share the oppression of God's people instead of enjoying the fleeting pleasures of sin.**[NLT] Moses' great faith was also revealed through his difficult decision. Moses became one of Israel's greatest prophets and a lawgiver. When Moses was born, the Jews, his people, were slaves in Egypt, and Pharaoh had ordered that all Hebrew baby boys were to be killed. Moses was spared, however, and through God's providence was raised by Pharaoh's daughter as a member of Pharaoh's own household (Exodus 1–2)! Although Moses had been given a great Egyptian education, wealth, and status, he rejected this heritage and *chose to share the oppression of God's people instead of enjoying the fleeting pleasures of sin.* Moses knew he could not participate in a comfortable and easy life while his fellow Hebrews were enslaved. Because of his faith, Moses knew that earthly comfort was not the ultimate purpose of his life.

TOUGH CHOICES

Moses made a tough choice. It took faith for Moses to give up his place in the palace, but he could do it because he saw the transitory nature of great wealth and prestige. It is easy to be deceived by the temporary benefits of wealth, popularity, status, and achievement, and to be blind to the long-range benefits of God's kingdom. How many Christians today would choose personal sacrifice or oppression rather than enjoy the fleeting pleasure of sin? Faith helps us look beyond the world's value system to see the eternal values of God's kingdom. We must choose friends, careers, and lifestyles that please God.

11:26-27 He thought it was better to suffer for the sake of Christ than to own the treasures of Egypt, for he was looking ahead to his great reward. It was by faith that Moses left the land of Egypt, not fearing the king's anger. He kept right on going because he kept his eyes on the one who is invisible.[NLT] Moses' great secret was that he looked ahead to the fulfillment of God's promises. This chapter teaches that the promises of God will not be received until after death. The promise of receiving the Promised Land and salvation was better than owning *the treasures of Egypt.* Here Moses illustrates that faith requires individuals to put their own desires aside for the sake of Christ. He was motivated by *looking ahead to his great reward.* Since this reward would come from his Lord, Moses was willing to *suffer for the sake of Christ.* Although Moses did not personally know Jesus Christ, Moses suffered for the sake of doing God's will and for the sake of proclaiming God's way of redemption to the Hebrews; thus, this passage speaks of Moses' suffering for the sake of Christ. Because God's history of salvation and redemption continued until Christ, Moses' suffering is linked to the cause of Christ.

Rather than make Egypt and this world his home, Moses was looking ahead to the great reward that God would give him. The reward that would come was more than honor or a new homeland. It was God's eternal home rewarded to people of faith. In the Bible, God gives rewards to his people according to his justice. In the Old Testament, obedience often brought reward in this lifetime (Deuteronomy 28), but obedience and immediate reward do not necessarily go hand in hand. If they did, good people would always be rich, and suffering would always be a sign of sin. Our true reward is God's empowering presence through the Holy Spirit. Later, in eternity, we will be rewarded for our faith and service.

ETERNAL WEALTH
True wealth is eternal. Consider the most powerful or well-known people in our world—how many got where they are by being humble, self-effacing, and gentle? Not many! But in the life to come, the last will be first—if they got in last place by choosing to follow Jesus. Hebrews has a critical message for earth-loving Christians. Don't forfeit eternal rewards for temporary benefits. Be willing to make sacrifices now for greater rewards later (see Matthew 6:19-21). Be willing to accept human disapproval because you know that you have God's approval.

11:28 It was by faith that Moses commanded the people of Israel to keep the Passover and to sprinkle blood on the doorposts so that the angel of death would not kill their firstborn sons.[NLT] Moses' faith encouraged him to be God's spokesman to the Hebrews. Through this faith, *Moses commanded the people of Israel to keep the Passover.* The Feast of the Passover was to be an annual holiday in honor of the night when the Lord "passed over" the homes of the Israelites. This incident occurred as the last of a series of plagues that devastated Egypt. The Hebrews followed God's instructions, given through Moses, *to sprinkle blood on the doorposts so that the angel of death would not kill their firstborn sons.* The "blood" was from a lamb slain as part of the Passover meal. That night the firstborn son of every family who did not have blood on the doorposts was killed. The lamb had to be killed in order to get the blood that would protect them. (This foreshadowed the blood of Christ, the Lamb of God, who gave his blood for the sins of all people.)

11:29 It was by faith that the people of Israel went right through the Red Sea as though they were on dry ground. But when the Egyptians tried to follow, they were all drowned.[NLT] *The people of Israel* leaving Egypt provide the next example of faith. It was *by faith* that they *went right through the Red Sea as though they were on dry ground.* The sight of the Red Sea parting and the requirement to walk into the seabed between walls of water must have been terrifying. But through Moses' leadership and their own faith, the people of Israel walked ahead and were delivered from Egypt.

As the people of Israel took the path through the Red Sea, the Egyptians tried to follow, but not in faith. Both the Israelites and the Egyptians followed the same path through the Red Sea, but Israel traveled in faith; the vast Egyptian army believed in their own power and strength. As a result, all the soldiers in the army *drowned* (see Exodus 14:5-31). This example of the Egyptians would be a warning to those who considered drifting from Christ. God severely punishes those who do not live by faith in him. Those who walk in faith, even into "seas" of difficulty or fear, will find their faith rewarded.

11:30 It was by faith that the people of Israel marched around Jericho seven days, and the walls came crashing down.[NLT] The wilderness wandering of the Israelites is skipped because it did not demonstrate the faith of the Israelites. In fact, Hebrews 3–4 points out that the people did not exercise faith during this time and therefore received God's punishment.

After the wandering, however, the people exercised faith and obeyed God when they *marched around Jericho seven days, and the walls came crashing down.* The command to march around the city for seven days must have seemed ridiculous (see Joshua 6), but the people believed God and followed his instructions. Their faith encouraged them to obey God. When they obeyed God, they won their first victory.

11:31 By faith the prostitute Rahab, because she welcomed the spies, was not killed with those who were disobedient.[NIV] When Joshua planned the conquest of Jericho, he sent spies to investigate the fortifications of the city. The spies met Rahab, who hid them. *Rahab* is an odd entry in this "hall of faith" because she was a Gentile and a *prostitute* (read the story in Joshua 2 and 6). But she demonstrated her faith in God by welcoming the spies and by trusting God to spare her and her family when the city was destroyed. Rahab's words to the spies reflect that faith: "I know that the LORD has given you the land. . . . The LORD your God is indeed God in heaven above and on earth below" (Joshua 2:9, 11 NRSV).

Faith helps us turn around and do what is right regardless of our past or what others may think. Those who disobeyed were killed. These people did not have faith and therefore faced God's punishment. Rahab's faith was rewarded: she and her family were saved. Even more important, she became an ancestor of Jesus. We read her name in Matthew 1:5—she was the mother of Boaz. Rahab's faith, despite her past sins, is contrasted with those who refused to turn to God and obey him. God's work in history is not limited by human failures or sins, and he works through ordinary people. Just as God used all kinds of people to bring his Son into the world, he uses all kinds today to accomplish his will.

11:32-34 And what more shall I say? I do not have time to tell about Gideon, Barak, Samson, Jephthah, David, Samuel and the prophets, who through faith conquered kingdoms,

administered justice, and gained what was promised; who shut the mouths of lions, quenched the fury of the flames, and escaped the edge of the sword; whose weakness was turned to strength; and who became powerful in battle and routed foreign armies.NIV The roll call of heroes continues with the words "what more shall I say?" The Old Testament records the lives of many people who experienced great victories; a few are selected for mention here. None of these people were perfect; in fact, many of their sins are recorded in the Old Testament. But these were among those who believed in God:

- *Gideon,* one of Israel's judges, was known for conquering the Midianite army with only three hundred men who were armed with trumpets and jars (Judges 6:11–8:35).
- *Barak* served with Deborah (another judge of Israel) in conquering the army of General Sisera from Hazor (Judges 4:4-23).
- *Samson,* another judge, was a mighty warrior against God's enemies, the Philistines (Judges 13–16).
- *Jephthah,* still another judge, delivered Israel from the Ammonites (Judges 11:1-33).
- *David,* the beloved king of Israel and a great warrior, brought peace to Israel, defeating all of his enemies.
- *Samuel,* the last judge of Israel, was a very wise leader. He also was a prophet. Samuel, along with all *the prophets,* served God selflessly as they conveyed God's words to an often rebellious people.

These persons were of every age and temperament—shepherds, statesmen, prime ministers, psalmists, poets, border chieftains, prophets, women martyrs—but they are all trophies of faith. . . . Their circumstances and trials were widely different, but in all the talisman of victory was faith's watchword—"God is able." There is no kind of need, trial, persecution, experience for which faith is not the sufficient answer. It is the master key for every lock of difficulty.
F. B. Meyer

These people demonstrated that faith will accomplish much:

- They *conquered kingdoms.* Throughout their years in the Promised Land, the Israelites had great leaders who brought victory against their enemies. People such as Joshua, all of the judges, and King David were great warriors.
- They *administered justice.* Many of the judges, as well as leaders such as Nehemiah, administered justice to the people.

- They *gained what was promised.* Some people actually did see the fulfillment of some of God's promises, such as possession of the Promised Land.
- They *shut the mouths of lions.* Daniel was saved from the mouths of lions (Daniel 6). This statement could also refer to Samson (Judges 14:6) or to David (1 Samuel 17:34-35).
- They *quenched the fury of the flames.* Shadrach, Meshach, and Abednego were kept from harm in the furious flames of a fiery furnace (Daniel 3).
- They *escaped the edge of the sword.* Elijah (1 Kings 19:2-8) and Jeremiah (Jeremiah 36:19, 26) had this experience.
- Their *weakness was turned to strength.* Hezekiah was one who regained strength after sickness (2 Kings 20).
- They *became powerful in battle and routed foreign armies.* This refers to Joshua, many of Israel's judges, and King David.

We, too, can experience victory through faith in Christ. We may have experiences similar to those of the Old Testament saints; more likely, however, our victories will be directly related to the role God wants us to play. Your life may not include the kinds of dramatic events recorded here, but it surely includes moments where faith is tested. Give testimony to those moments, publicly and honestly, and thereby encourage the faith of others. Even though our bodies deteriorate and die, we will live forever because of Christ. In the promised resurrection, even death will be defeated, and Christ's victory will be made complete.

STEADFAST

This chapter summarizes the lives of great men and women of faith. Some experienced outstanding victories, even over death. But others were severely mistreated, tortured, and even killed. Having a steadfast faith in God does not guarantee a happy, carefree life. On the contrary, our faith almost guarantees some form of abuse from the world. On earth we may never see the purpose of our suffering. But we know that God will keep his promises to us. Hold on to God; never give up; never give in. The Old Testament people of faith are cheering you on.

11:35 **Women received their dead by resurrection. Others were tortured, refusing to accept release, in order to obtain a better resurrection.**NRSV Other great accomplishments that came through faith are listed: *women received* their children back from the dead when they were resurrected. The widow from Zarephath received her son back from the dead (1 Kings 17:17-24), and so did the Shunammite woman (2 Kings 4:8-37). Others *were tortured* but refused to give in in order to gain their release because these martyrs wanted *to obtain a better resurrection.* This may be a reference to 2 Maccabees 6–7 (an apocryphal book), which explains the benefits of Jewish martyrdom. These people placed their hope in God's promises rather than seeking release from torture.

> Faith is a living, daring confidence in God's grace. It is so sure and certain that a man could stake his life on it a thousand times.
> *Martin Luther*

All these faithful people experienced the blessings and endured persecution because they placed their hope in the resurrection. These people lived by faith because they knew that gaining the world and achieving this world's success was not their objective. They waited for a better life that would begin after death. This promise of a better life encouraged them during persecution and other difficulties.

"WHY ME?"
Many think that pain is the exception in the Christian life. When suffering occurs, they say, "Why me?" They feel as though God deserted them, or perhaps they accuse him of not being as dependable as they thought. In reality, the world is sinful, so even believers suffer. God allows some Christians to die as martyrs for the faith, and he allows others to survive persecution. Rather than asking, "Why me?" we should ask, "Why not me?"

Our faith and the values of this world are on a collision course. If we expect pain and suffering to come, we will not be shocked when they occur. But we can also take comfort in knowing that Jesus also suffered. He understands our fears, our weaknesses, and our disappointments (see 2:16-18; 4:14-16). He promised never to leave us (Matthew 28:18-20), and he intercedes on our behalf (7:24-25). In times of pain, persecution, or suffering, trust confidently in Christ.

11:36 Some were jeered at, and their backs were cut open with whips. Others were chained in prisons.NLT These descriptions could apply to many people who lived by faith—including some who were part of the community of the original readers of this epistle. Many Christians were persecuted and punished for their faith in the ways listed in verses 36-37. They were

- *jeered at*—like Elisha (2 Kings 2:23-25), Nehemiah (Nehemiah 2:19; 4:1), and Jeremiah (Jeremiah 18:12);
- *cut open with whips*—like Jeremiah (Jeremiah 37:15);
- *chained in prisons*—like Joseph (Genesis 40:15), Samson (Judges 16:21), Micaiah (1 Kings 22:26-27), Hanani (2 Chronicles 16:10), and Jeremiah (Jeremiah 37:16; 38:6).

> Scars are the price which every believer pays for his loyalty to Christ.
> *William Hendricksen*

11:37-38 They were stoned; they were sawed in two; they were put to death by the sword. They went about in sheepskins and goatskins, destitute, persecuted and mistreated—the world was not worthy of them. They wandered in deserts and mountains, and in caves and holes in the ground.[NIV] More examples of unwavering faith included other people:

- *They were stoned*—like Zechariah (2 Chronicles 24:20-21); according to Jerome, Jeremiah was stoned at the hands of Jewish Egyptians because he denounced their idolatry.
- *They were sawed in two*—like Isaiah, presumably. Although we do not know for sure, tradition (from the apocryphal book, The Ascension of Isaiah, chapters 1-5) says that the prophet Isaiah was sawed in half at the command of King Manasseh because Isaiah had predicted the destruction of the temple. Isaiah had at first escaped and hid in the trunk of a tree while in the hill country. Manassah supposedly had the tree sawed in half with Isaiah in it.
- *They were put to death by the sword*—although some prophets did escape death by the sword, others did not (see 1 Kings 19:10).

Many of God's followers who lived before Christ and many who have lived after Christ have been persecuted. When they were *destitute, persecuted and mistreated* they were sometimes forced to live in the wilderness apart from others. Despite their difficult lot, the writer of Hebrews claims that *the world was not worthy of them.* These people were great men and women of faith.

11:39 These were all commended for their faith, yet none of them received what had been promised.[NIV] All of the above people mentioned by name and those alluded to *were all commended for their faith.* These people looked forward to a better day and salvation, but *none of them received what had been promised* in this life. Of course, they saw some of God's promises fulfilled, but not the promises that referred to the new covenant and the promised eternal kingdom. These people did not live to see the kingdom arrive, but their future citizenship was secure there. Thus, they were able to endure suffering. God did not forget or neglect them; "all" were commended for their faith. They maintained their faith because they were not content with the success of the visible world. They maintained their faith by continually looking forward to the fulfillment of God's promises.

Hebrews 11 has been called faith's "hall of fame." No doubt the author surprised his readers by this conclusion: these mighty Jewish heroes did not receive God's full reward because they died before Christ came. In God's plan, they and the Christian believers (who were also enduring much testing) would be rewarded together.

11:40 **God had planned something better for us so that only together with us would they be made perfect.**NIV The *something better* that God has in mind refers to the new covenant, *so that only together with us would they be made perfect.* The forefathers did not receive this "something better"; rather, it is experienced by those who live after the death and resurrection of Christ, for he is the one who introduced the new covenant and the new promises (see commentary on 1:2).

There is a solidarity among believers (see 12:23). Old and New Testament believers will be glorified together. Not only are we one in the body of Christ with all those alive, but we are also one with all those who ever lived. One day all believers will share in the promised blessing with Christ. We will then be complete and perfect in him.

FAITH'S OTHER DIMENSION

We often consider faith as intensely personal and largely private. In many churches, in fact, the adjective "personal" precedes faith as a sign it is true and right. But real faith involves the entire community of believers. Get connected today:

- to a church, through regular worship and service;
- to Christian friends, through small group prayer and Bible study;
- to Christians overseas, through support of missions;
- to believers of the past, through study of Christian history.

As you take your stand for faith in Christ, make sure you don't stand alone.

HEBREWS 12

GOD'S DISCIPLINE PROVES HIS LOVE / 12:1-13

The book of Hebrews has, up to 10:19, described the superiority of Jesus Christ and of the new covenant. Hebrews 10:19 through 13:20 describes the church's responsibility in light of Christ's superiority. In chapter 11, faithful people from Jewish history are held up as examples of patient perseverance as they awaited the promises of God.

Chapter 12 contains clues regarding the situation of the believers to whom this letter was written. They have been encouraged not to drift away (2:1), but in this chapter we perceive a community weary of persecution, struggling to stay strong in an increasingly hostile environment, but weakening perhaps to the point of giving up and turning away from their faith. All that has been addressed so far comes to focus as these weary believers are encouraged to look not around them but at Jesus, their ultimate example of faithfulness and endurance in the face of hatred and humiliation. Not only is Jesus Christ superior to all that the Jews had previously known, but he also had suffered just as they were presently suffering—in fact, Jesus had suffered even more deeply. Yet Christ is now enthroned in the heavens, and the believers can trust that this will be their future as well.

Believers were also encouraged to look upon their suffering as though it were the discipline of a loving Father, not for wrong actions but for helping them to mature spiritually. God alone can take unbelievers' hostility and turn it into an avenue of blessing and growth for his children. It would be important for believers to carry that perspective into the coming days.

12:1 **Therefore we also, since we are surrounded by so great a cloud of witnesses, let us lay aside every weight, and the sin which so easily ensnares us, and let us run with endurance the race that is set before us.**[NKJV] After hearing the roll call of faithful believers throughout the centuries, illustrating true faith (chapter 11), the readers are challenged to also persevere in their faith. These faithful people from the past now stand as *so great a cloud of witnesses.* Hebrews uses the athletic imagery of a Greek amphitheater that has rows and rows of spectators, a "great cloud" or a large group. They do not "witness" as if they were merely spectators, looking down from heaven and watching believers' lives; instead, they witness through the historical record of their faithfulness that constantly encourages those who follow them. We do not struggle alone, and we are not the first to struggle with problems, persecution, discouragement, even failure. Others have "run the race" and crossed the finish line, and their witness stirs us to run and win also. What an inspiring heritage we have! These great believers' lives, examples, and faithfulness in God, without seeing his promises, speak to all believers of the rewards of staying in "the race." This metaphor of a footrace run "with endurance" describes a marathon, a test of stamina and commitment. This provided an apt description of the lives of these suffering believers.

Three aspects to this "race" are set before all believers:

1. *Preparation.* The first step of preparation to run the race requires that each racer *lay aside every weight.* This had two meanings for the racers of the ancient world: the clothes that hold back (races often were run naked) or the fat or superfluous weight that would keep an athlete from running efficiently. Christians must be "spiritually trim" and able to run the race unencumbered (see 1 Corinthians 9:25; 2 Timothy 2:3-4). Many "weights" may not be necessarily sinful acts, but could be things that hold us back, such as use of time, some forms of entertainment, or certain relationships. The second step of preparation requires believers to avoid *the sin which so easily ensnares.* Classical Greek runners would race nude so that a garment would not impede or slow them down. Spiritually speaking, Christians should put away any sin that might entangle, impede, or trip them up. Sins such as greed, pride, arrogance, lust, gossip, dishonesty, and stealing can cause believers to drift off spiritual course.
2. *Participation.* After Christians prepare, they must participate in the race—they must *run.* Hebrews gives examples of what it means to "run": having faith, visiting prisoners, entertaining strangers, believing God, trusting God, worshiping God, knowing Christ, having courage, praying, encouraging others, and confessing sin. These can be summarized as loving God and loving others.
3. *Perseverance.* The race that we run is not our own. We did not select the course; it is God who marks it out before us. We should be running for Christ, not ourselves, and we must always keep him in sight. The "race that is set before us" refers to the trials Christians will experience as outlined in 12:4-11. Finally, Christians persevere, running *with endurance the race that is set*

before [them]. The writer has often referred to having endurance, being diligent, and persevering (see 2:1; 4:11; 6:11; 10:34, 36; 11:27; 12:7; 13:14). The Christian life involves opposition and suffering, requiring believers to give up whatever endangers their relationship with God, to run patiently, and to struggle against sin with the power of the Holy Spirit. To live effectively, believers must keep their eyes on Jesus. We will stumble if we look away from him to stare at ourselves or at the circumstances surrounding us.

Running a race requires preparation, participation, and perseverance. Christians prepare to run the race through daily training. We pray, read the word of God, and examine our life for habits that would impede us in the race. We participate in worship, and we persevere by maintaining a Christlike and God-honoring attitude even when the trials are strong and we feel weak.

SHEDDING WEIGHT
To run the race set before us, we must train. Long-distance runners work hard to build endurance and strength. On race day, their clothes are lightweight and their bodies lean.

Since shedding "sin weight" is important to your spiritual run, how can you do it?

- Choose friends who are also committed to the race. Wrong friends will have values and activities that may deter you from the course. Much of your own weight may result from the crowd you run with. Make wise choices.
- Drop certain activities. That is, for you at this time these may be a weight. Try dropping them for a while; then check the results. If TV consumes precious time, try doing without it. If shopping is your stress relaxer, try something else.
- Get help for addictions that disable you. If you have a secret "weight" such as pornography, gambling, or alcohol, admit your need and get help today.

12:2 **Looking to Jesus the pioneer and perfecter of our faith, who for the sake of the joy that was set before him endured the cross, disregarding its shame, and has taken his seat at the right hand of the throne of God.**NRSV Jesus, our example, perfectly finished his race. Because he stands at the finish line, Christians should *fix [their] eyes on Jesus,* looking away from other distractions or options (see also 3:1). This is the same focused attention Moses had, as recorded in 11:26, "He was looking ahead to his reward" (NIV). Jesus is the

> Christ's followers cannot expect better treatment in the world than their Master had.
> *Matthew Henry*

ultimate "hero of faith" as carried over from the list of heroes in chapter 11. We look to him as the supreme model of persevering faith (11:26-39). We should have single focus on him. We cannot look in two different directions at the same time. The use of the name "Jesus" focuses on Jesus' humanity; in the flesh, he faced suffering and thus is able to help us. Each member of the "great cloud of witnesses" can be inspiring, but Jesus provides the ultimate example. Jesus is described in two ways:

1. *Pioneer.* The Greek word is *archegon;* it means pioneer, pathfinder, or leader. Perhaps "champion" conveys the best meaning. Jesus is our hero, the first who obeyed God perfectly and thus began the new covenant (see also 2:10). He set the course of faith, ran the race first (6:20), and now waits for us to join him at the end, encouraging us all the way.
2. *Perfecter of our faith.* "Perfecter" is *teleioten* in Greek, meaning finisher, the one who brings us to our intended goal. Jesus is our perfecter, both because he was made the perfect High Priest through suffering and obedience (see 2:10, 5:8) and because he perfects us as we draw closer to him.

After explaining some of Jesus' credentials and reasons for keeping our eyes him, Hebrews tells how Jesus must be the believers' example in facing trials. He *endured the cross, disregarding its shame.* Crucifixion was a horrible and shameful way to die. Jesus endured this disgraceful and degrading death; even more, he "disregarded" the shame it represented, despising and scorning it. The human shame amounted to nothing compared to the shame that Jesus felt when he took on the sins of the world. So great were the sins that even the Father had to turn his face away from his Son.

Yet Jesus endured all this suffering on account of *the joy that was set before him.* He kept his eyes focused on the goal of his appointed course, the accomplishment of his priestly work, and his seat at the right hand of God. Knowing that a great reward was coming for God's people gave Jesus great joy. He did not look at his earthly discomforts, but he kept his eyes on the spiritual, invisible realities.

When the suffering was complete and Jesus had finished the race appointed for him, he took *his seat at the right hand of the throne of God.* Again Hebrews returns to the focus of Psalm 110 (see commentary on 1:13; 8:1). Christ "sat down" because when he offered up his life, he completed his work. He no longer needs to provide sacrifices or pave a way to God. Just as Christ, our forerunner, received great reward for finishing the race before him and now sits enthroned by God, exalted to a place of highest honor, Christians will also share his reward when they finish the race set before them (see Luke 22:28-30). So, like Christ, we should persevere in times of suffering, looking to Christ as our model and concentrating on our heavenly destination.

12:3 **Think of all the hostility he endured from sinful people; then you won't become weary and give up.**[NLT] Christ endured great suffering to finish his race. As a result, he can be an inspiring example for believers who face suffering and persecution. When these believers were tempted to focus on their trials, even to the point of considering renouncing their faith, Hebrews encouraged them to *think of all the hostility [Jesus] endured from sinful people.* Christ was ridiculed, whipped, beaten, spit upon, and crucified. Even so, he did not give in to fatigue, discouragement, or despair.

By focusing on Christ and what he did on our behalf, we won't *become weary and give up.* Trials can cause us to become discouraged and even to despair. During these difficult times, we can remember how Christ endured, and that endurance can inspire us. Throughout the history of the church, meditation on the suffering of Christ has helped countless martyrs, prisoners, and those being persecuted. Christ's suffering surpassed any suffering we humans might face. We can also remember the great cloud of witnesses who demonstrated faith (chapter 11), and they can inspire us. Facing hardship and discouragement, we must not lose sight of the big picture. We are not alone; Jesus stands with us. Many have endured far more difficult circumstances than we have experienced. Suffering trains us for Christian maturity, developing our patience and making our final victory sweet.

WHEN YOU'RE TIRED

Weariness takes a great toll on the lives of "people helpers." Mothers of young children know the feeling. So do social workers, teachers, and anyone for whom work never seems to end. How does "focusing on Christ" relieve stress from constant work responsibility and fatigue?

- Jesus did not try to do it all. His ministry was less than three years long. He left a lot of work for disciples to do. Ask for help, and don't be afraid to depend on others.
- Jesus took breaks. Often he went alone to pray, sometimes during his busiest weeks. In your life, schedule breaks for prayer, reading, and learning.
- Jesus remained faithful. He trusted God through all his ordeals; he did not abandon his mission or those who believed in him. He stands beside us in our troubles. Trust him.

12:4 **In your struggle against sin, you have not yet resisted to the point of shedding your blood.**[NIV] Here we find a clue about the present situation of the readers in that the writer mentions their *struggle against sin.* This "struggle" refers not to personal struggles against temptation, but rather to their struggle against sinful people. Just as Christ struggled against sinful people (12:3), so Christians struggle against opposition from hostile nonbelievers and sometimes even from fellow believers. Jesus had told his disciples, "Remember the word that I said to you, 'Servants are not greater than their master.' If they persecuted me, they will persecute you" (John 15:20 NRSV).

During their struggle, the Jewish Christians had *not yet resisted to the point of shedding [their] blood.* These readers were facing difficult times of persecution, but none of them had yet died for their faith. As difficult as these times were, they did not compare with the difficulties that Christ faced. These living believers were urged to continue to run their race. Just as Christ did not give up, neither should they. Their suffering might one day lead them to death, so the text says "not yet."

12:5-6 **And have you forgotten the encouraging words God spoke to you as his children? He said, "My child, don't make light of the LORD's discipline, and don't give up when he corrects you. For the LORD disciplines those he loves, and he punishes each one he accepts as his child."**[NLT] Hebrews explains that difficult times may come as a result of God's discipline. In reality, it is a sign of God's love. In fact, discipline is so important that the writer explains it as the normal experience of believers. The believers should have remembered the words of Proverbs 3:11-12, which say, *My child, don't make light of the LORD's discipline, and don't give up when he corrects you. For the LORD disciplines those he loves, and he punishes each one he accepts as his child.* Proverbs contains many words of wisdom regarding discipline, both earthly and spiritual. In these verses, both kinds of discipline are combined. This quotation teaches that God's discipline comes from his love. God's discipline, although difficult, should encourage us that God loves us. He cares about us enough to help us mature. Like a loving father, he wants us to stay away from what would hurt us and to move along the path toward maturity. Sometimes that involves discipline.

The question becomes: how do we know whether the difficult times we face are part of the discipline of the Lord or something else? For example, they could be the result of our own foolish behavior or attacks by Satan. Regardless of their sources, we can treat all difficulties as opportunities for us to grow and learn from

God. The context of this chapter shows that these words apply to the suffering that believers face from hostile nonbelievers, those who mistreat Christians who stand for their faith. In many parts of the world, Christians face persistent persecution. Even if we are not experiencing persecution (and perhaps we should be if we are truly standing for Christ), we can pray for those who are.

Much of the force of this verse is lost to modern readers in an age of permissiveness. Such harsh discipline (the Greek word for "punishes" literally means "to whip") seems cruel to many, and the point of these verses may be overlooked. Discipline is a responsibility for human fathers; thus, the father who does not provide it shows indifference and lack of love to his children. Human parents should learn from the way God disciplines. Parents discipline their children because they love them and because correction and teaching help train and educate children. The goal of correction shouldn't be merely punishment, but to help teach important lessons and to help them become more responsible and mature. When we discipline our children, that correction should have the same loving purpose and self-restraint that God shows with us.

NEED PROOF?
Who loves his child more—the father who allows the child to do what will harm him, or the one who corrects, trains, and even punishes the child to help him learn what is right? It's never pleasant to be corrected and disciplined by God, but his discipline is a sign of his deep love for us. When God corrects you, see it as proof of his love, and ask him what he is trying to teach you. If you believe that a sovereign God disciplines his beloved children, turning problems into moments of growth and finally joy, you will overcome fear and shame.

12:7-8 **As you endure this divine discipline, remember that God is treating you as his own children. Who ever heard of a child who is never disciplined by its father? If God doesn't discipline you as he does all of his children, it means that you are illegitimate and are not really his children at all.**[NLT] Because God promises to discipline his children, believers must *endure this divine discipline.* The only other choice would be to refuse to endure it, to pout, to grow depressed, or to give up completely. How much better to remember that, when God disciplines you, he *is treating you as his own children.*

> God will go to any lengths to bring us to an acknowledgement of who he is.
> *Elisabeth Elliot*

The rhetorical question, *Who ever heard of a child who is never disciplined?* pictures the Jewish fathers of the day who were responsible for the training, education, and discipline of their children. Proverbs explains that "those who spare the rod hate their children, but those who love them are diligent to discipline them" (Proverbs 13:24 NRSV). Indeed, to refuse discipline would be tantamount to hating one's children! While we may indeed know of some children who were never disciplined, we also know what kind of children they are—unruly, destructive, mean, and lacking self-control (the book of Proverbs also attests to this; see Proverbs 5:22-23; 10:17; 12:1; 13:18; 15:5).

Jesus died on the cross for sinners. Those who believe in him still battle a sinful nature and need guidance in order to stay on course (12:1). Sometimes we need God's discipline in order to learn the tough lessons and not repeat the same mistakes. It works for our earthly children; it works for God's spiritual children.

Therefore, Christians will experience God's discipline. Those who are not disciplined are *illegitimate and are not really his children at all.* "Illegitimate children" were those born of a slave or concubine. In that culture, only illegitimate children received no discipline, attention, or education. Under Roman law, illegitimate children also did not receive any inheritance or recognition that came with being a genuine child. When we experience God's discipline, we can be encouraged that we really are God's children.

12:9 Moreover, we have all had human fathers who disciplined us and we respected them for it. How much more should we submit to the Father of our spirits and live!NIV The analogy between human fathers and the heavenly Father figures often in Jesus' teachings (see Matthew 7:9-11; 21:28-31; Luke 15:11-32). Here *human fathers* are compared to *the Father of our spirits,* that is, to the Creator himself. Verses 7-8 describe the value of discipline and that all of God's children will endure discipline; verses 9-10 teach the parallel between God's discipline and earthly parental discipline. All people (or at least the vast majority) *had human fathers who disciplined* them. Rarely did that discipline occur out of cruelty; instead, loving fathers would discipline with the children's best interests in mind. As a result, *we respected them for it.*

If this is true with earthly fathers, *how much more* it is so of our heavenly Father. If we respected the discipline of our earthly parents, how much more *should we submit to the Father of our spirits and live.* Submission to God's discipline means not trying to wriggle out of it by making excuses or hardening our hearts;

instead, it means allowing the discipline to drive us to our knees before God so that he can teach us the lessons he has for us. This phrase recalls the challenge to covenant obedience recorded in Deuteronomy: "For I command you today to love the LORD your God, to walk in his ways, and to keep his commands, decrees and laws; then you will *live* and increase, and the LORD your God will bless you in the land you are entering to possess" (Deuteronomy 30:16 NIV, italics ours). Submitting to God means being willing to obey him. When we have this attitude toward God's discipline, we will "live"—referring to our ability to truly enjoy this life and to look forward to eternity with God.

REAL LIVING

The book of Hebrews stresses the importance of submitting to God. The consequences of rebelling are disastrous. A biography of the great essayist Ralph Waldo Emerson describes the change that came over him when his first wife died young. He withdrew from the ministry and from Christian faith and became famous for advocating the glory of self. By the time he reached midlife, he had "died" emotionally and spiritually. The fire he sought in his own soul had become a dim flicker on a wet wick.

Instead of rebelling when life's adversity rolls over you, regard your problems as God's opportunities to shape your character. Depend on God for relief and deliverance. Trust God for vision to see beyond the bleakness. Believe God to be the loving parent he is. And live.

12:10 **For our earthly fathers disciplined us for a few years, doing the best they knew how. But God's discipline is always good for us, so that we might share in his holiness.**[NLT] *Earthly fathers* are imperfect. Sometimes they discipline when they shouldn't or in the wrong way, and sometimes they fail to discipline when they should. But most of them did *the best they knew how* for the *few years* during which they had responsibility for us. Their effort reminds us of the perfection of God's discipline. God always exercises the right discipline, in the right way, at the right time. His *discipline is always good for us.* His discipline is always to our advantage (see Romans 8:28-29; 1 Corinthians 10:13).

> It is doubtful if God can bless a man greatly without hurting him deeply. *A. W. Tozer*

God's discipline also means that *we can share in his holiness.* Discipline may not be enjoyed, but it brings great reward. Earlier in this book, the Christians were said to be partakers of God's holiness (3:14). Christians already share in God's holiness as a result of Christ's work. Here, however, sharing in holiness refers to our growth. God's discipline helps Christians become more and more like Christ, mature and complete (see Matthew 5:48; 1 John 3:2). Only God, the loving Creator and Father, could take the suffering brought upon his children by sinful unbelievers and turn it into a blessing for his children—drawing us ever closer to his holiness.

THEOLOGY OF TRIALS IN THE NEW TESTAMENT

As we live for Christ, we will experience troubles because we are trying to be God's people in a perverse world. Some people say that troubles are the result of sin or lack of faith, but the Bible teaches that they may be a part of God's plan for believers. Our problems can help us look upward and forward, instead of inward. They can build strong character, and they can provide us with opportunities to comfort others who are also struggling. Your troubles may be an indication that you are taking a stand for Christ.

Suffering is not always the result of sin. "His disciples asked him, 'Rabbi, who sinned, this man or his parents, that he was born blind?' 'Neither this man nor his parents sinned,' said Jesus, 'but this happened so that the work of God might be displayed in his life'" John 9:2-3 (NIV).

God provides hope and love in suffering. "We also rejoice in our sufferings, because we know that suffering produces perseverance; perseverance, character; and character, hope. And hope does not disappoint us, because God has poured out his love into our hearts by the Holy Spirit, whom he has given us" Romans 5:3-5 (NIV).

Problems help us trust in God's sovereignty for our lives. "We know that all things work together for good for those who love God, who are called according to his purpose. For those whom he foreknew he also predestined to be conformed to the image of his Son, in order that he might be the firstborn within a large family" Romans 8:28-29 (NRSV).

Suffering enables us to comfort others. "Praise be to the God and Father of our Lord Jesus Christ, the Father of compassion and the God of all comfort, who comforts us in all our troubles, so that we can comfort those in any trouble with the comfort we ourselves have received from God. For just as the sufferings of Christ flow over into our lives, so also through Christ our comfort overflows" 2 Corinthians 1:3-5 (NIV).

Our eternal reward outweighs our suffering. "For this slight momentary afflicton is preparing us for an eternal weight of glory beyond all measure, because we look not at what can be seen; for what can be seen is temporary, but what cannot be seen is eternal" 2 Corinthians 4:17-18 (NRSV).

Problems open up opportunities for service. "I want you to know, beloved, that what has happened to me has actually helped to spread the gospel" Philippians 1:12 (NRSV).

Problems may be a confirmation that we are living for Christ. "This is evidence of the righeous judgment of God, and is intended to make you worthy of the kingdom of God, for which you are also suffering" 2 Thessalonians 1:5 (NRSV).

12:11 **No discipline seems pleasant at the time, but painful. Later on, however, it produces a harvest of righteousness and peace for those who have been trained by it.**NIV All Christians will experience God's discipline, and all Christians should endure that discipline because the results are worth it. While *no discipline seems pleasant at the time, but painful,* Christians can respond

God uses suffering in his plan for our lives. Finally, brothers and sisters, pray for us, so that the word of the Lord may spread rapidly and be glorified every-where, just as it is among you, and that we may be rescued from wicked and evil people; for not all have faith. But the Lord is faithful; he will strengthen you and guard you from the evil one" 2 Thessalonians 3:1-3 (NRSV).

Through his suffering, Jesus fully identified with us. "Because he himself was tested by what he suffered, he is able to help those who are being tested" Hebrews 2:16 (NRSV).

Jesus was willing to obey God even when it meant suffering. "Although he was a Son, he learned obedience through what he suffered" Hebrews 58:8 (NRSV).

Trials help train us to be more fruitful. "No discipline seems pleasant at the time, but painful. Later on, however, it produces a harvest of righteousness and peace for those who have been trained by it" Hebrews 12:11 (NIV).

Problems help us mature. "My brothers and sisters, whenever you face trials of any kind, consider it nothing but joy, because you know that the testing of your faith produces endurance; and let endurance have its full effect, so that you may be mature and complete, lacking in nothing" James 1:2-4 (NRSV).

Trials help refine our character. "In this you greatly rejoice, though now for a little while you may have had to suffer grief in all kinds of trials. These have come so that your faith—of greater worth than gold, which perishes even though refined by fire—may be proved genuine and may result in praise, glory and honor when Jesus Christ is revealed. Though you have not seen him, you love him; and even though you do not see him now, you believe in him and are filled with an inexpressible and glorious joy, for you are receiving the goal of your faith, the salvation of your souls" 1 Peter 1:6-9 (NIV)

When we suffer, we share in the suffering of Christ. "Dear friends, do not be surprised at the painful trial you are suffering, as though something strange were happening to you. But rejoice that you participate in the sufferings of Christ, so that you may be overjoyed when his glory is revealed. If you are insulted because of the name of Christ, you are blessed, for the Spirit of glory and of God rests on you" 1 Peter 4:12-14 (NIV).

to it by remembering the end result of the discipline. After the fact, the benefits will be clear. Certainly discipline is painful; if it weren't, it would have little effect in combatting sin or changing us from within. When brought in the form of suffering or persecution, the pain may be extreme. By painful discipline, however, believers will be made more like their heavenly Father who disciplines them, sharing in his holiness (12:10). We may respond to discipline in several ways:

- we can accept it with resignation;
- we can accept it with self-pity, thinking we really don't deserve it;
- we can be angry and resentful toward God;
- we can accept it graciously, letting it accomplish its purpose in us.

The result of discipline, however, makes the pain worthwhile: *It produces a harvest of righteousness and peace for those who have been trained by it.* The "harvest of righteousness" evokes the imagery of pruning. By pruning a plant, greater fruitfulness occurs (see John 15:2). God's discipline strengthens our faith and character (see also Romans 5:1-5). The "training" referred to is continuous, strenuous training that requires perseverance. This is an athletic term from which our word "gymnasium" comes. The training received in discipline helps us stand strong and firm for the faith so that we live righteous lives in an unrighteous world. When discipline cleans up sin in our lives, it moves us on the pathway toward righteousness and holiness. The promised peace refers both to an inward tranquility and contentment (Philippians 4:11-12; James 1:4) in any circumstance (Philippians 4:6-7).

12:12-13 So take a new grip with your tired hands and strengthen your weak knees. Mark out a straight path for your feet so that those who are weak and lame will not fall but become strong.[NLT] This passage vividly pictures God as a challenging coach who pushes us to our limits, encouraging us beyond what we think we can attain. When the pressure and opposition build, we must not be paralyzed with fear and inaction. We must get involved in the challenging contest. Although we may not feel strong enough to push on to victory, we will be able to accomplish it as we follow Christ and draw on his strength. Then we can use our growing strength to help those around us who are weak and struggling. Apparently these readers were low in spirits and weak in their resolve; therefore, the writer introduces a series of concluding commands (reminiscent of Isaiah 35:3 and Proverbs 4:26):

- *Take a new grip with your tired hands.* Tired hands want to stop working. The Christians were at the point of sheer exhaustion;

morale was low. Rather than concede defeat, Christians must continue to make the effort and always be ready to endure.

- *Strengthen your weak knees.* Discipline or persecution should not cause Christians to fear; instead, difficult times should encourage them to endure. Rather than dropping in defeat, Christians should stand firm—even when knees are weak and legs are shaky—in their confident expectation of Christ's return (see 10:37).
- *Mark out a straight path for your feet so that those who are weak and lame will . . . become strong.* Most "paths" encountered in nature wind and dip along with the terrain. A "straight path," however, has most likely been constructed by someone who took the effort to move the rocks, level out the holes, and even clear away little pebbles that would be hard on one's feet. This picture of making a straight path ties in with the "righteousness" (12:11) that results in the life of a person who has faced discipline and has worked to remove any stumbling blocks that would impede progress. Hard work obviously helps, but it has another benefit for those who follow behind. Some who follow may indeed be *weak and lame.* We can help them not to *fall* by encouraging them and working hard to remove the obstacles that may be in the path. We must not ignore the spiritual and moral fatigue of other believers. Though they are weak and lame (disabled or out of joint), God will heal them so they can follow.

As said throughout this epistle, Christians have the responsibility to encourage one another and to help those who are weak. If the original readers were contemplating a return to Jewish practices, their example would prove discouraging to new Christians. Instead of running in a straight, clear path, they would be adding hindrances and obstacles to the already difficult trip. Believers must not live with only survival in mind—others will follow their example. Does your example make it easier for others to believe in and follow Christ, and to mature in him? Or would those who follow you end up confused and misled?

MOVING ON

How can we get a new grip and stand firm? We can reconsider our purpose. Is your purpose continued misery, or progress? Another day of self-pity, or a breakthrough into joy?

If your purpose is misery, then try this: Get bitter about your problems, escape through some chemical addiction, and die snarling that life should have been better.

If your purpose is progress, try this: Get adjusted to the reality that God knows what he is doing, agree to cooperate with God's agenda, and live in the light of God's promises.

WARNING AGAINST REFUSING TO LISTEN / 12:14-29

Parents claim their children never listen to them; siblings complain to each other that their parents ignore all they say; one spouse shouts at the other, "Listen to me!" Listening is a skill that is seldom perfected or rarely practiced. Listening, however, could solve a host of relational problems. The book of Hebrews states emphatically, "See to it that you do not refuse him who speaks."

12:14 **Pursue peace with all people, and holiness, without which no one will see the Lord.**NKJV Believers have been encouraged to endure suffering as part of God's plan for them and to continue to walk with God in holiness and righteousness. They must also carry certain attitudes and responsibilities to people in this

PEACE WITH ALL PEOPLE?

We cannot get around it. Believers, as the salt and light in the world, must pursue peaceful relationships. Verbs such as "pursue" and "seek" show us that it may not necessarily be easy to do, but God calls us to do it. (Verses are quoted from NRSV.)

Psalm 34:14	"Depart from evil, and do good; seek peace, and pursue it."
Matthew 5:9	"Blessed are the peacemakers, for they will be called children of God."
Mark 9:50	"Salt is good; but if salt has lost its saltiness, how can you season it? Have salt in yourselves, and be at peace with one another."
Romans 12:18	"If it is possible, so far as it depends on you, live peaceably with all."
Romans 14:19	"Let us then pursue what makes for peace and for mutual upbuilding."
2 Corinthians 13:11	"Finally, brothers and sisters, farewell. Put things in order, listen to my appeal, agree with one another, live in peace; and the God of love and peace will be with you."
1 Thessalonians 5:13	"Be at peace among yourselves."
2 Timothy 2:22	"Shun youthful passions and pursue righteousness, faith, love, and peace, along with those who call on the Lord from a pure heart."
Hebrews 12:14	"Pursue peace with everyone, and the holiness without which no one will see the Lord."
1 Peter 3:11	"Let them turn away from evil and do good; let them seek peace and pursue it."

world—both fellow believers as well as nonbelievers (some of whom may even be their persecutors).

First, believers must *pursue peace with all people.* Believers are to have as peaceful relations as possible with their unbelieving neighbors and associates, as well as harmonious relationships within the church. In a perfect world, all people could live peacefully together. Of course, this is impossible in our imperfect world. However, believers should do their best to at least "pursue" peace and reconciliation. Believers certainly should not cause dissension. Christian fellowship should be characterized by peace and building up one another (see 1 Thessalonians 5:11).

PURSUE PEACE

How can we be holy? The readers were familiar with the ceremonial cleansing ritual that prepared them for worship, and they knew that they had to be holy or clean in order to enter the temple. Sin always blocks our vision of God; so if we want to see God, we must renounce sin and obey him (see Psalm 24:3-4).

This holy living will result in peaceful living. A right relationship with God leads to right relationships with fellow believers. Rather than pursuing peace, it is often easier to irritate others who are abrasive to us. Although we will not always feel loving toward all other believers, we must pursue peace as we become more Christlike.

In addition to seeking peace, believers must also pursue *holiness, without which no one will see the Lord* (see also 12:10). "Holiness," when applied to God, means his moral perfection and the fact that he is totally separate from humanity in his holiness—his separateness. "Holiness," when applied to us, means devoted or consecrated to his service. Of course, Christians are made holy once for all by the onetime sacrifice of Jesus Christ. We are perceived by God as holy because of what Christ has done on our behalf. In a practical way, our holiness means honoring God in how we treat others—friends, neighbors, spouse, children, even enemies—and in how we run our businesses, finances, etc. Holiness causes the behavior, thoughts, and attitudes of Christians to be different from unbelievers. So, while Christians must pursue peace, at the same time they should be separate from the world. Our holiness, provided for us by the death and resurrection of Christ, will allow us to "see the Lord" as he really is, when we go to be with him forever. John wrote, "Beloved, we are God's children now; what we will be has not yet been revealed. What we do know is this: when he is revealed, we will be like him, for we will see him as he is" (1 John 3:2 NRSV).

12:15 **Look after each other so that none of you fails to receive the grace of God. Watch out that no poisonous root of bitterness grows up to trouble you, corrupting many.**[NLT] As believers deal with interpersonal relationships in the local church, they should *look after each other.* Christians are commanded to look out for each other and not just be focused on themselves. We look after others so that

- we can help those who might be in danger of drifting away (see 2:1-4);
- we can, through our love and example of faithfulness, soften the heart of those who might become hardened (3:12);
- we can encourage those who may need help enduring God's discipline (12:8);
- we can help remove obstacles from the path of those coming along behind us (12:13).

By these actions, we can help our fellow believers *so that none of you fails to receive the grace of God.* The word "grace" here refers to all the benefits that God has bestowed on his children. Believers should encourage each other to appropriate these blessings, for these will help them stand firm. Too often believers "miss out" because they are not aware of certain of God's promises, teachings, or guidance.

The allusion to the "poisonous root of bitterness" comes from the language of Deuteronomy 29:18-19:

> *Make sure there is no man or woman, clan or tribe among you today whose heart turns away from the LORD our God to go and worship the gods of those nations; make sure there is no root among you that produces such bitter poison. When such a person hears the words of this oath, he invokes a blessing on himself and therefore thinks, "I will be safe, even though I persist in going my own way." This will bring disaster on the watered land as well as the dry.* (NIV)

This "poisonous root" refers to unbelief, as seen in the Deuteronomy quotation. Moses cautioned that the day the Hebrews chose to turn from God, a root would be planted that would produce bitter poison. If such a person assumes to have God's blessing and then proceeds to disobey, this plants an evil seed that begins to grow out of control, eventually yielding a crop of sorrow and pain—*corrupting many.* But believers can *watch out* that this doesn't happen. If the "bitter root" never finds fertile soil, its bitter fruit will never develop. Christians must watch out for these false roots because they do not really belong among God's people. Christians should not allow people who undermine faith to remain in the church. Their influence may not be noticeable at first, but it will come (see also 2 Peter 2).

12:16-17 See that no one is sexually immoral, or is godless like Esau, who for a single meal sold his inheritance rights as the oldest son. Afterward, as you know, when he wanted to inherit this blessing, he was rejected. He could bring about no change of mind, though he sought the blessing with tears.[NIV] Part of the believers' looking after one another and watching out for the bitter root means that they need to *see that no one is sexually immoral.* Though there is no mention of Esau's immorality in the Old Testament, certain Jews regarded his marriages to Hittite women as being immoral (Genesis 26:34-35; 28:49). Sexual immorality has no place among Christians and should not be tolerated in the church (see commentary on 13:4; see also 1 Corinthians 5:1-11; 7:2; 10:8; 2 Corinthians 12:21). God expects his people to maintain the standards of morality found in his Word. God forbids sexual sin because he knows its power to destroy us physically and spiritually. No one should underestimate the power of sexual immorality. It has devastated countless lives and destroyed families, churches, communities, and even nations. God wants to protect his people from damaging themselves and others.

Believers are also commanded to see that no one is *godless like Esau.* Esau did not follow the examples of those who kept their eyes focused on heavenly rewards (see chapter 11). Rather than take interest in his birthright, which had great spiritual value, he *for a single meal sold his inheritance rights as the oldest son* (see Genesis 25). A birthright (here called "inheritance rights") was a special honor given to the firstborn son. It included a double portion of the family inheritance along with the honor of one day becoming the family's leader. The oldest son could sell his birthright or give it away if he chose, but in so doing, he would lose both material goods and his leadership position. By trading his birthright, Esau showed complete disregard for the spiritual blessings that would have come his way if he had kept it. In effect, Esau "despised" his birthright (Genesis 25:34). Esau's sin was impulsiveness and complete disregard for his spiritual heritage. Just as Esau had little regard for spiritual matters, the church should be on the lookout for people who join the church but have no real concern for spiritual matters.

The result of Esau's "godless" attitude and behavior was that *when he wanted to inherit this blessing, he was rejected.* The word "godless" *(bebelos)* can be translated "profane" or "irreligious." There is no direct reference to Esau being godless in the story in Genesis, but he surely rejected his religious heritage. He disregarded the covenant promises of God for him as worth no more than a meal of stew. Esau becomes an example in the way that the Hebrew people became an example in Hebrews 3–4. Esau rejected God's plan and could not undo his actions. The Hebrew people rejected God's offer of the Promised Land and could not undo their actions. These served as examples to the present readers not to reject God's plan. If they rejected God's means of salvation, nothing could save them. Just as Esau found that *he could bring about no change of mind, though he sought the blessing with tears,* so those who reject God's way will not be given a second chance when it comes time for others to inherit his spiritual blessing. No amount of pleading before God's throne will change his mind about the fate of those who rejected him while alive on earth.

Esau's story shows us that mistakes and sins sometimes have lasting consequences (Genesis 25:29-34; 27:36). Repentance and forgiveness do not always eliminate the consequences of sin. How often do you make decisions based on what you want now, rather than on what you need in the long run? Evaluate the long-range effects of your decisions and actions. Impulsiveness can bring heartache and grief.

12:18-21 You have not come to a mountain that can be touched and that is burning with fire; to darkness, gloom and storm; to a trumpet blast or to such a voice speaking words that those who heard it begged that no further word be spoken to them, because they could not bear what was commanded: "If even an animal touches the mountain, it must be stoned." The sight was so terrifying that Moses said, "I am trembling with fear."NIV Again Hebrews contrasts the old and new covenant. This time the contrast is between the earthly Mount Sinai (12:18-21) and the heavenly Mount Zion (12:22-24). The awesome scene at Mount Sinai was so terrifying that even Moses said, *"I am trembling with fear."*

The scene described in this passage comes from Exodus 19. As the Israelites were camped at the foot of Mount Sinai, God was preparing the nation for receiving his Ten Commandments. God commanded that no one, not even an animal, should touch the mountain, under penalty of death (Exodus 19:12-13). The *fire, ... darkness, gloom and storm* describe the awesome scene on the mountain, for God himself descended there to speak with Moses (Exodus 19:18-21). A blazing fire engulfed the top half of the mountain; this illustrated the Lord's presence. The loud *trumpet blast* came from the mountain and caused the people to tremble (Exodus 19:16, 19). They *begged that no further word be spoken to them,* terrified by the awesome sight before them (Exodus 20:18-19). The fear caused the people to beg that Moses be the lone mediator. They thought they would die if God were to speak directly to them (see Deuteronomy 5:25-27). Moses entered this "thick darkness" and met with God (Exodus 19:19; 20:21).

The old covenant, with its display of God's awesome power, still was not superior to what God had planned in the new covenant. The old covenant caused only fear from the people; they begged that they would not have to approach God themselves. God, in turn, did not allow them to approach him. *[They] have not come to a mountain that can be touched,* or they would die. God has offered something new (12:22). Returning to this old way would be foolish.

GOD ISN'T SCARY?

How can we approach a holy and awesome God?

God is holy, awesome, and omnipotent—but not scary.

God is frightening—nothing can oppose his will and plan. But his plan is good.

God strikes terror since his judgment is decisive and irrevocable. But Jesus is the world's Savior, and we are God's beloved children.

God is God, and you are not—the thought alone can be frightening. But God is your God, your loving parent, your problem solver, your hope. Don't be afraid. Approach him in confidence and with love.

12:22 **No, you have come to Mount Zion, to the city of the living God, the heavenly Jerusalem, and to countless thousands of angels in a joyful gathering.**[NLT] *No,* instead of coming to a threatening mountain of fear and death, *you have come to Mount Zion.* Two mountains, both extremely significant in Israel's history, are used here to describe the two covenants. Mount Sinai was a place of fear, which separated God from his people. Mount Zion represents a new community and a new relationship with God. Throughout the Old Testament, Mount Zion (another name for Mount Moriah, the hill on which the temple was built) was the home of God and his glory. This Mount Zion was the center of Israel's worship in the Old Testament. Psalm 9:11 says, "Sing praises to the LORD, who dwells in Zion. Declare his deeds among the peoples" (NRSV). God did not live only in Zion; he is everywhere all the time. Later, the focal point of Israelite worship became Jerusalem and its beautiful temple. God was present in the tabernacle (Exodus 25:8-9) and in the temple built by Solomon (2 Chronicles 7:16). Now access to him was made available to all believers through Christ.

By faith (see 11:1), we lay hold of that which is yet to come, so that we can say that we *have come* already to *Mount Zion,* the *city of the living God, the heavenly Jerusalem.* This is the "new Jerusalem" (described in Revelation 3:12; 21:2). Here believers live with God and can worship him without reserve. In this city, *thousands of angels in a joyful gathering* continually worship God. The new Jerusalem is the future dwelling of the people of God. All Christians will have a new citizenship in God's future kingdom. Everything will be new, pure, and secure.

What a contrast between the people's terrified approach to God at Mount Sinai and their joyful approach at Mount Zion! What a difference Jesus has made! Before Jesus came, God seemed distant and threatening. Now God welcomes us through Christ into his presence. As Christians, we are citizens of the heavenly Jerusalem right now. Because Christ rules our lives, the Holy Spirit is always with us, and we experience close fellowship with other believers. The full and ultimate rewards and reality of the heavenly Jerusalem are depicted in Revelation 21. (For more on the contrast of the old and new covenants, see the chart "The Old and New Covenants" on page 122.)

12:23 **You have come to the assembly of God's firstborn children, whose names are written in heaven. You have come to God himself, who is the judge over all things. You have come to the spirits of the righteous ones in heaven who have now been made perfect.**[NLT] Christians do not enter a covenant in which someone like Moses must go up the mountain to meet with God. Rather, we *have come to the assembly of God's firstborn children.*

The "assembly" means the church or congregation, referring to the gathering of believers who have been called out by God for the special purpose of loving, obeying, and worshiping him. We are no longer separated from the angels, but join them in praising God.

All believers are God's "firstborn," for all are promised his inheritance (Ephesians 1:11). "Firstborn" refers to the privileged position of the firstborn son in every family; it was he who received the blessing (see 12:16-17). But now every believer is a "firstborn son." There is no longer only one for each family. All believers are on the same level. We are all heirs of God's promise (Romans 8:17). In Colossians 1:15 there is only one true firstborn *(prototokos),* referring to Christ, but in and through him we participate in his privileged position. We become members of God's family and can approach God our Father at any time.

We do not need an intermediary; we *have come to God himself.* This means we have been given free access to God through Christ himself (4:16; 6:19-20; 7:25; 10:19-21).

As his children, our *names are written in heaven,* presumably in the Book of Life (Luke 10:20; Philippians 4:3; Revelation 3:5; 13:8; 17:8; 20:12, 15; 21:27). Christians are heavenly citizens, officially registered and recorded. Although Christians worship God in spirit now, one day they will take up residence in heaven and worship him face-to-face. Because our names are written, we have no fear of his judgment. God is *the judge over all things,* but Christians need not fear that judgment. Although Christians will be judged (9:27), we do not need to fear it because Christ has taken our punishment. The judgment believers face will be for receiving rewards based on what we have done in our lives. We can look forward to a glorious eternity, for we are promised that when we die, we will *come to the spirits of the righteous ones in heaven who have now been made perfect.* "Spirits" refers to spiritual beings of people (see 12:9) but not angels, for believers have "now been made perfect" by the Savior's death (12:2). This is the day we anticipate, when all believers will have been made complete and will have reached their fulfillment. At death, Christians reach the finish line of their race. At the end is not fear but joy, justice, God's favor, and eternal life in God's heavenly city.

The paradox in all of this is that we have come to the city, yet the city is still to come. We are already there in spirit, yet we are still pilgrims. This is the journey of faith.

12:24 You have come to Jesus, the one who mediates the new covenant between God and people, and to the sprinkled blood, which speaks of forgiveness instead of crying out for vengeance like the blood of Abel.[NLT] "You have come to God himself" (12:23); *you have come to Jesus, the one who mediates the new covenant between God and people.* The only access to God is through Jesus Christ, who is "the way" (John 14:6). This new covenant far surpasses the old covenant; no person who understood the new covenant could ever intelligently choose to

A BETTER WORD

In contrast to Abel's blood, Christ's blood made a "good word" for us and our salvation.

Good words are clear.	Abel's death left the idea of justice quite ambiguous.	Jesus' death showed clearly the mercy of God to you.
Good words are complete.	Abels' death was unresolved.	Jesus' death was followed by resurrection.
Good words make powerful messages.	Abels' death was tragic. Yet no one says, "I'm a follower of Abel."	Jesus' death was also tragic, yet it saved us. Millions follow him.
Good words explain confusion and point to hope.	Abel's death left humanity with no hope.	Jesus had the most wonderful words of hope for you today. Listen, believe, and obey.

revert to the old way. Rather than offer sacrifices year after year, Christ offered one sacrifice. We come *to the sprinkled blood* because through it alone can we receive God's gracious forgiveness. Christ's sacrifice cleanses the conscience rather than convicting it. Jesus alone was worthy to mediate the new covenant (8:6; 9:15).

In contrast with Christ's redeeming blood, *the blood of Abel* is pictured as *crying out for vengeance.* Abel is referred to here because his sacrifice is the first one mentioned in the Bible and because it provided the impetus for the sacrifice system in the old covenant. In the NRSV, this verse reads, "And to Jesus, the mediator of a new covenant, and to the sprinkled blood that speaks a better word than the blood of Abel." Abel's blood cried out for vengeance; Christ's blood speaks a "better word," calling all people to repentance. Christ's death brought peace and hope. Christ's blood brought the end of the old covenant and sealed the new one.

12:25-26 **See to it that you do not refuse him who speaks. If they did not escape when they refused him who warned them on earth, how much less will we, if we turn away from him who warns us from heaven? At that time his voice shook the earth, but now he has promised, "Once more I will shake not only the earth but also the heavens."**[NIV] If people refuse to follow God's new covenant, they reject his plan. But more than the plan, they reject God himself. To do so is final and tragic, so the writer again warns his readers: *See to it that you do not refuse him who speaks.*

This continues to reflect the awesome picture of Mount Sinai mentioned in 12:18-21. At that time God *warned them on earth,* giving them the covenant and outlining his expectations for them. Those who *refused* to listen and obey *did not escape* just punishment. If they did not escape, then *how much less will we, if we turn away from him who warns us from heaven,* meaning Jesus Christ, who died for us.

When God gave the first covenant, *his voice shook the earth* (Exodus 19:18). Psalm 68:8 also describes an earthquake accompanying God's revelation at Mount Sinai. God promises that he will *once more . . . shake not only the earth but also the heavens* (quoting from Haggai 2:6). At the end of the world, God will shake the earth again. This shaking stands for another major cataclysm in the earth to go along with God's revelation to all the nations. But God's revelation as reported by Haggai will shake not only the earth but the heavens as well. This divine judgment will terrify those who have refused to listen to him and who face his judgment. But to those who follow God and are members of the new covenant, this will be a moment of glorious expectation, as we wait for our King to return and set up his eternal kingdom.

12:27 **The words "once more" indicate the removing of what can be shaken—that is, created things—so that what cannot be shaken may remain.**[NIV] When God shakes the world again, he will do it for a final time. The phrase "once more" alludes to that one final time. One day, God will shake this world, and it will come apart completely (Mark 13:31; 2 Peter 3:7). At that time, all *created things* will be destroyed—the earth, the universe, animals, people, and everything else that can be seen. Only what belongs to God's kingdom will be unshakable. These will *remain,* for they belong to the heavenly city.

Eventually the world will crumble, and only God's kingdom will last. Those who follow Christ are part of this unshakable kingdom, and they will withstand the shaking, sifting, and burning. When we feel unsure about the future, we can take confidence from these verses. No matter what happens here, our future is built on a solid foundation that cannot be destroyed. Don't put your confidence in what will be destroyed; instead, build your life on Christ and his unshakable kingdom. (See Matthew 7:24-27 for the importance of building on a solid foundation.)

12:28 **Therefore, since we are receiving a kingdom that cannot be shaken, let us be thankful, and so worship God acceptably with reverence and awe.**[NIV] Because this world will one day disappear, faith concentrates on the heavenly promises. The future, unseen world is actually more real than this present one. This one can be shaken and destroyed, but believers *are receiving a kingdom that cannot be shaken.* This kingdom exists now in the hearts of believers and will become a physical reality when the present world disappears. Although this world will be shaken apart, God's kingdom can never be shaken.

This is a kingdom that we "are receiving." Christians receive it by God's grace, not through their own effort or by any means other than God's kindness. Because we have this kind of kingdom, we should *be thankful.*

In addition to being thankful, we should *worship God acceptably with reverence and awe.* When we truly worship God, we do it all the time—not just in a Sunday morning worship service that has a few hymns, an offering, a sermon, and a time of prayer. True worship includes every action of every day. By obeying God, our lives become living sacrifices of worship (see Romans 12:1-2).

THANK YOU, GOD

The book of Hebrews tells us to be thankful. How do we show thanks to God? In simple ways—because even the most elaborate ceremony isn't enough. In honest ways—by expressing thanks for his creation, his provision, and his protection of us. In loving ways—not from duty only or fear, as if God has to be placated. Jesus has already done that.

12:29 **For our God is a consuming fire.**[NKJV] God is worthy of our thanks and worship because he is *a consuming fire.* This description may be taken from Deuteronomy 4:24. God reigns over and will destroy everything that is temporary. Everything that is imperfect and bound by time will end. Only the new covenant and those who are part of it will survive.

The words "our God" refer to that relationship. He is the focal point of our worship. We may have a personal relationship, but this awesome privilege must never be taken lightly. God's power provides sufficient reason for us to fear and stand in awe of him. "Fire" is a metaphor for judgment—severe, total, and complete judgment. This fire is not the flame of a candle, but it is the roaring blast of a raging fire that consumes everything in its path. Even with sophisticated fire-fighting equipment, a consuming fire is often beyond human control. God is not within our control,

FIVE WAYS WE CAN BE THANKFUL

We can be thankful that God answers our prayers.	Psalm 3:4; Isaiah 65:24; John 11:41; 2 Corinthians 1:11
We can be thankful for God's provision for our needs.	Matthew 14:19; 26:26-27; Acts 27:35; Romans 14:6; 1 Cornthians 10:30; 1 Thessalonians 5:18; 1 Timothy 4:4-5
We can be thankful for God's blessings	1 Chronicles 16:34; Daniel 6:10; Philippians 4:6; Colossians 1:10
We can be thankful for God's character and wondrous works.	Psalm 7:17, 75:1; 2 Cornthinans 9:15; Colossians 1:12; Revelation 11:17
We can be thankful for our brothers and sisters in Christ.	1 Corinthians 1:4; Ephesians 1:16; Philippians 1:3-5; Colossians 1:3-4; 1 Thessalonians 1:2; 2 Timothy 1:3; Philemon 1:4-5

either. We cannot force him to do anything; he cannot be contained. Yet, he is a God of compassion. He has saved us from sin, and he will save us from death. But everything that is worthless and sinful will be consumed by the fire of his wrath. Only what is good, dedicated to God, and righteous will remain.

There could hardly be a more startling conclusion to this letter for these Jewish Christian readers who were considering turning away from the faith. Failure to listen to God, refusing to accept all that he has done, will bring catastrophe.

HEBREWS 13

HOLY AND OBEDIENT LIVES / 13:1-17

This final chapter presents a series of exhortations regarding believers' social, private, and religious lives. The readers are encouraged to make a final break with Judaism. Changes in industrial development, transportation methods, and electronic technology have crescendoed throughout recent decades. Fortunately, Jesus has not changed at all. People have created some remarkable items, yet nothing can or will approach the majesty of God's creation.

The changeless Christ remains both our great High Priest and the perfect sacrifice. Regardless of how far industrial manufacturing methods develop, how fast we can travel from one place to another in the future, or how rapidly we can process information in the years to come, all people still need the salvation available only through the Lord Jesus.

13:1 Keep on loving each other as brothers and sisters.[NLT] After giving commands to pursue peace and holiness (12:14-29), the book of Hebrews presents three commands that deal with the social life of a Christian (13:1-3).

The first command is: *Keep on loving each other as brothers and sisters.* The early Christians faced persecution and hatred from the world; hopefully, within the church and in the fellowship of believers, they should be able to find love and encouragement. The church ought to be a haven for believers. The command for believers to love one another was not new; it had been around since God had given the law through Moses (see Leviticus 19:18). To love as Christian "brothers and sisters" means loving others the way Christ loves us. Jesus had told his followers on the night before he died, "A new command I give you: Love one another. As I have loved you, so you must love one another. By this all men will know that you are my disciples, if you love one another" (John 13:34-35 NIV). Believers are to love one another based on Jesus' sacrificial love for them. Such love brings people to Christ and will keep believers strong and united in a world hostile to God. Jesus was a living example of God's love, and we are to be living examples of Jesus' love (see also Romans 12:10; 1 Thessalonians 4:9; 1 Peter 1:22; 2 Peter 1:7).

Such love is more than simply warm feelings; it is an attitude that reveals itself in action. How can we love others as Jesus loves us? By helping when it's not convenient, by giving when it hurts, by devoting energy to others' welfare rather than our own, by absorbing hurts from others without complaining or fighting back. This kind of loving is hard to do. That is why people notice when you do it and know you are empowered by a supernatural source.

With this kind of love, believers can look out for one another (12:14-17) and help those who feel discouraged or weak, and those who are in danger of turning away from the faith. Real love for others produces tangible actions: kindness to strangers (13:2); empathy for those who are in prison and those who have been mistreated (13:3); respect for your marriage vows (13:4); and contentment with what you have (13:5). Make sure that your love runs deep enough to affect your hospitality, empathy, fidelity, and contentment.

13:2 Do not forget to entertain strangers, for by so doing some have unwittingly entertained angels.[NKJV] The second command is to *entertain strangers.* This kind of hospitality was important because inns of that day were expensive, as well as being centers for pagan practices and criminal activities. This hospitality also helped spread the gospel because traveling missionaries would be able to go to more places and minister to more people if they did not have to stay in inns. These "strangers" to be entertained, however, were *not* to be people who worked against God's kingdom; that is, believers were not to welcome false teachers into their homes. Second John 10-11 says, "Do not receive into the house or welcome anyone who comes to you and does not bring this teaching; for to welcome is to participate in the evil deeds of such a person" (NRSV). The book of 3 John focuses on hospitality, and Gaius is commended:

> *You are faithful in what you are doing for the brothers, even though they are strangers to you. They have told the church about your love. You will do well to send them on their way in a manner worthy of God. It was for the sake of the Name that they went out, receiving no help from the pagans. We ought therefore to show hospitality to such men so that we may work together for the truth.* (3 John 5-9 *NIV*)

A further encouragement to this kind of hospitality comes from the biblical record that, through their hospitality, *some have unwittingly entertained angels.* This happened to Abraham

(Genesis 18:1-14) and Lot (Genesis 19:1-3). That hospitality was given to and received by angels shows the importance of the hospitality Christians ought to give one another. It is better to offer hospitality generously than to miss the chance to entertain angels.

COME ON OVER

Christian hospitality differs from social entertaining. Entertaining focuses on the host—the home must be spotless; the food must be well prepared and abundant; the host must appear relaxed and good-natured. Hospitality, by contrast, focuses on the guests. Their needs are the primary concern. Hospitality can happen in a messy home. It can happen around a dinner table where the main dish is canned soup. It can even happen while the host and the guest are doing chores together. Offer hospitality even if you are tired, busy, or not wealthy enough to entertain.

Share a meal with visitors to your church. Invite single people over for an evening of conversation. Think of how you could use your home to meet the needs of traveling missionaries. Hospitality simply means making other people feel comfortable and at home.

13:3 **Remember those in prison as if you were their fellow prisoners, and those who are mistreated as if you yourselves were suffering.**NIV The third command focuses on *those in prison.* This instruction was already alluded to in 10:32-34. Believers are to have empathy for prisoners, especially for (but not limited to) Christians imprisoned for their faith. Jesus said that his followers would represent him as they visited people in prison (Matthew 25:36). The apostle Paul encouraged people to empathize and to share the suffering of others (1 Corinthians 12:26; 2 Timothy 1:16). Having this loving attitude is often more difficult than showing hospitality, which requires only that the home be open. Visiting prisoners requires the Christian to make plans and to go to the prison. This effort honors God and demonstrates his love.

We should remember those in prison *as if [we] were their fellow prisoners.* These believers knew that at any time any of them could be imprisoned for his or her faith. They could become one another's "fellow prisoners" in a very real sense. Those who were sent to prison ought to be remembered by those who were still free. Prisoners were often beaten, abused, or neglected, and they depended on the help, prayers, and visits of fellow believers in order to survive.

Others who were *mistreated*—beaten, robbed, assaulted, humiliated—also needed to be remembered by their fellow believers as if they *were suffering* too.

HELPING PRISONERS

The Bible instructs us to remember those in prison. Where Christians are detained and imprisoned merely for being Christians, those outside prison should assume the care of those inside. But today's situation calls for extended meaning:

- Prisons are a mission field. Send in evangelists and Bible teachers. Care for all, regardless of their criminal record.
- Prison systems are a political project. Justice and mercy in funding, staff training, and rehabilitative programs need a strong Christian voice.
- Prisons are an international problem. Through large multination agencies, Christians can help victims of foreign gulags. Compassion for suffering people demands no less. We must do more than just remember; we must actively help and encourage those in prison.

13:4 Give honor to marriage, and remain faithful to one another in marriage. God will surely judge people who are immoral and those who commit adultery.[NLT] In addition to commands for the social life of Christians (13:1-3), Hebrews also includes commands for private lives. Believers had a responsibility to *give honor to marriage, and remain faithful to one another in marriage.* This would include promises to love continually, to remain faithful in thought, attitude, and action, and to support and provide for each other.

Hebrews presents two specific ways to "remain faithful." Believers can stay away from *immoral* behavior and *adultery.* Immorality and adultery have split marriages for thousands of years. God's commands against such actions (given for people's own good) have been in place for just as long (see Exodus 20:14, 17; Job 24:15-24; Proverbs 5:15-23). Christians, however, are to maintain high standards (Matthew 5:27-28). Hebrews makes the point that even if no consequences are seen right away, promiscuous people will incur God's wrath—*God will surely judge* them.

Why is integrity in marriage so important for the church? Honesty, moral purity, and faithfulness are essential to the proper worship of God (see also 12:16). Because the marriage relationship often illustrates the relationship of God with his people, a relationship on earth with one's spouse ought to illustrate the love, trust, and devotion available with the Creator (see the book of Hosea; Revelation 18:23; 19:7; 21:2, 9; 22:17). Also, in times of persecution and pressure, a believer needs help and encouragement from his or her spouse. A good marriage relationship provides one of the best deterrents against apostasy.

HONORING YOUR SPOUSE

Giving honor to marriage will require the utmost in Christian conviction and sensitivity. Modern social theory may redefine the family, and the new definitions may be far from its biblical foundation. What can you do?

- Witness to the depth of God's love for you by keeping your marriage happy and strong.
- Pray for your spouse. Take delight in him/her.
- Honor biblical marriage (consenting, man-woman unions) by resisting political pressure to recognize and legalize other sexual preferences.
- Teach children the meaning of marriage. Pray early for their own eventual partners and family.
- Make marriage enrichment the goal of your small group discussions and study.

13:5 **Don't love money; be satisfied with what you have. For God has said, "I will never fail you. I will never abandon you."**[NLT] Another command for the believers' private lives concerned material needs: *Don't love money.* This was also commanded by Jesus (Matthew 6:24; Luke 16:13) and Paul (1 Timothy 3:3; 6:10). Materialistic cravings and greed are a great evil because they show dependence on money rather than on Christ. Materialism is the antithesis of chapters 11–12, where a life pursuing heavenly rather than earthly rewards is extolled. Materialism also demonstrates that someone cares more about items they can see than about spiritual promises that they cannot presently see.

> It is possible to love money without having it, and it is possible to have it without loving it.
> *J. C. Ryle*

The antidote to greed is contentment, so the writer says, *be satisfied with what you have.* Again, this teaching was given by Jesus (Matthew 6:31-34) and Paul (Philippians 4:11; 1 Timothy 6:6). Our contentment should be in what Christ gives, not in what we can achieve for ourselves. Money cannot save a soul from God's punishment. Money cannot even bring contentment. Rather than bring contentment, most people find that money often fails to live up to their expectations. Money is also difficult to keep. Where money fails, God does not. *For God has said, "I will never fail you. I will never abandon you."* When faith reminds us that God is in control, we remember that we have all we need.

13:6 **So we can say with confidence, "The LORD is my helper, so I will have no fear. What can mere people do to me?"**[NLT] Money cannot give security (13:5); only God can truly help us. While we are not guaranteed to have earthly possessions, we are guaranteed that God is our helper. He watches over his people and gives them what they need. Every believer, along with the psalmist (see Psalm 118:7), *can say with confidence* that *the LORD is my helper.* It must have been wonderful for these Jewish believers to realize that, when they became believers, the promises in the psalms could still be used as songs of praise!

TRUE CONTENTMENT

How can we learn to be content? Strive to live with less rather than desiring more; give away out of your abundance rather than accumulate more; relish what you have rather than resent what you're missing. See God's love expressed in what he has provided, and remember that money and possessions will all pass away.

We become content when we realize God's sufficiency for our needs. Christians who become materialistic are saying by their actions that God can't take care of them—or at least that he won't take care of them the way they want. Insecurity can lead to the love of money, whether we are rich or poor. The only antidote is to trust God to meet all our needs.

When we are confident that God is our helper, we need *have no fear.* If the king of the universe is on our side, *what can mere people do?* Granted, humans can take our possessions, mistreat us, throw us into prison, or even kill us. But Jesus has said, "Do not fear those who kill the body but cannot kill the soul; rather fear him who can destroy both soul and body in hell" (Matthew 10:28 NRSV). Humans cannot hurt our souls or affect our salvation. With God as our helper, we truly have nothing to fear! Death will only bring us that much sooner into God's immediate presence. Believers need not be afraid.

13:7 **Remember your leaders, who spoke the word of God to you. Consider the outcome of their way of life and imitate their faith.**[NIV] Next follows instructions about the religious life of his readers (see also 13:17, 24). Their religious *leaders* had provided examples for others to follow. The leaders referred to here were most likely the founding Christians, the elders of the group *who spoke the word of God* to them. Although these men had died, their influence remained, as evidenced by the existence of the communities of believers. Thus, the passage states, *consider the outcome of their way of life and imitate their faith.* These leaders had copied Christ's example and the example of the great cloud of witnesses (12:1-2). Because they were imitating Christ and godly heroes, their lives were worth imitating.

The New Testament places strong emphasis on imitating

leaders. It also gives strong words to those leaders that they be worthy of emulation (Scripture quotations are from the NIV):

- Matthew 11:29—"Take my yoke upon you and learn from me." Jesus told his followers to learn from his example of gentleness and humility.
- Philippians 3:17—"Join with others in following my example." Paul urged believers to follow his example of enthusiasm, perseverance, and maturity.
- 1 Thessalonians 1:6-7—"You became imitators of us and of the Lord. . . . And so you became a model to all the believers." The new Christians at Thessalonica received training in discipleship from Paul, and even in suffering, they modeled before others what they had learned.
- 1 Timothy 1:16—"In me . . . Christ Jesus might display his unlimited patience as an example for those who would believe on him." Paul used his unworthiness to receive Christ as an example of grace so that no one would hold back from coming to Christ.
- 1 Peter 5:3—"Not lording it over those entrusted to you, but being examples to the flock." Peter taught Christian leaders to lead by example, not by commands.
- See also 1 Corinthians 4:16 and Hebrews 6:12.

If you are a Christian, you owe much to others who have taught you and have modeled for you what you need to know about the gospel and Christian living. Continue following the good examples of those who have invested themselves in you by investing your life through evangelism, service, and Christian education. In turn, you must also become a model worth emulating.

FOLLOW THE LEADER
Becoming a good leader is the goal of most Christian training programs. Following a leader is not so often the point of focus. But the first requires the second. Great followers give leaders the "advantage of the doubt." In judgment calls, speak your piece, then give your leadership team lots of support. Great followers also hold leaders accountable. Leaders don't need marshmallow groupies. Be an active follower who expects and appreciates energetic, wise leadership. Finally, great followers should learn from their leaders. Be mentored by people of compassion, vision, generosity, judgment, temperance, knowledge, and enthusiasm. You will become like the leader you follow.

13:8 **Jesus Christ is the same yesterday, today, and forever.**[NKJV]
Though times and leaders change, Jesus Christ does not. Christ

is the same all the time. He served faithfully *yesterday* (dying on the cross to make atonement for our sins; see 2:17-18). He serves faithfully *today* (interceding for us at the right hand of God; see 4:14-16; 7:25). He will remain faithful *forever.* Because of what he has done in the past and what he does in the present, he is sufficient for any need any believer will ever have. (See also 1:12.)

Human leaders have much to teach us and we can learn much from emulating them (13:7), but we must keep our eyes on Christ, our ultimate leader. Unlike any human leaders, he will never change. Christ has been and will be the same forever. In a changing world we can trust our unchanging Lord.

TRUST IN SOMETHING SURE

How do people cope with change?

1. *Encyclopedias.* Great books collect the stream of changing knowledge; now electronic systems deliver it. The Bible is God's changeless word to us. Its message: Jesus saves us.

2. *Storage tanks.* People will store anything of value. Today, store Jesus' words in your heart and mind. Their value is supreme and constant.

3. *Life insurance.* Because everyone dies, insurance is big business. Jesus takes the fear out of an unknown future. His work for us is good forever. Trust him with your fears today.

13:9 **Do not be carried away by all kinds of strange teachings. It is good for our hearts to be strengthened by grace, not by ceremonial foods, which are of no value to those who eat them.**[NIV]
If Christ never changes, neither can the new covenant that he initiated. Be careful, the passage warns, *do not be carried away by all kinds of strange teachings* (see 1 Timothy 4:16; 6:3; Titus 1:9). In order to resist "strange teachings," believers must be familiar with the correct teachings. Christians today have an advantage of having the entire Bible and Bible study tools. When we hear an interesting new doctrine, we should be sure to study it ourselves and become certain it is true before we are "carried away."

Many "strange teachings" arose during the days of the early church. One of these "strange teachings" may have concerned *ceremonial foods.* Apparently some false teachers had been teaching these Jewish converts that they still needed to keep the Old Testament ceremonial laws and rituals (such as not eating certain foods). But these laws were useless for conquering a person's evil thoughts and desires (Colossians 2:23). The believers' *hearts* (referring to their inner selves) should *be strengthened by grace,* not by the foods they did or did not eat. Laws could influence conduct, but they could not change the heart. The ceremonial foods might fulfill a ritual, but they *are of no value to those who eat them.* Lasting changes in conduct begin when the Holy Spirit lives in each person. Since God's approval is secured by grace, it was valueless to keep these ceremonial laws.

STRANGE TEACHINGS

In the search for answers to important questions, some ideas will emerge, some organizations will form, and some movements will result. And some of these will distort the Bible's message and disrupt people's faith. Watch out. Don't be "carried away by all kinds of strange teachings" (13:9).

Find a church whose teaching is Christ-centered, where the Bible is believed. Commit yourself to lifelong learning. Understand Christian theology so you can tell "strange teachings" from truth. The best defense against disruptive ideas is not the absence of learning, but constant learning. Faith grows when people say, "Lord, what can I discover today?" Find a small group unafraid of open talk, where questions are welcome and discussion is vigorous.

13:10-12 We have an altar from which those who minister at the tabernacle have no right to eat. The high priest carries the blood of animals into the Most Holy Place as a sin offering, but the bodies are burned outside the camp. And so Jesus also suffered outside the city gate to make the people holy through his own blood.[NIV] Returning to similar arguments used throughout the book, Hebrews again compares Christ and the new covenant with the old covenant. Here are further analogies between the Day of Atonement ceremony and Christ's once-for-all sacrifice on the cross (for more on the Day of Atonement, see commentary on chapters 9–10). We read how *the high priest carries the blood of animals into the Most Holy Place as a sin offering* (see 9:7). This would occur one day each year when the high priest would enter God's presence to atone for the sins of the entire nation. The new detail included here reminds the readers that *the bodies* (of the slain animals) *are burned outside the camp.* The priests could eat the meat of the sacrifices that were offered on a daily basis, but not on the Day of Atonement; on that day, the remainders of the slain animals were burned outside the camp.

In a similar way, *Jesus also suffered outside the city gate* (see Matthew 21:39; 27:31-33; John 19:20); this refers to Jesus' crucifixion, which occurred outside the city walls. Just as the Day of Atonement had an activity outside the camp, so Jesus' sacrifice was outside the gate. The writer of Hebrews used "typology" to show the connection of Christ to the Day of Atonement.

However, the writer did not just compare these sacrifices, he also contrasted them. Christ's sacrifice could *make the people holy through his own blood.* Christ's sacrifice was final, once and for all. The priests' sacrifices were not final. They performed many sacrifices that could never fully do the job. Those who still hold on to the old covenant and its trappings (sacrifices, ceremonial foods) *have no right to eat* (or to participate) in the new covenant that Christ sealed with his death. People cannot partake of both covenants. This was an important point for the Hebrew Christians, who were considering practicing Jewish ceremonial laws in addition to their faith in Christ. To revert to Jewish practices in order to gain God's approval, these people would lose their right to participate in the new covenant. They would have "no right to eat" in the new covenant.

13:13 So let us go out to him, outside the camp, and bear the disgrace he bore.[NLT] When Christians suffer persecution, they join Christ in his suffering. When Christians suffer for the cause of Christ they *go out to him, outside the camp, and bear the disgrace he bore.* Christ existed outside of the comfort and security of the Jewish system. Believers must go and stand with him. The original readers might experience disgrace because they seemed to be abandoning their Jewish roots, but they could not cling to their roots and still worship at the cross of Christ. The ridicule and persecution came from Jews who didn't believe in Jesus the Messiah. Most of the book of Hebrews explains how Christ is greater than the sacrificial system. Here is the practical implication of this lengthy argument: It may be necessary to leave the "camp" and suffer with Christ. In the days of the Exodus, those who were ceremonially unclean had to stay outside the camp. But Jesus had suffered humiliation and uncleanness outside the Jerusalem gates on their behalf. It was time for Jewish Christians to declare their loyalty to Christ above any other loyalty, to choose to follow the Messiah whatever suffering that might entail, to "go out to him outside the camp." They needed to move outside the safe confinement of their past, their traditions, and their ceremonies to live for Christ. Since Jesus was rejected by Judaism, they should reject Judaism.

13:14 For this world is not our permanent home; we are looking forward to a home yet to come.[NLT] The reason given for joining the suffering of Christ is that *this world is not our permanent home.* This is more than a passing point; it provides a key New Testament theme on our true citizenship. Philippians 3:19-21 teaches that our citizenship is in heaven. We should not be so tied to earthly privileges that we forget our heavenly loyalties. First Peter 1:17 and 2:11 teach us to live as foreigners and strangers in the world. We should not be so attached to our worldly possessions that we forget to obey Christ. Life on earth is temporary; Christians live here as foreigners (11:10). It would not be appropriate for Christians to grow comfortable here. Jobs, money, homes, and hobbies should not become the most important parts of their lives.

Instead, Christians should be like the heroes of faith discussed in chapter 11 and spend their lives *looking forward to a home yet to come.* This means that we should not be content or attached to this world, because all that we are and have here is temporary. Rather, we should eagerly expect the coming kingdom. Only our relationship with God and our service to him will last. We shouldn't store our treasures here; we should store them in heaven (Matthew 6:19-21).

LOOKING AHEAD

Christians love their families, spouses, jobs, and churches—but their sights should be set ahead beyond the horizon.

Christians are activists, invested in witnessing to a needy world—but they take frequent glances toward a promised community still to come.

Christians are gardeners and builders, shaping environments, turning weed pits into floral splendor, painting and patching and clearing—but they know God is building something far more beautiful and breathtaking for us.

Christians should be characterized by looking forward to the future. We should not love our present home so much that we lose sight of God's future blessing. Do earthly pleasures and treasures keep you from seeking heavenly ones?

13:15 Through Jesus, therefore, let us continually offer to God a sacrifice of praise—the fruit of lips that confess his name.[NIV]
The need for blood sacrifices ended with Jesus' death on the cross. But Christians do have a sacrifice that they can bring *continually*—called here *a sacrifice of praise.* God wants us to offer ourselves, not animals, as living sacrifices—daily laying aside our own desires so that we can follow him. We do this out of gratitude that our sins have been forgiven. We do this *through* Jesus because he alone makes our sacrifices acceptable. We do this with praise because we have been made acceptable to God through Jesus' sacrifice on our behalf. By continually offering this sacrifice of praise, we *confess his name* and thereby show that we are loyal to him. The sacrifices discussed

> We should be always wearing the garment of praise, not just waving a palm branch now and then. *Andrew Bonar*

TWENTY-FIVE REASONS FOR PRAISING GOD

We praise God for . . .

his splendor and majesty.	Psalm 104:1
giving us salvation	Psalm 96:2; Luke 1:68; 1 Peter 1:3-6
bearing our burdens	Psalm 68:19
hearing our prayers	Psaslm 66:20
giving us his strength.	Psalms 59:17; 68:35
his marvelous deeds	Psalms 9:1; 26:7; 52:9; 72:18
his guidance	Psalm 16:7
his compassion	Psalm 28:6; 2 Corinthians 1:3
his righteousness.	Palm 48:10
his enduring love	Psalm 106:1
his enduring faithfulness	Psalm 117:1-2; Isaiah 25:1
his comfort.	Isaiah 12:1; 2 Corinthians 1:3
his wisdom.	Daniel 2:20
his spiritual blessings.	Ephesians 1:3-6
forgiving our sins	Hosea 14:2; Ephesians 1:7

We praise God because . . .

he made us	Psalm 139:14
he is worthy of praise.	2 Samuel 22:4; 1 Chronicles 16:25; Psalm 48:1
he keeps his promises.	1 Kings 8:15, 46
he is in control	Ezra 7:27
he is eternal.	Nehemiah 9:5
he is powerful and mighty	Psalm 21:13
he is sovereign	Psalms 47:7; 66:4
he is trustworthy	Psalm 56:4
he is holy	Psalm 99:3
he is preparing a glorious future for us	Isaiah 61:11; 62:7-9; Revelation 21-22

here are also described in Romans 12:1-2, "I appeal to you therefore, brothers and sisters, by the mercies of God, to present your bodies as a living sacrifice, holy and acceptable to God, which is your spiritual worship. Do not be conformed to this world, but be transformed by the renewing of your minds, so that you may discern what is the will of God—what is good and acceptable and perfect" (NRSV).

Since these Jewish Christians, because of their belief in Jesus as the Messiah, no longer worshiped with other Jews, they could consider praise and acts of service their sacrifices. These were sacrifices that they could offer continually, anywhere, anytime. This must have reminded them of the prophet Hosea's words, "Forgive all our sins and receive us graciously, that we may offer the fruit of our lips" (Hosea 14:2 NIV). The phrase "fruit of lips" refers to real and heartfelt love and confession of faith. A "sacrifice of praise" today would include thanking Christ for his sacrifice on the cross and telling others about it.

PRAISE GOD!

Our lips should confess God's name in praise. Yet, in your typical day, how many times do you hear God's name used profanely? Christians should tilt the frequency toward praise!

How many times in your town today is God addressed obliquely, casually, or politically? Christians should tilt the numbers toward personally!

Praise God early in the day before the rush, then again in the hurried middle, and at the end as business winds down.

Praise God as the "firstfruits" of all your spoken words today, an offering that says, "God loves me, and I love God."

13:16 **And don't forget to do good and to share with those in need. These are the sacrifices that please God.**NLT The sacrifice referred to in 13:15 focuses on believers' praise to God. Just as praise to God flows from Jesus' sacrifice for us, so should our works of love. We know that loving service cannot save anyone from sin; rather, it is the overflow of the love of God in a person's heart. Another "sacrifice" that pleases God focuses on service to others. Acts of kindness and sharing our resources are particularly

DON'T FORGET TO DO GOOD

We are saved by faith in Jesus Christ, but faith ought to result in a changed life and a willingness to do good to others.

What Jesus said . . .	Matthew 5:14-16; 6:1; John 3:21
What Paul said	2 Corinthians 9;8; Ephesians 2:10; 2 Thessalonians 2:16-17; 1 Timothy 6:17-19; 2 Timothy 3:16-17; Titus 3:14
What James said . . .	James 1:22; 2:14-26; 3:13
What Peter said	1 Peter 1:14; 2:12
What John said	1 John 2:6; Revelation 14:13

pleasing to God, even when they go unnoticed. In times of persecution especially, Christians depend on one another (see 10:24; 13:20). Doing *good* to others improves a believer's ability to respond quickly and effectively. Another side of doing good is a willingness *to share with those in need.* This strikes a blow at the self-centeredness of our times. By sharing with others, we get by with less for ourselves so that others may have their basic needs met.

Believers experience fellowship with other believers when they make their resources available to those in need. Being rich in good works may not necessarily benefit our financial statement, but in the long run it will be a far more valuable asset in God's eyes. Taking care of each other's emotional, financial, and physical needs are *sacrifices that please God.* In Philippians 4:18, Paul refers to the financial gifts brought to him by Epaphroditus as an acceptable sacrifice that pleases God.

13:17 Obey your leaders and submit to their authority. They keep watch over you as men who must give an account. Obey them so that their work will be a joy, not a burden, for that would be of no advantage to you.[NIV] Members in the church have the responsibility to *obey* their leaders and *submit to their authority.* While 13:7 referred to past leaders who had died and were to be remembered for their great examples, this verse refers to the present leaders in the various congregations. Wise and God-honoring leaders watch over the church and have the best in mind for their followers. They do not lead for their own sake but because God has called them to a position of helping people mature in Christ. These leaders are concerned for the deepest needs of those in their fellowship. These leaders also take on great responsibility. They must give an account to God. Yet what pressures our leaders feel to please their congregations more than God! *They keep watch over you as men who must give an account.* God will hold them accountable to care for those who are in their charge (see also 1 Peter 5:1-5).

Because of this grave responsibility, cooperative followers can greatly ease the burden of leadership. God ordained leaders in the church for the benefit of those who follow. That is why the book of Hebrews states, *Obey them so that their work will be a joy, not a burden, for that would be of no advantage of you.* Too many believers create problems and tension for their leaders through endless complaints and interpersonal conflicts. How welcome would cheerfulness, helpfulness, and loyalty be to your leaders? Does your conduct give your leaders reason to report joyfully about you?

FINAL WORDS / 13:18-25

Shepherds in Palestine today care for their flocks much as they did when this letter was written. Several flocks of various shepherds arrive at a well at the same time; when each shepherd decides to leave, he calls his sheep and they follow him. He doesn't "herd" them with a stick from behind; he strides away and only his sheep trail after, more or less in single file.

If those less-than-brilliant sheep leave cool, refreshing water to follow a human shepherd, we human and intelligent Christians should follow the "great Shepherd of the sheep" wherever he leads us.

The last few verses of this book (13:20-21) are utilized to conclude many worship services, providing a pattern for prayer on any occasion. The writer again mentions the "eternal covenant," a thread woven throughout these thirteen chapters, tying it to a vivid description of our Lord as the great Shepherd.

WANTED: PRAYERS
The writer of Hebrews recognized the need for prayer. Christian leaders are especially vulnerable to criticism from others. They also need prayer for pride (if they succeed) and discouragement (if they fail). They desperately need our prayers! The leaders in your church have been placed in that position by a loving God who has entrusted them with the responsibility of caring for you. Your leaders need your prayers. Pray regularly for them.

13:18-19 Pray for us, for our conscience is clear and we want to live honorably in everything we do. And especially pray that I will be able to come back to you soon.NLT Apparently the writer of this letter, like his readers, had come face-to-face with persecution. The writer says he has done nothing wrong—*our conscience is clear*—but requests prayers in order to continue *to live honorably in everything we do.* (The use of the plural *us* may imply a general willingness to pray for all leaders—the writer included.) "Live honorably" refers to the firm determination to live according to the highest ethical standards. Because of this purity before God and purity of motivation, the writer could freely request prayer from fellow believers. In fact, he depended on it. This offers a clue that the writer of Hebrews may have been a former leader of the church who was traveling in another area. This leader requested prayer to *come back* to the readers soon. We do not know what prevented the writer from returning, but it was apparently significant. Whatever the problem was, the writer depended on the support of this church by asking for their prayers.

The tense of the verb "pray" is present imperative, meaning a continual action of uplifting the writers in prayer before God. We should pray continually for Christians who are undergoing difficult times or who are working to spread the gospel. Instead of just praying once and considering our job finished, we should pray often for them.

13:20-21 Now may the God of peace who brought up our Lord Jesus from the dead, that great Shepherd of the sheep, through the blood of the everlasting covenant, make you complete in every good work to do His will, working in you what is well pleasing in His sight, through Jesus Christ, to whom be glory forever and ever. Amen.[NKJV] This doxology describes God as *the God of peace.* This characteristic of God may have been included to promote harmony and to heal the disunity among the readers. Perhaps the writer wanted to encourage those whose faith was wavering due to persecution or to stress the peace between people and God that Jesus established through the Cross (such peace should carry over among God's people).

The next part of the doxology, "who brought up our Lord Jesus from the dead," recalls the resurrection and exaltation of our Lord Jesus. These facts prove that Jesus was an effective sacrifice and High Priest and is superior to anyone or anything in the old covenant. In fact, without the Resurrection, there would be no new covenant. The resurrection of Jesus from the dead is the central fact of Christian history. On it, the church is built; without it, there would be no Christian church. Jesus' resurrection is unique. Other religions have strong ethical systems, concepts about paradise and afterlife, and various holy writings. Only Christianity has a God who became human, actually died for his people, and was raised again to life in power and glory to rule his church forever.

Called here *that great Shepherd of the sheep,* Christ is the greatest one. Israel's leaders were often portrayed as shepherds. Other "shepherds," including Aaron, Moses, Joshua, and David, were important figures in the Old Testament, but not one of them compares to Christ. Jesus called himself "the good shepherd" (John 10:11) and went on to explain, "The good shepherd lays down his life for the sheep."

Again Hebrews highlights the sacrificial imagery of Christ's once-for-all sacrifice: *through the blood of the everlasting covenant.* This new covenant was established and provides purification from sin and the ability of people to approach God. It is an "everlasting covenant," unlike the earlier covenant that Moses initiated (described in 7:22–8:13).

This closing prayer contains two requests: first, that God would *make you complete in every good work to do His will* (for more on good works, see 10:24 and 13:16); second, that God would continue *working in you what is well pleasing in His sight.* They had begun to do works that accompanied their salvation (6:9-10), but now they needed to mature in this area. So the writer prays for God to perfect them.

These final words emphasize Christ's mediating work: *through Jesus Christ, to whom be glory forever and ever.* Only through Christ and his priestly work on our behalf can we fulfill that for which God has called us.

These verses (which borrow in part from Isaiah 63:10-14 and Zechariah 11:4 in the Septuagint) include two significant results of Christ's death and resurrection: (1) God works in us to make us the kind of people who will please him; and (2) God equips us to do the kind of work that will please him. Let God change you from within and then use you to help others.

13:22 I urge you, dear brothers and sisters, to pay attention to what I have written in this brief exhortation.[NLT] This letter includes its share of commands, appeals, rebukes, and warnings. Readers are encouraged to take it all seriously, but in the right spirit, realizing that the writer loves them and has only their best in mind. The letter has encouraged the readers to understand Christ's role as priest and understand that the new covenant is superior to the old covenant. These important words could make the difference between their holding on to Christ or turning away—the difference, literally, between eternal life and eternal death. So the writer urged his readers to *pay attention.* Apparently, the writer could have written much more on these subjects, so he notes that it is merely a *brief exhortation.*

13:23 I want you to know that our brother Timothy has been released. If he arrives soon, I will come with him to see you.[NIV] Other than this statement, the New Testament does not record Timothy's imprisonment. He may have been imprisoned in Rome or Ephesus. This is probably the same Timothy who was the disciple of Paul, and to whom Paul wrote two letters that now appear in the New Testament. Timothy grew up in Lystra, a city in the province of Galatia. Paul and Barnabas visited Lystra on Paul's first missionary journey (see Acts 14:8-21). Most likely, Paul met the young Timothy and his mother, Eunice, and grandmother Lois (see 2 Timothy 1:5) on this journey, perhaps even staying in their home.

On Paul's second missionary journey, he and Silas traveled to several cities that Paul had already visited, including Lystra, "where there was a disciple named Timothy, the son of a Jewish woman who was a believer. . . . He was well spoken of by the believers in Lystra and Iconium. Paul wanted Timothy to accompany him" (Acts 16:1-3 NRSV). Timothy traveled the Empire with Paul, serving as his assistant and sometimes as his emissary. Timothy's name is included as cosender on many of Paul's letters to the churches. Timothy became an important leader in the early church, continuing the ministry of the word after Paul's death. Apparently he, too, was imprisoned at one point but was *released*. The writer knew Timothy, and if Timothy arrived in time, the writer would come with him to see the readers.

13:24-25 Greet all your leaders and all God's people. Those from Italy send you their greetings. Grace be with you all.[NIV] Most New Testament letters end with greetings from the writer to others in the church and from the Christians in one locality to the Christians receiving the letter. So this letter offers greetings from the writer to the *leaders* and to *all God's people.* At the time of this letter, most churches still met in people's homes. These house churches, situated in different localities, needed to be encouraged about their unity with all other believers. The call to greet all the leaders and all of God's people underscored the importance of unity.

There has been much controversy over the phrase "those from Italy send you their greetings." Some interpret this phrase to mean that: (1) the letter was going to Jewish Christians in Italy, and those believers who were presently with the writer but had come from Italy were sending their greetings to people they knew; (2) this letter was sent to an unknown location, but the recipients knew people from Italy and these people sent their greetings; or (3) the letter was being sent from Italy, and the believers there were sending their greetings. This last interpretation, although not conclusive, is the most natural.

A final benediction ends the letter: *Grace be with you all.* Concluding with "grace" is an appropriate ending for this letter. God's approval could not be won through ceremonies or through following the old covenant. Rather, God's grace comes through the new covenant.

Hebrews is a call to Christian maturity. It was addressed to first-century Jewish Christians, but it applies to Christians of any age or background. Christian maturity includes making Christ the beginning and the end of our faith. To grow in maturity, we must center our lives on him, not depending on religious ritual, not falling back into sin, not trusting in ourselves, and not letting anything come between us and Christ. Christ is sufficient and superior.

BIBLIOGRAPHY

Blanchard, John. *Gathered Gold.* Hertfordshire, England: Evangelical Press, 1984.

———. *More Gathered Gold.* Hertfordshire, England: Evangelical Press, 1986.

Bruce, F. F. *The Epistle to the Hebrews* in The New International Commentary on the New Testament. Grand Rapids: Eerdmans, 1964.

Guthrie, Donald. *Hebrews* in the Tyndale New Testament Commentaries. Grand Rapids: Eerdmans, 1988.

Hagner, Donald A. *Hebrews* in the New International Biblical Commentary Series. New Testament edited by W. Ward Gasque. Peabody, Mass.: Hendrickson Publishers, 1990.

Lane, William L. *Hebrews 1-8* in Word Biblical Commentary. Waco, Tex.: Word, 1991.

———. *Hebrews 9-13* in Word Biblical Commentary. Waco, Tex.: Word, 1991.

Morris, Leon. "Hebrews." In *The Expositor's Bible Commentary.* Vol. 12. Edited by Frank E. Gaebelein. Grand Rapids: Zondervan, 1981.

Turner, George Allen. *The New and Living Way.* Minneapolis: Bethany Fellowship, 1975.

INDEX